COMPANY LAW

Colin Thomas, LLB(Hons.), Dip. Ed., is a Barrister and Senior Lecturer in the School of Legal Studies at the University of Wolverhampton. He specialises in company law and employment law, and is the author of *Employment Law*, also published in the Teach Yourself series.

To Rita, Dawn and Catherine

Of the first edition:

'. . . a succinct and orderly summary of a large and complex subject. Company formation, finance, control and liquidation are covered in a clear and methodical fashion . . .'
Personnel Executive

'. . . an excellent introduction to the complex subject of Company law . . . For students who seek a comprehensive introduction to Company Law there is no better textbook.'
The Society of Commercial Teachers

TEACH YOURSELF

COMPANY LAW

Colin Thomas

Hodder & Stoughton
LONDON SYDNEY AUCKLAND

British Library Cataloguing in Publication Data
Thomas, Colin
 Company law. – 4th ed. – (Teach yourself books).
 1. Great Britain. Companies. Law
 I. Title
ISBN 0 340 58603 6

First printed 1982
Second edition 1985
Third edition 1990
Fourth edition 1993
Impression number   10 9 8 7 6 5 4 3 2
Year   1998 1997 1996 1995 1994 1993

Copyright © 1982, 1985, 1990, 1993 Colin Thomas

All rights reserved. No part of this publication may be reproduced or transmitted in any form or by any means, electronic or mechanical, including photocopy, recording, or any information storage and retrieval system, without permission in writing from the publisher or under licence from the Copyright Licensing Agency Limited. Further details of such licences (for reprographic reproduction) may be obtained from the Copyright Licensing Agency Limited, of 90 Tottenham Court Road, London W1P 9HE.

Typeset by Rowland Phototypesetting Ltd, Bury St Edmunds, Suffolk.
Printed in Great Britain for the educational publishing division of Hodder & Stoughton Ltd, Mill Road, Dunton Green, Sevenoaks, Kent TN13 2YA by Clays Ltd, St Ives plc.

CONTENTS

Preface	ix
Index of Cases	1
Table of Main Statutes	7
1 History and Development	13

The joint stock company. The South Sea Bubble. Company legislation. Company law and community law.

2 Incorporation 23
Forming a company. Companies and partnerships.

3 Company Classification 33

4 Memorandum of Association 44
Form. Content.

5 Articles of Association 57

6 The Promoter 63

7 Raising Capital 68

8 Share Offers 71
Offer of listed securities. Offers of unlisted securities. Offers of shares on admission to an approved exchange. Other offers of shares. Contents of a prospectus. Underwriting. Brokerage.

9	**Liability for False Statements in a Public Offer of Shares**	79
	Civil liability. Exemptions from liability to pay compensation. Negligence. Criminal liability.	
10	**Membership of a Company**	87
	How persons become members. Who may become members? Rights and liabilities of members. Termination of membership. Register of members. Register of interests in shares. The annual return.	
11	**Share Capital**	99
12	**Shares**	111
	Application. Allotment. Certificates. Transfer of shares.	
13	**Dividends**	129
14	**General Meetings**	133
	Types of meeting. Notice of general meeting. Voting at the meeting. Adjournment of general meetings. Resolutions.	
15	**Directors**	152
	Appointment of directors. Power of management. Managing director. Remuneration of directors. Vacation of office.	
16	**Directors' Duties**	165
17	**Directors' Business Interests**	175
	Contracts with the company. Directors' interests in shares or debentures. Insider dealing.	
18	**Majority Rule**	186
	The rule in *Foss v. Harbottle*. Statutory protection of the minority. Investigations of companies and their affairs.	
19	**Borrowing Powers**	199
20	**Debentures**	203
21	**Accounts**	217

CONTENTS

Accounting reference period. The balance sheet. Profit and loss account. Group accounts. Auditors' report. Directors' report.

22 Auditor and Company Secretary — 236
The auditor. The secretary.

23 Compulsory Liquidation — 247
Striking off the register. Winding up by the Court. The liquidator. The creditors. Termination of office of liquidator. Dissolution of the company.

24 Voluntary Liquidation — 267

25 Voluntary Arrangements — 272
Voluntary Arrangements. Administration orders. Powers of administrator. Duties of administrator.

26 The Reconstruction and Amalgamation of Companies — 281
Sale under the memorandum. Reconstruction under Insolvency Act section 110. Scheme of arrangement. Takeovers. Sections 428–430.

27 Mergers and the City Code — 291
Mergers. The City Code on takeovers and mergers.

Index — 299

Abbreviations

CA	Companies Act 1985
CDDA	Company Directors Disqualification Act 1986
CSIDA	Company Securities (Insider Dealing) Act 1985
FSA	Financial Services Act 1986
IA	Insolvency Act 1986

PREFACE

I have often told my students that the study of company law is similar to completing a jigsaw puzzle. Although each piece is looked at separately, at the end of the course the pieces fit into place and the overall picture can be seen. So it is with company law.

My aim in writing this book is to show in as concise a manner as possible how companies are formed, financed, controlled and liquidated. I have quoted many cases, as these illustrate the many facets of company law.

My thanks to my wife, Rita, for her encouragement, patience, and for being such a good listener.

The fourth edition incorporates recent case law and changes effected by the Companies Act 1989, which amends various sections of the Companies Act 1985 and introduces new radical concepts (see page 18).

I trust that this edition reflects my original aim in writing the book and that it will be of assistance to students and of interest to the general reader.

Colin Thomas
January 1993

INDEX OF CASES

Page references are given in bold type

Aaron's Reef v. Twiss [1896] AC 273 **79**
Aberdeen Railway Co v. Blaikie Bros [1854] 1 Macq 461 **175**
Adams v. Cape Industries [1991] 1 ALLER 929 **26**
Alexander v. Automatic Telephone Company [1900] 2 Ch 56 **125**
Allen v. Gold Reefs of West Africa [1900] 1 Ch 656 **59**
Allen v. Hyatt [1914] 30 TLR 444 **167, 169**
Al Saudi Banque v. Clarke Pixley [1990] 2 WLR 344 **241**
Andrews v. Mockford [1896] 1 QB 372 **82**
Arenson v. Casson, Beckman, Rutley and Co [1977] AC 405 **241**
Ashbury Railway Carriage and Iron Co v. Riche [1875] LR 7 HL 653 **49**
Atkins and Co v. Wardle (1889) 58 LJQB 377 **48**
Bahia and San Francisco Railway, Re [1868] LR 3 QB 584 **117, 124**
Baillie v. Oriental Telephone and Electric Co [1915] 1 Ch 503 **138, 187**
Bamford v. Bamford [1970] Ch 212 **168, 169**
Barnett, Hoares and Co v. South London Tramway Co [1887] 18 QBD 815 **246**
Beattie v. E & F Beattie [1938] CL 708 **61**
Bede Steam Ship Co, Re [1917] 1 Ch 123 **119**
Bell Houses v. City Wall Properties [1966] 2 QB 656 **51**
Bloomenthal v. Ford [1897] AC 156 **118**
Bondina Ltd v. Rollaway Shower

— 1 —

Blinds Ltd, [1986] IWLR 517 **48**

Borland's Trustee *v.* Steel Brothers and Co Ltd, [1901] 1 Ch 279 **61**

Boston Deep Sea Fishing and Ice Co *v.* Ansell [1888] 39 Ch D **165**

Bradman *v.* Trinity Estates plc [1989] BCLC 757 **137**

Brinsmead (T. E.) and Sons, *Re* 1897 1 Ch 406 **253**

Brown *v.* British Abrasive Wheel Co Ltd, [1919] 1 Ch 290 **59**

Bugle Press, *Re* [1961] Ch 270 **30**

Bushell *v.* Faith [1970] AC 1099 **141, 162**

Cane *v.* Jones [1980] 124 SJ 542 **147**

Caparo Industries plc *v.* Dickman [1990] 1 All ER 568 **241**

City Equitable Fire Insurance, *Re* [1924] 2 All ER 485 **171**

Clemens *v.* Clemens Bros Ltd, [1976] 2 All ER 268 **188**

Coles *v.* White City (Manchester) Greyhound Assoc. Ltd, [1929] 45 TLR 230 **80**

Company, *Re* A [1986] PCC 296 **191**

Company, *Re* (ex p Broadhurst) [1990] BCLC 384 **191**

Cook *v.* Deeks [1916] IAC 554 **166**

Copal Varnish Co *Re* [1917] 2 Ch 349 **119**

Cotman *v.* Brougham [1918] AC 514 **51**

Cumana Ltd, *Re* [1986] BCLC 430 **192**

Cumbrian Newspapers Group *v.* Cumberland and Westmoreland Newspapers Ltd [1986] 3 WLR 26 **109**

Daimler Co Ltd *v.* Continental Tyre and Rubber Co (GB) Ltd, [1916] 2 AC 307 **28**

Daniels *v.* Daniels [1978] 2 All ER 89 **187**

Derry *v.* Peek [1889] 14 App Cas 337 **81**

DHN Food Distributors Ltd *v.* Tower Hamlet BC [1976] 3 ALLER 462 **29**

Diamond Manufacturing Co Ltd *v.* Hamilton [1969] 2 LR 609 **85**

Duomatic Ltd, *Re* [1969] 2 Ch 365 **162**

Eaton *v.* Robert Eaton Ltd **171**

Edwards *v.* Halliwell [1950] 2 AER 1064 **187**

Eley *v.* Positive Government Security Life Assurance Co [1875] 45 LJQB 451 **61**

Elkington's Case. *Re* Richmond Hill Hotel Co [1867] LR 2 Ch 511 **112**

El Sombrero, *Re* [1958] Ch 900 **139**

English and Colonial Produce Co, *Re* [1906] 2 Ch 435 **66**

Erlanger *v.* New Sombrero Phosphate Co [1878] 3 App Cas 1218 **64**

Esparto Trading Co, *Re* [1879] 12 Ch D 191 **127**

Estmanco (Kilner House) Ltd *v.* Greater London Council [1982] 1 All ER **188**

Europemballage Corpn and Continental Can Co Inc *v.* EC Commission [1973] CMLR 199 (Court of Justice) **293**

Evans *v.* Brunner, Mond and Co Ltd [1921] 1 Ch 359 **52**

Ewing *v.* Buttercup Margarine Co [1917] 2 Ch 1 **47**

Express Engineering Works, *Re* [1920] 1 Ch 466 **147**

Exxon Corporation *v.* Exxon Insurance Consultants Ltd [1982] Ch 119 **47**

Folami *v.* Nigerline (UK) Ltd **170**

Fomento (Sterling Area) *v.* Selsdon Fountain Pen Co [1958] 1 All ER 11 **238**

Foss *v.* Harbottle [1843] 2 Hare 461 **187, 189**

Freeman and Lockyer *v.* Buckhurst Park Properties [1964] 2 QB 480 **201**

Galloway *v.* Hallé Concerts Society [1915] 2 Ch 233 **125**

German Date Coffee Co, *Re* [1882] Ch D 169 **51, 252**

Gerrard (Thomas) and Son Ltd, *Re* [1968] Ch 455 **239**

Gilford Motor Co Ltd *v.* Horne [1933] Ch 935 **30**

Gluckstein *v.* Barnes [1900] AC 240 **64**

Greenhalgh *v.* Arderne Cinemas Ltd [1951] Ch 286 **59**

Guinness Plc *v.* Saunders [1990] 1 WLR 324 **176**

Harmer (H. R.) Ltd, *Re* [1959] 1 WLR 62 **191**

Hedley Byrne Co *v.* Heller and Partners [1964] AC 465 **85**

Hely-Hutchinson *v.* Brayhead Ltd, [1968] 1 QB 549 **200**

Hickman *v.* Kent or Romney Marsh Sheep Breeders Association [1915] 1 Ch 881 **60**

Holdsworth (Harold) and Co Ltd *v.* Caddies [1955] 1 All ER 725 **158**

Horsley and Weight Ltd, *Re* [1982] Ch 442 **52**

Household Fire Insurance Co *v.* Grant [1879] 4 Ex D 216 **112**

Howard *v.* Patent Ivory Manufacturing Co [1888] 38 Ch D 156 **201**

Industrial Development Consultants Ltd *v.* Cooley [1972] 2 All ER 162 **166**

Introductions Ltd, *Re* Introductions Ltd *v.* National Provincial Bank [1970] Ch 199 **50**

Island Export Finance Ltd *v.* Umunna [1986] BCLC 460 **167**

Jones *v.* Lipman [1962] 1 ALL ER 442 **30**

Kaye *v.* Croydon Tramways Co [1898] 1 Ch 358 **138**

Kelner *v.* Baxter [1866] LR 2 CP 174 **66**

Kingston Cotton Mill Co (No 2), *Re* [1896] 2 Ch 279 **240**

Lagunas Nitrate Co v. Lagunas Syndicate [1899] 2 Ch 392 **172**
Lee v. Lee's Air Farming Ltd, [1961] AC 12 **25, 159**
Leeds and Hanley Theatre of Varieties Ltd, *Re* [1902] 2 Ch 809 **65**
Lee Panavision Ltd v. Lee Lighting Ltd [1992] BCLC 22 **168**
Leitch, *Re* [1932] 2 Ch 71 **260**
Lemon v. Austin Friars Investment Trust Ltd, [1926] Ch 1 **203**
Levy v. Abercorris Slate and Slab Co [1887] 37 Ch D 260 **203**
Limpus v. London General Omnibus Co [1862] 1 H & C 526 **26**
Loch v. John Blackwood Ltd, [1924] AC 783 **253**
London and General Bank, *Re* [1895] 2 Ch 166 **239**
London and Northern Bank, *Re* Mack's Claim [1900] WN 114 **162**
London Pressed Hinge Co Ltd, *Re* [1905] 1 Ch 576 **214**
London School of Electronics, *Re* [1986] Ch 211 **193**
McNaughton (James) Ltd v. Hicks Anderson & Co [1991] 2QB 113 **242**
Macaura v. Northern Assurance Co Ltd, [1925] AC 619 **25**
Menier v. Hooper's Telegraph [1874] 9 Ch App 350 **187**
Merchandise Transport v. British Transport Commission [1962] 2 QB 173 **29**

Middlesborough Assembly Rooms Co, *Re* [1880] 14 Ch D 104 **252**
Morgan Crucible v. Hill Samuel Ltd [1991] Ch 295 **242**
Morris v. Kanssen [1946] AC 459 **201**
Moseley v. Koffyfontein Mines [1904] 2 Ch 108 **114, 204**
Natal Land and Colonisation Co v. Pauline Colliery and Development Syndicate [1904] AC 120 **67**
New British Iron Co, *ex p.* Beckwith [1898] 1 Ch 324 **62**
New Finance and Mortgage Co Ltd, *Re* [1975] Ch 420 **51**
New Mashonaland Exploration Co, *Re* [1892] 3 Ch 577 **172**
Ocean Coal Co v. Powell Dyffryn Steam Coal Co [1932] 1 Ch 654 **120**
Opera Photographic Ltd, *Re* [1989] 1WLR 634 **139**
Panorama Developments (Guildford) Ltd v. Fidelis Furnishing Fabrics Ltd [1971] 2 QB 711 **245**
Parke v. Daily News Ltd [1962] Ch 927 **170**
Parker v. McKenna [1874] 10 Ch App 96 **175**
Parsons v. Albert J. Parsons and Sons Ltd **170**
Patent Paper Manufacturing Co, *Re* Addison's Case [1875] 5 Ch App 294 **93**

INDEX OF CASES

Paul (HR) and Son Ltd, *Re* [1935] 1 KB 26 **139**
Pavlides *v.* Jensen [1956] Ch 565 **173, 186**
Payne *v.* Cork Co Ltd, [1900] 1 Ch 308 **284**
Peake and Hall, *Re* [1985] PCC 87 **260**
Peek *v.* Gurney [1873] LR 6 HL 377 **80**
Pender *v.* Lushington [1877] 6 Ch D 70 **189**
Percival *v.* Wright [1902] 2 Ch 421 **168**
Peso Silver Mines *v.* Cropper [1966] 56 DLR 117 **167**
Phonogram Ltd *v.* Lane [1981] 3 All ER 182 **66**
Piercy *v.* Mills and Co [1920] 1 Ch 77 **165**
Produce Marketing Consortium, *Re* [1989] 5 BCC 569 **261**
Prudential Assurance Co Ltd *v.* Newman Industries Ltd, [1979] 3 All Er 507 **189**
R *v.* Kylsant [1932] 1 KB 442 **80, 86**
Ramsgate Victoria Hotel Co *v.* Montefiore [1866] LR 1 Ex 109 **113**
Rayfield *v.* Hands [1960] Ch 1 **61**
Regal (Hastings) Ltd *v.* Gulliver [1942] 1 All ER 378 **166**
Roith (W & M) Ltd, *Re* [1967] 1 WLR 432 **52, 165**
Rolled Steel Product (Holdings) Ltd *v.* British Steel Corporation [1986] ch 246 **50**
Royal British Bank *v.* Turquand [1856] 6 EEB 327 **200**
Ruben *v.* Great Fingall Consolidated [1906] AC 439 **117, 201**
Ryder Installations, *Re* [1966] 1 WLR 524 **251**
Salomon *v.* Salomon and Co [1897] AC 22 **25**
Scott *v.* Scott [1943] 1 All ER 582 **156**
Scottish Co-operative Wholesale Society *v.* Meyer [1959] AC 324 **191**
Sevenoaks Stationers (Retail) Ltd, *Re* [1991] 3 ALLER 578 **155**
Sheffield Corporation *v.* Barclay [1905] AC 392 **118**
Sidebottom *v.* Kershaw, Leese and Co, [1920] 1 Ch 154 **59**
Simmonds *v.* Heffer [1983] BCLC 298 **52**
Simpson *v.* Molson's Bank [1895] AC 270 **95**
Smith and Fawcett, *Re* [1942] Ch 304 **119**
Smith (Howard) Ltd *v.* Ampol Petroleum Ltd [1974] AC 821 **168**
Smith, Stone and Knight Ltd *v.* Birmingham Corporation [1939] 4 All ER 116 **28**
Smith's (John) Tadcaster Brewery, *Re* [1953] Ch 308 **110**
Southern Foundries (1926) Ltd *v.* Shirlaw [1940] AC 701 **60, 159**

Steinberg v. Scala (Leeds) Ltd [1923] 2 Ch 452 **91**
Swaledale Cleaners, Re [1968] 3 All ER 619 **119**
Taupo Totara Timber Co Ltd v. Rowe [1978] AC 537 **163**
Tesco Supermarkets v. Nattrass [1972] AC 153 **27**
Twycross v. Grant [1887] 2 CPD 469 **63**
Underwood (AL) Ltd v. Bank of Liverpool and Martins Ltd [1924] 1 KB 775 **201**
Union Accident Insurance Co Ltd, Re [1972] All ER 1105 **254**
Unit Construction Co Ltd v. Bullock [1960] AC 351 **29**
Vickers and Bott Ltd, Re [1968] 2 All ER 264 **248**
Wall v. London and Northern Assets Corporation [1898] 2 Ch 469 **140**
Wallersteiner v. Moir [1975] QB 373 **189**
Welfab Engineers Ltd, Re [1990] BCLC 833 **262**
Weller (Sam) and Sons Ltd, Re [1990] Ch 682 **192**
West Canadian Collieries Ltd, Re [1962] Ch 370 **137**
White v. Bristol Aeroplane Co Ltd [1953] 1 Ch 65 **110**
Whitechurch (George) v. Cavanagh [1902] AC 117 **245**
Wood v. Odessa Waterworks Co [1889] 42 Ch D 636 **61, 130**
Yenidje Tobacco Co Ltd, Re [1916] 2 Ch 426 **30, 253**
Yorkshire Woolcombers Association, Re [1903] 2 Ch 284 **206**

TABLE OF MAIN STATUTES

Companies Act 1985

Page references are given in bold type.

section 1 **37**	section 26 **46**	section 55 **39**
section 2 **44**	section 28 **46, 48, 145**	section 80 **113, 121, 148**
section 3 **44**	section 29 **46**	
section 3A **50**	section 30 **148, 53**	section 84 **113**
section 4 **53, 145**	section 32 **46, 150**	section 88 **114**
section 5 **54, 193**	section 33 **46, 47**	section 89 **121**
section 6 **54**	section 35 **50, 53**	section 91 **121**
section 7 **58**	section 36 **24**	section 94 **121**
section 9 **59, 145**	section 39 **25**	section 95 **121, 145, 148**
section 10 **153**	section 41 **25**	
section 13 **153**	section 43 **37, 150**	section 97 **78, 115**
section 14 **60**	section 44 **150**	section 99 **113**
section 16 **60**	section 47 **38**	section 100 **114**
section 17 **56, 145**	section 48 **37, 38**	section 101 **113**
section 18 **150**	section 49 **36**	section 102 **114**
section 22 **87**	section 51 **37, 145**	section 103 **114**
section 23 **90**	section 53 **39, 145**	section 104 **150**
section 24 **27, 55**	section 54 **39, 193**	section 110 **174**

— 7 —

section 111 **150**
section 117 **24**
section 120 **145**
section 121 **53, 103**
section 125 **108, 109, 146**
section 127 **193**
section 128 **109, 114**
section 130 **115**
section 131 **115**
section 132 **115**
section 135 **53, 104, 145**
section 136 **105**
section 137 **105**
section 138 **106**
section 139 **105**
section 142 **136**
section 146 **88, 128**
section 147 **150**
section 150 **128**
section 151 **89**
section 153 **89**
section 154 **89**
section 155 **89, 145, 148**
section 156 **90**
section 157 **90, 193**
section 159 **102**
section 160 **102**
section 162 **106, 107**
section 163 **106**
section 164 **106, 148**
section 165 **106, 148**
section 166 **81, 150**
section 167 **107, 148**
section 168 **107**
section 169 **107**
section 171 **107**

section 173 **107, 148**
section 175 **145**
section 176 **108**
section 178 **108**
section 182 **111**
section 183 **119**
section 184 **123**
section 185 **116**
section 186 **116**
section 190 **205**
section 191 **205**
section 192 **211**
section 198 **97**
section 202 **97**
section 203 **96**
section 204 **97**
section 205 **97**
section 206 **97**
section 208 **96**
section 211 **96**
section 212 **193**
section 214 **193**
section 221 **217**
section 222 **217**
section 224 **218**
section 225 **218**
section 227 **218, 220, 225, 230**
section 229 **231**
section 232 **160**
section 233 **217**
section 235 **235, 239**
section 236 **233, 239**
section 237 **233, 239**
section 238 **217**
section 240 **235**
section 245 **109**
section 246 **41, 43**
section 247 **42**

section 251 **218**
section 252 **149**
section 258 **230**
section 263 **131**
section 264 **131**
section 269 **137**
section 270 **131**
section 272 **132**
section 282 **152**
section 283 **244**
section 286 **245**
section 291 **156**
section 293 **154**
section 303 **161**
section 306 **55**
section 307 **145**
section 308 **154**
section 309 **169**
section 310 **174**
section 311 **159**
section 312 **162, 163**
section 313 **163**
section 314 **163**
section 315 **162**
section 316 **163**
section 317 **176**
section 318 **181**
section 319 **181, 148**
section 320 **177**
section 321 **177**
section 322 **178**
section 323 **180**
section 324 **182, 192**
section 325 **183**
section 327 **180, 197**
section 328 **182, 197**
section 330 **178**
section 331 **179**
section 332 **179**

TABLE OF MAIN STATUTES

section 333 **179**
section 334 **180**
section 335 **179**
section 337 **179, 148**
section 338 **179**
section 349 **30, 48**
section 350 **48**
section 352 **95**
section 356 **95**
section 359 **95**
section 360 **126**
section 363 **97, 98**
section 364 **98**
section 366 **134**
section 366A **134,**
se 149 ɿ 431
section 367 **134, 128**
section 368 **135, 193**
section 370 **138, 139**
section 371 **139**
section 372 **142, 143**
section 373 **141, 193**
section 376 **149**
section 377 **149**
section 378 **145, 146**
section 379 **147**
section 379A **148**
section 380 **150**
section 381 **59**
section 381A **148**
section 381B **148**

section 382 **151**
section 383 **151**
section 384 **236**
section 385 **237**
section 385A **237**
section 386 **149, 237, 243**
section 388 **237**
section 389 **238**
section 390 **243**
section 391 **244**
section 395 **208**
section 398 **208**
section 409 **215**
section 425 **136, 284, 285, 286**
section 426 **285**
section 427 **287**
section 428 **30, 94, 287, 288, 289**
section 429 **289**
section 430 **290**
section 431 **194**
section 432 **194**
section 433 **194**
section 434 **195**
section 435 **195**
section 436 **195**
section 437 **195**
section 438 **195**
section 440 **195**
section 442 **196**

section 444 **196**
section 446 **180, 197**
section 447 **197, 198**
section 448 **197, 198**
section 450 **198**
section 451A **197**
section 454 **196**
section 456 **196**
section 459 **190**
section 460 **190**
section 461 **190**
section 651 **248**
section 652 **248**
section 653 **248**
section 654 **248**
section 691 **40**
section 711 **151, 254**
section 714 **46**
section 719 **52, 169, 170**
section 722 **95**
section 727 **174, 243**
section 730 **289**
section 735 **203**
section 736 **28**
section 741 **152**
Schedule 5 **231**
Schedule 6 **160, 164, 207, 231**
Schedule 7 **234**
Schedule 13 **182, 183**
Schedule 15A **148**

Company Directors (Disqualification) Act 1986

section 2 **155**
section 3 **155**
section 4 **155, 260**

section 6 **155**
section 8 **155**
section 10 **155, 260**

section 11 **91, 154**

Company Securities (Insider Dealing) Act 1985

section 1 **183**
section 5 **184**

section 4 **184**
section 9 **184**

section 10 **183**

Financial Services Act 1986

section 47 **86**
section 48 **37**
section 143 **69, 71**
section 144 **71**
section 146 **72**
section 147 **72**
section 148 **72**
section 149 **73**

section 150 **81, 82, 83**
section 151 **85**
section 152 **82**
section 159 **74**
section 160 **75**
section 161 **74, 76**
section 162 **76**
section 165 **77**

section 166 **81, 83**
section 167 **85**
section 168 **82**
section 170 **69**
section 177 **185, 194**
section 178 **185**

Insolvency Act 1986

section 1 **273**
section 2 **273**
section 4 **273**
section 5 **274**
section 6 **274**
section 7 **274**
section 8 **212, 275**
section 9 **212**
section 10 **275**
section 11 **193, 276**
section 12 **276**
section 14 **277**
section 15 **278**
section 17 **278**
section 19 **280**
section 20 **280, 95**
section 21 **278**
section 22 **278**
section 23 **278, 279**
section 24 **278**
section 26 **279**
section 27 **279**
section 30 **213**
section 31 **213**
section 32 **214**
section 38 **215**
section 39 **215**
section 42 **25**
section 44 **44, 214**
section 76 **108**
section 79 **251**
section 84 **146, 267, 150**

section 85 **268**
section 87 **270**
section 88 **270**
section 89 **268**
section 91 **268, 271**
section 93 **268**
section 95 **268**
section 96 **268**
section 98 **268**
section 99 **270**
section 101 **270**
section 105 **270**
section 110 **145, 281, 282, 283, 286**
section 111 **283**
section 122, **30, 145, 251**
section 123 **250, 252**
section 124 **212, 251**
section 127 **254**
section 128 **254**
section 129 **254**
section 130 **254**
section 132 **255**
section 133 **255**
section 135 **254, 256**
section 136 **254, 255**
section 137 **256**
section 139 **256**
section 140 **254, 256**
section 141 **256**
section 144 **254**

section 145 **257**
section 165 **146, 257, 271**
section 167 **257**
section 174 **265**
section 177 **254**
section 178 **262**
section 187 **170**
section 201 **269, 270**
section 202 **249**
section 203 **249**
section 205 **266**
section 212 **173**
section 213 **30, 173, 260**
section 214 **30, 173, 261**
section 216 **48**
section 238 **208, 258**
section 239 **207, 208, 261**
section 240 **207, 208, 262**
section 244 **208, 259**
section 245 **207, 208**
section 315 **92, 123**
section 386 **207, 264**

Schedule 1 **276**
Schedule 4 **257, 271**
Schedule 6 **264**

Other Statutes

Apportionments Act 1970 **160**
Competition Act 1980 **291**
Fair Trading Act 1973 **29, 291**
Forged Transfer Acts
    1891, 1892 **124**
Law of Property Act 1925 **213**
Limitation Act 1980 **168**

Limited Partnership Act
    1907 **31**
Stock Exchange
    (Completion of Bargains)
    Act 1976 **122**
Theft Act 1968 **86**

1
HISTORY AND DEVELOPMENT

The medieval guild was one of the earliest forms of business association. The guilds sought to preserve a monopoly of trade in a particular area by regulating the activities of their members, and were therefore monopolistic and restrictive in character.

With the growth of trade in the Middle Ages traders found it advantageous to combine with one another in trading ventures. They were able to bring together large amounts of capital and they would share in the profits of such ventures. This form of partnership had no legal existence apart from the individual partners, as the property and debts of the partnership were regarded as the property and debts of the individual partnership. Such a partnership ceased to exist on the death of any one partner.

Although the Crown had granted charters to individual companies since the fourteenth century, it was only when the Tudor monarchs granted charters of incorporation to trading companies in the sixteenth century that the movement towards merchant investment and capitalism gained momentum. Companies sought Royal charters in order to obtain a monopoly of trade in certain areas of the world, for example, in Africa and the Indies. The Crown also benefited in that it was able to control trade in these areas.

The joint stock company

Two types of oversea trading companies emerged during this period – the regulated company and the joint stock company.

The earliest form of company was the regulated company, which was a loose association of traders and merchants who traded with their own stock on their own account, for example, the Baltic and the Levant companies. They were, however, subject to the discipline of the governing bodies of these companies.

At a later date there evolved the joint stock company, such as the East India Company and the African Company. Traders operated on a joint stock and each contributed to the merchandise to be sold at the end of the voyage (i.e. the stock) and would share rateably in the profits at the conclusion of the venture.

A considerable amount of capital was raised for financing these ventures. The East India Company, formed to trade with the Indies, attracted £1 500 000 by public subscription for its voyages in 1617.

The incorporated company was seen to possess certain characteristics and advantages. The company's property was under the control of the board of governors or directors; it had a common seal; it was capable of existing in perpetuity; and an individual member was not liable for the debts of the company.

The end of the seventeenth century marked a decline in the number of companies formed for foreign trade, but the number of domestic companies increased. These companies had a permanent fixed capital and encouraged investment by having shares which could be freely sold and transferred. Many of these companies were formed without being incorporated by Royal Charter or Acts of Parliament but merely by executing deeds of settlement. The provisions contained in those deeds were similar to the provisions of incorporated companies.

Other companies purchased the charters of moribund companies and engaged in any venture or trade which appeared profitable – for example, a banking company acquired the charter of the Sword Blade Company which had been incorporated in 1690 to manufacture hollow sword blades.

Another form of enterprise which appeared at the end of the seventeenth century was that of lending money at interest to the State. The

Bank of England was formed in 1694 when the government incorporated a group of its creditors.

The South Sea Bubble

In 1719 the Bank of England was outbid by the South Sea Company which offered £7 500 000 to acquire the whole of the national debt of £31 000 000. The South Sea Company considered that a loan which carried interest, owned by the State, would enable it to raise large sums of money to work its monopoly of the South American trade. In 1720 Parliament passed the Bubble Act which prohibited unincorporated trading companies from acting or presuming to act as corporations. It also prohibited the use of charters other than for the purposes for which they were originally granted. The Act was passed for the benefit of the South Sea Company. It was expected that the prosecution of the four other companies operating with obsolete charters, who were trespassing on the South Sea Company's preserves, would result in more capital being invested in the South Sea Company. These prosecutions led to widespread panic and loss of public confidence. South Sea stock fell in six months from 1000 per cent to 125 per cent. The company was then rescued by government intervention and remained in existence until 1807.

The combined effect of the loss of public confidence and the restrictions contained in the Bubble Act made it almost impossible for companies to raise further capital by public subscription for the next 100 years. During that time capital was obtained almost exclusively from affluent private investors. A few companies were incorporated by special Acts of Parliament from 1760 onwards to finance the construction of canals, and later the construction of railways – between 1758 and 1802 £13 000 000 was subscribed for canal construction.

As the Bubble Act had made the privilege of incorporation too costly or impractical, businessmen had to devise a new form of business association. They formed unincorporated companies which were associations formed by deeds of settlement, under which members agreed to take shares and abide by the regulations. The management of the company was entrusted to directors, and provision was made for the transfer of shares. Although the undertaking thereby had perpetual succession, the Courts treated it as a partnership and its members were liable for its debts. It would appear that there was little litigation relating to these companies in the eighteenth century and that most of the disputes were submitted to arbitration.

The Bubble Act was repealed in 1825, and although it was a purely negative measure it was soon established that unincorporated associations were lawful at common law.

Company legislation

In 1841 a committee, under the chairmanship of W. E. Gladstone, was set up to consider company law reform. Its recommendations led to the passing of the Joint Stock Companies Act 1844, which provided a simple method of incorporation for a joint stock company.

Certain documents giving details of the company's organisation and membership had to be registered with the Register of Joint Stock Companies and were open to public inspection. Although the company could hold property and take legal proceedings in its own name, its members remained personally liable for the company's debts. The 1844 Act provided that a 'full and fair' balance sheet should be presented at the annual general meeting; that an auditor should be appointed to report on the balance sheet; and that an audited balance sheet should be filed with the Registrar.

The Joint Stock Companies Act 1855 introduced the principle of limited liability, despite warnings that such a change would encourage fraud and reckless conduct by promoters and directors. Three-quarters of the company's capital had to have been subscribed, and the company could not continue in business if it lost three-quarters of its capital.

A further Joint Stock Companies Act was passed in 1856, which consolidated the Acts of 1844 and 1855, and thenceforward made company formation simple and inexpensive. A mere seven signatures were required for a document called the *memorandum*, and a company no longer required a deed of settlement. It could register its own articles or adopt a model set of articles which were attached to the Act. Once registered, a certificate of incorporation would be granted and the company could then commence business.

Five other Acts were passed between 1856 and 1862, when the first Companies Act was passed which consolidated the previous Acts relating to companies. Provision was made for guarantee and unlimited companies, and the provisions relating to the winding up of companies were extended. The model set of articles attached to the Act was called Table A.

This remained the principal Act until the Companies Act 1908 which consolidated previous company legislation. Some eighteen Companies Acts had been passed since the Act of 1862, and had introduced various new concepts such as the private company, the auditing and publication of company accounts, the registration of mortgages and requirements dealing with prospectuses.

The next landmark in company legislation is to be found in the 1929 Companies Act. This consolidated previous company legislation and introduced certain modern innovations including the emergence of the redeemable preference share, minority protection rights and accounting provisions dealing with holding and subsidiary companies.

Companies Act 1948 and subsequent legislation

The 1948 Companies Act adopted most of the recommendations of the Cohen Committee on company law amendment, which recommended that information should be readily available to a company's shareholders and creditors, and to the public, and suggested that means should be found to make it easier for shareholders to exercise a greater degree of control over the company's management. Provision was made for greater disclosure in balance sheet and profit and loss accounts, and for group accounts. The Board of Trade was given wider powers for company investigation, whilst minority rights were also extended.

The 1967 Companies Act gave effect to some of the recommendations of the Jenkins Committee on company reform which presented its report in 1962. The exempt private company was abolished, and important new provisions were introduced in connection with company accounts, directors' reports, re-registration of companies, and Department of Trade investigations and inspections.

The 1976 Companies Act amended various accounting provisions and made new provisions for the appointment, qualifications and powers of auditors. It also required a greater degree of disclosure of interests in a company's shares.

The Companies Act 1980 amended certain aspects of company law. New definitions were introduced for public and private companies, and provision made for the registration and re-registration of companies. New requirements were set out for the issue, payment and maintenance of capital. New pre-emption rights were given to shareholders, and provision was made for variation of certain classes of shares. Restrictions were imposed on the distribution of profits and assets, while numerous sections dealt with directors' duties and conflict of interests. 'Insider dealing' became a criminal offence, while new safeguards were introduced to protect the interests of employees and members.

The Companies Act 1981 included provisions dealing with company accounts, thus implementing the European Community's fourth directive. In particular it reduced the amount of information required from small and medium-sized companies when filing their accounts. The arrangements for the approval of company names were simplified. Companies were permitted to purchase their own shares, 'management buy-outs' were facilitated, and restrictions on the use of the share premium account were relaxed, while the law on the disclosure of interests in shares was strengthened. The powers of investigation and enquiry of company inspectors were strengthened and further restrictions imposed on the activities of fraudulent directors.

Companies Act 1985 and recent legislation

The Companies Acts of 1948, 1967, 1976, 1980 and 1981 were consolidated in the 1985 Companies Act. The provisions in the 1980 Act relating to insider dealing are now to be found in a separate Act, the Company Securities (Insider Dealing) Act 1985, while the provisions relating to the use of business names, formerly in the 1981 Act, are now contained in the Business Names Act 1985.

The Insolvency Act 1985 repealed certain sections of the Companies Act 1985 relating to corporate insolvency and introduced new concepts, e.g. administration orders.

The Insolvency Act 1986 repealed its 1985 predecessor and consolidated the provisions relating to winding up, receivership, administration and voluntary arrangements.

The Company Directors Disqualification Act 1986 consolidated the provisions relating to the disqualification of persons from being company directors or otherwise concerned with a company's affairs.

The Financial Services Act 1986 dealt with the regulation of the investment business. This Act was to a large extent based on Professor Gower's review of investor protection and recommendations for legislative reform. It provided regulations for the investment of company securities and new rules for the public issue of shares.

The Companies Act 1989 amended the law relating to company accounts and made new provisions for the appointment of auditors – thus implementing the European Community's seventh and eighth directives. It included new provisions relating to the registration of company charges, the investigation of a company's affairs, the *ultra vires* rule, references to the Monopolies and Mergers Commission, the de-regulation of private companies, and so on.

— Company law and community law —

As a result of becoming a member of the European Community, the United Kingdom has become subject to the provisions of community law which consist of original and amending treaties and secondary legislation.

The most important sources of secondary legislation are regulations, which are binding on the member states 'without further enactment', and directives which are binding in principle, although the member states have to legislate to bring them into operation.

The Council of Ministers of the European Economic Community has approved a number of directives on the harmonisation of company law within the European Community, and other draft directives are under consideration.

The first directive deals with disclosure of information and the validity of obligations entered into by the company. Section 9 of the European Communities Act 1972 (now section 35 Companies Act) gave effect to most of the proposals of the first directive and introduced changes giving protection to third parties dealing with the company and its directors; it also provided for the disclosure of certain documents and information, and regulated pre-incorporation contracts.

COMPANY LAW

The second directive deals with the formation of companies, the maintenance of capital and the increase and reduction of capital. The Companies Act 1980 implemented the second directive.

The third directive deals with the internal mergers of companies. This includes takeovers, mergers by forming a new company, and the takeover of a company by another which is its sole shareholder. This was implemented by the Companies (Mergers and Divisions) Regulations 1987.

The fourth directive deals with the contents of the annual accounts, with particular reference to the balance sheet and profit and loss account. It also deals with the disclosure of financial information. This directive was implemented by the Companies Act 1985.

The fifth draft directive deals with the structure of the limited liability company, with some form of employee participation.

The sixth directive deals with the transfer by a public limited company of its assets and liabilities to a number of companies, within the same member state, in exchange for shares. This was implemented by the Companies (Mergers and Divisions) Regulations 1987.

The seventh and eighth directives on consolidated accounts and the qualifications of auditors have been implemented by the Companies Act 1989.

The proposed ninth directive on the conduct of groups of companies has not been adopted by the EC Commission.

The proposed tenth directive governs mergers between public limited companies in different member states and enables public companies to effect mergers with companies in other states without the need to go into liquidation.

The eleventh directive lays down the requirements for overseas companies establishing a branch in a member state or non EC country. Separate accounts will not be required for branches incorporated in other member states but disclosure will be required in the member state in which the branch is active.

The twelfth directive allows a private limited company to be registered with one member who could be either a natural or legal person. It applies to companies formed and owned by a sole member and to companies whose shares have come to be owned by one shareholder. The sole member or his representatives would exercise the powers of a general meeting and minute decisions he would make.

The proposed thirteenth directive specifies the minimum requirements in the conduct of takeover bids to ensure equal treatment for shareholders. There are also directives on the disclosure of major shareholdings in listed companies, disclosures in company prospectuses, coordinating regulations on insider dealing, while a proposed directive deals with the formation of a European company (see below).

The three directives on Stock Exchange listing, the contents of listing particulars and the supply of information by listed companies have been implemented by the Financial Services Act 1986.

The European Company

The European Commission has published proposals for the creation of a new form of business organisation within the European Community – the European Company. The proposals consist of a Regulation setting out the legal framework for establishing a European Company and a directive requiring member states to establish one form of the proposals for employee participation.

The aim of the proposals is to provide national companies, already operating within several member countries, with a single unified legal framework. Such a company would have the status of a national company in every member state.

It is envisaged that such a company could only be formed when two or more existing companies, registered in different member states, either amalgamate or form a holding company or a joint subsidiary, and would be subject to a European statute covering the major areas of company law. It would have corporate personality, limited liability and a minimum capital of 100 000 ECU in registered bearer shares.

The company would either have a single board of directors with a majority of non-executive directors who delegate the day to day running of the company to executive directors, or a two tier board comprising a management board and a supervisory board. The supervisory board would be appointed by the general meeting and by employees and would not be able to participate in the company's management or represent it in dealings with third parties. It would appoint the management board and would be able to remove its members at any time.

Provision is also made for a large degree of employee participation which would take one of the following forms:

(a) at board level; or
(b) at a separate representative body; or
(c) by a collective agreement.

(a) Participation at board level would involve the election of representatives to the supervisory board (or to the single board) from the whole of the company's workforce within the Community. The employee representation would amount to between one third and one half of the board membership. Certain major decisions, e.g. plant closures, organisational changes, etc., would only be made with the consent of the supervisory board (or the single board).

(b) A separate representative body would have similar rights as in *(a)* to information and consultation.

(c) Any other form of employee participation agreed upon by a company and its employees which would give the same rights to consultation and information as *(a)* or *(b)*.

2
INCORPORATION

Forming a company

A company is formed by delivering certain documents to the Registrar of Companies and paying certain fees and stamp duties.

The documents which must be delivered are:

(a) a memorandum of association;
(b) the articles of association (unless the company intends to adopt Table A as the company's articles);
(c) a statutory declaration by either a solicitor engaged in the formation of the company, or by a director or secretary of the company that requirements as to registration have been complied with;
(d) a statement of the intended situation of the company's registered office;
(e) a statement containing the names and particulars of the first directors and first secretaries of the company.

If a company is formed as a public company it must deposit further documents to satisfy the Registrar that it meets the capital requirements of public companies, that is that the amount of share capital stated in its memorandum is not less than the authorised minimum – an allotted share capital of £50 000.

The Registrar will sign and issue a certificate of incorporation if he is satisfied that the documents are in order. He must also publish in the *Gazette* a notice of the issue of a certificate of incorporation. The issue of this certificate is conclusive evidence that the requirements in respect of registration have been complied with, and that the company is duly registered under the Act. If the certificate contains a statement that the company is a public company, this is conclusive evidence of that fact.

A private company can commence business immediately upon receipt of a certificate of incorporation.

A public company is prohibited from doing business or exercising any borrowing powers unless the Registrar has issued an additional certificate that the company's allotted share capital is not less than the authorised minimum, and the company has received at least one quarter of the nominal value of each issued share, plus the whole of any premium payable on such a share (section 117). If a company enters into a transaction or exercises its borrowing powers without a section 117 certificate the transaction is valid but the company and any officer of the company in default is guilty of an offence. If a company fails to meet its obligations under such a transaction, within 21 days of being requested to do so by the other party, the company's directors are jointly and severally (collectively and individually) liable to indemnify the other party for any loss or damage resulting from the company's failure to meet those obligations (section 117).

The seal

A company may enter into contracts in the same way as a private individual – orally, in writing if the contract is required to be in writing, or if the contract is required to be made by deed, it may be made under the company's common seal. A company, however, need not have a common seal and a document signed by a director and secretary, or by two directors, and expressed to be executed by the company has the same effect as if issued under seal. If a document makes clear that it is intended to be a deed it takes effect as a deed (sections 36, 36A).

Only certain documents are required to be under seal. They are deeds, contracts which have to be in the form of a deed if entered into by a private individual, share certificates and share warrants.

A document requiring authentication by a company need not be under its seal. It may be signed by a director, secretary or other authorised officer (section 41).

A company whose objects include transacting business in foreign countries may, if authorised by its articles, have an official seal for use in any place outside the United Kingdom. This is a facsimile of the company seal, with the addition on its face of the name of the place where it is to be used (section 39).

The consequences of incorporation

From the date of incorporation a company becomes a body corporate or corporation. It is an artificial legal person with rights and duties distinct from its members or shareholders. This was established in the nineteenth century in the case of *Salomon v. Salomon and Co.*. Salomon was a prosperous leather merchant living in Leicester who sold his business to a limited company, formed for the purpose, for £39 000. Salomon was given 20 000 £1 shares, debentures to the value of £10 000 and the balance in cash. His wife and five children were given one share each. A year later the business foundered with assets of £6000 and liabilities of £17 500, of which £10 000 was owed to Salomon for the debentures. (In a winding up, a debenture holder is paid in priority to unsecured creditors.) The unsecured creditors claimed that as Salomon Ltd was in reality the same person as Salomon, their debts should be paid first. It was held that Salomon was entitled to the £6000, as the company had been validly formed and was therefore an independent legal person. The business belonged to the company, that is to Salomon Ltd and not to Salomon.

In *Lee v. Lee's Air Farming Ltd*, Lee held 2999 of the company's 3000 shares. He was the company's governing director and was also employed as the company's chief pilot at a salary to be determined by himself. He was killed in an air crash and it was held that his widow was entitled to compensation as her husband was employed by the company.

In *Macaura v. Northern Assurance Co.*, Macaura formed a company and sold his timber estate to the company, receiving shares as payment for the sale. However, he insured the timber in his own name. A fire destroyed most of the timber and it was held that he could not claim under his policy as the timber was owned by the company.

In *Adams v. Cape Industries plc* a company and its subsidiaries were incorporated in the United Kingdom. The plaintiff who had been injured by exposure to asbestos dust in a factory to which the company had supplied asbestos, sought to enforce in England a US judgment. He could only succeed if he could show that the company had been present in the USA when proceedings commenced. The company marketed asbestos in the USA through a US subsidiary and an independent Illinois corporation. It was held that he could not succeed as the presence of the subsidiary and the independent corporation could not be treated as that of the defendant company.

A corporation also has perpetual succession in that its existence is maintained by new members who replace those who have died or transferred their interests. Should the membership fall below the statutory minimum of two, the company continues in existence. In such a case application may be made to the Court to convene a meeting of the company.

Certain consequences follow from this fictional legal personality of a company. A company may enter into contracts in the same way as a natural person, provided that it is not acting *ultra vires* (i.e. beyond its powers). If a contract is required to be under seal, that is in the form of a deed, a company's seal has to be affixed. If a contract is required to be in writing, a person acting under the company's authority may sign the contract. Should it be an oral contract, a duly authorised person may contract on the company's behalf.

A company may be a founder member, shareholder, director, secretary, manager and auditor of another company. It may also be a partner in a partnership, and a partnership may be formed where all the partners are companies.

A company has the capacity to commit torts, or civil wrongs, and is liable for the torts of its employees or agents as long as they are acting in the course of their employment (i.e. vicarious liability). In *Limpus v. London General Omnibus Co.*, the drivers of the horse drawn buses had been expressly forbidden by their employer, the company, to race against buses of other companies. In one race, a bus overturned and Limpus and other passengers were injured. Nevertheless, the company was liable.

INCORPORATION

It is uncertain if a company is liable for the torts of an employee whose acts are *ultra vires* the company. This can only arise if the company has expressly authorised those acts. A widely held view is that the company is not liable as it cannot authorise an act which is beyond its powers. A company may also be prosecuted for the crimes of its employees, if the statute imposes liability on the employer as well as on the employees, despite the fact that the offences have required *mens rea* (i.e. a guilty mind) which the company, as an abstract personality, could not have and which the board of directors did not have. Nevertheless, in recent cases, the Courts have held that an act cannot impose criminal liability on a company unless the person or persons who manage its affairs are directly participating in the criminal act. In *Tesco Supermarkets v. Nattrass* a shop manager charged an old age pensioner the full price for a box of washing powder, despite the fact that the company had advertised the powder at a lower price. The company was held not liable under the Trade Descriptions Act, as the manager, according to Lord Denning, was one of the hands of the company and not part of its brain.

There are obviously certain crimes which a company *cannot* commit, such as perjury, bigamy, and offences for which the only punishment is imprisonment. A company *can* be charged with a variety of offences such as conspiracy to defraud, using a motor vehicle on a road contrary to the Road Traffic Act 1972, and offences under the Unsolicited Goods and Services Act 1971.

Lifting the veil of incorporation

A result of incorporation is that a veil is drawn between the persons dealing with a company and its members. Proceedings may not be taken against the members by third parties, as a company is 'a legal person just as much as an individual'.

However, the Courts have not hesitated to lift the veil of incorporation and examine the realities of a company's ownership and control if the need should arise. It has been lifted in the following cases:

If the number of members of a company falls below two, and the company carries on business for more than six months, the remaining member (if aware of it) is liable for the payment of the company's debts contracted after the six month period (section 24).

If control of a company registered in England is believed to be in enemy hands, it may be necessary to examine the reality of the situation. In *Daimler Co. Ltd v. Continental Tyre and Rubber Co.*, the members of the company were a company incorporated in Germany, and five other individuals. Four of the individuals were German and the other, a British subject, held one share out of the total 25 000. It was held that the company would be regarded as an enemy company.

Where one company is a holding company and it has a subsidiary or subsidiaries, the Court may decide that the subsidiary is an agent for the holding company. In *Smith, Stone and Knight Ltd v. Birmingham Corporation* certain premises were owned by a subsidiary of the parent company. The parent company had complete control of the subsidiary and kept its books and accounts. Only the holders of annual tenancies were entitled to compensation if their property was compulsorily acquired. Although it was the subsidiary that had the annual tenancy, it was nevertheless held that the parent company was entitled to compensation.

The Courts will lift the veil to determine whether one company is a subsidiary of another. Section 736 stipulates that a company is a subsidiary if the first company:

(a) holds a majority of the voting rights in the second company;
(b) is a member of the second company and has the right to appoint or remove a majority of its board of directors; or
(c) is a member of the second company, and alone controls a majority of its voting rights, because of an agreement with the other shareholders or members (section 736).

New definitions of holding and subsidiary companies are used for accounting purposes (see page 229).

The relationship of a holding company to its subsidiary is of importance in certain instances. As a general rule a subsidiary may not hold shares in its holding company. If a company has a subsidiary or subsidiaries, it must lay group accounts before the general meeting together with its own balance sheet and profit and loss accounts. An inspector appointed by the Department of Trade to investigate a company's affairs may investigate the affairs of a related company, either a subsidiary or holding company as applicable.

In certain instances the courts have recognised group enterprises despite the separate interests of individual companies within the group.

In *DHN Food Distributors v. Tower Hamlets Borough Council* a company carried on business through two subsidiaries. One subsidiary owned the premises from which the business was conducted while the other dealt with the distribution of goods. The holding company and the subsidiaries had the same directors. The local authority compulsorily purchased the business property and the three companies went into liquidation. It was held that compensation should be paid to the group as the companies should be regarded as carrying on business as a single economic entity.

The Courts will lift the veil in some revenue cases in order to establish in what country a company is resident, and where its management lies. In *Unit Construction Co. Ltd v. Bullock*, a United Kingdom company had three Kenyan subsidiaries which were, in theory, completely separate from the parent company. The parent company nevertheless controlled their activities, although it had no constitutional right to do so. It was held that, for tax purposes, the Kenyan subsidiaries were resident in the United Kingdom where their control and management were located.

The veil of incorporation is lifted if a proposed merger has to be examined by the Courts. Under the Fair Trading Act a merger arises if two or more enterprises cease to be distinct enterprises in that they are brought under common ownership or common control, or one of them ceases to be carried on at all, as a result of an agreement to prevent competition between the enterprises. Although the EEC Treaty does not expressly provide for a system of merger control, the Commission and the Court of Justice have taken the view that Article 86 may in certain circumstances be used to control mergers. Article 86 prohibits any abuse by any undertaking of its dominant position within the Common Market in so far as it may affect trade between member states. Secondary legislation has also decreed that a holding company and its subsidiary should be treated as an economic unit.

Occasionally the device of incorporation has been used for some improper or illegal purpose and the courts have lifted the veil. In *Merchandise Transport v. British Transport Commission*, a transport company applied for licences through its subsidiary company as it was unlikely to obtain these licences if it applied in its own name. It intended transferring its vehicles to its subsidiary. The Court refused to treat the application as one by the subsidiary, as it regarded the subsidiary and its holding company as one commercial entity.

The courts will also lift the veil where an individual attempts to shelter behind the concept for the purposes of fraud. In *Gilford Motor Co. Ltd v. Horne*, an employee covenanted that after leaving the firm he would not solicit his previous employer's customers. Shortly after leaving his employment he formed a company with his wife and one other person, and this company sent out circulars to his previous employer's customers. The Court granted an injunction against the ex-employee and his company. In *Jones v. Lipman* an individual who had entered into an agreement to sell land attempted to avoid the contract by transferring the land to a company in which he was the controlling shareholder. It was held that a decree of specific performance would be granted compelling him to fulfil his obligations as the company was 'a device and a sham'.

The Courts will prevent an abuse of section 428, by prohibiting the formation of a new company by members holding 90 per cent of the shares in the existing company, if the new company is formed solely to expropriate the shares of minority shareholders (*Re Bugle Press*).

The Courts will also, in certain instances, have regard to the substance of an association rather than its particular form. This applies especially to small private companies which are founded on a personal relationship between their members. Some are to all intents 'partnerships' which are formed as companies. The Court may, if the personal relationship between members has foundered or soured, order such a company to be wound up under the just and equitable clause of IA section 122g (*Re Yenidje Tobacco Co. Ltd*).

A liquidator of an insolvent company may apply to the court to declare that a director contribute to a company's assets in that he knew or ought to have known before the company's liquidation that there was no prospect of avoiding insolvent liquidation and that the director failed to take steps to minimise the loss to the creditors (1A 214).

A person may be guilty of fraudulent trading if in the course of liquidation it appears that the company's business has been carried on with intent to defraud creditors or for any fraudulent purpose. The persons responsible may be liable to make such contributions to the company's assets as the court thinks proper (1A section 213).

An officer of a company who signs a bill of exchange, cheque, promissory note or order for money or goods may incur personal liability if the company's name is omitted or incorrectly mentioned (section 349).

INCORPORATION

Companies and partnerships

The characteristics and attributes of a company can be conveniently compared with an alternative form of business association, the partnership.

A company is a corporation, a separate legal person, while a partnership is no more than the sum of its members. Although a partnership can sue and be sued in its own name, it is the partners who are liable for the firm's debts and contracts. The debts and contracts of a company are those of the company, and not its members.

The members of a company are not its agents and may not enter into contracts on a company's behalf, although its directors are limited agents. A partner is normally an agent for the partnership and may bind the firm by his acts. A member of a company may enter into a contract with a company, but a partner is not permitted to make a contract with the firm.

Shares in a company are freely transferable, unless a company's articles decree otherwise. A partner cannot transfer his shares in a firm without the consent of the other partners. A partner may assign his share in a firm, but the assignee does not become a partner and is merely entitled to the assigning partner's share of the profits. Different rights can also be attached to different classes of shares issued by companies. This degree of flexibility is not found in partnerships, although certain partners may be given certain rights and powers in a partnership agreement, for example to purchase a deceased partner's share. A company may now purchase the shares of its members.

A limited company is subject to rules regarding the raising and maintenance of its share capital, which can only be increased or reduced in accordance with the provisions of the Companies Acts. Partners may alter the amount of capital in a partnership without any such restrictions.

The property of a company is vested in the company. Partnership property belongs to the partners and any change in the constitution of the partnership, such as on death or retirement of a partner, is a change in the ownership of the partnership property.

The liability of a member of a company may be limited either by shares or by guarantee. The liability of a partner for the partnership debts is unlimited, with the exception of a limited partner under the Limited Partnerships Act 1907.

A company's powers are determined by the objects clause in its memorandum of association and by the Companies Acts in general. The doctrine of *ultra vires* does not apply to partners, who may carry on any activity which the partners have agreed to enter into, as long as it is legal.

A company must have a minimum of two members. There is no maximum. Partnerships may not consist of more than twenty partners, with the exception of partnerships of certain groups of professional men, such as solicitors, accountants, consulting engineers, stockbrokers and surveyors.

A company has perpetual succession so that any circumstance affecting a member – insanity, death, bankruptcy – does not directly affect the life of a company. On the death or bankruptcy of a partner the partnership is automatically dissolved. A partnership may also be dissolved at any time by a partner, unless entered into for a fixed time, but no one member of a company may wind up a company.

If an insolvent company is wound up, this does not make its members bankrupt; but the bankruptcy of a partnership means the bankruptcy of every partner (except for a limited partner).

A company's accounts are open to inspection by the general public, with the exception of the accounts of an unlimited company; partnership accounts are never subject to public scrutiny.

There are fewer formalities to be observed with partnerships, as a partnership agreement may be in the form of a deed, in writing, oral or even implied by conduct. In forming a company, certain documents must be delivered to the Registrar, and stamp duty, registration fees and legal costs are payable.

3
COMPANY CLASSIFICATION

The modern company is a form of business organisation which has proved attractive to businessmen and investors seeking the benefits of incorporation and limited liability. The present statutes governing companies are the Companies Act 1985, the Insolvency Act 1986, the Company Directors Disqualification Act 1986 and the Financial Services Act 1986. References in this book to the Act and to sections are references to the Companies Act 1985. References to other Acts are stated as such.

The Act recognises five main types of companies:

1. chartered
2. statutory
3. registered
4. oversea
5. partnership

1 Chartered companies

Chartered companies are incorporated by the grant of a charter from the Crown. In previous centuries trading concerns were granted royal charters and some of these companies are still in existence at the present time – for example, the Hudson Bay Company was granted a charter by Charles II in 1670, while the Bank of England was granted a charter in 1694. The Stock Exchange Year Book lists seven chartered companies. Charters are now used to incorporate non-commercial bodies, universities and colleges.

There is no restriction on the number of members in this type of company, and unless otherwise stated, the members are not personally liable for the company's contracts. The creditors' remedy lies against the company.

2 Statutory companies

These companies are formed by special Acts of Parliament. This method of company formation was frequently used in the past for the formation of public utilities such as railway, gas, canals, electricity and water companies. These companies often required special powers, such as compulsory purchase of land, and were usually granted a monopoly in a particular locality. As a result of nationalisation most statutory companies have been taken over by Public Boards, and by Corporations set up by Public Acts. Of the fifty-two remaining statutory companies quoted on the Stock Exchange, twenty-eight are water companies.

A statutory company must have a minimum of two members. A member whose shares are not fully paid up may be liable for the company's debts if the company has insufficient assets to satisfy its creditors.

3 Registered companies

These are companies formed under the Act or one of the earlier Companies Acts. A registered company may or may not have a share capital, for although a share capital is essential for a trading company it may not be required by other companies.

The Act provides for three basic types of registered company: *(a)* companies limited by guarantee, *(b)* unlimited companies, *(c)* companies limited by shares; and two forms of company: public and private companies.

(a) Companies limited by guarantee

A company limited by guarantee has 'the liability of its members limited by the memorandum to such amount as the members may . . . undertake to contribute to the assets of the company in the event of its being wound up'. It may be either a private or a public company.

Such a company is usually formed by trade associations, professional associations, clubs and societies who wish to obtain the advantages of incorporation without incurring personal liability. A large number of guarantee companies obtain dispensation by making a statutory declaration and are permitted to register their name without the addition of the word 'limited'.

It is similar to a share company (see below) in that it has legal personality, and that the liability of its members is limited. It differs in that a member of a share company may be called upon at any time during the existence of the company to pay the amount outstanding on his share, while a member in a guarantee company may be called upon to honour his guarantee only if the company is wound up and is unable to meet its debts.

A past member may be liable if he ceased to be a member within a year of the commencement of the winding up, but only for the debts and liabilities contracted by the company before he ceased to be a member.

The amount of the guarantee must be stated in the memorandum and is frequently as little as £1, although it may be greater.

A guarantee company does not usually have a share capital. Its memorandum and articles must correspond with the form set out in Table C of the Act and it must register its articles of association. A guarantee company having a share capital usually requires this initial capital to purchase business premises. Its memorandum and articles must correspond with Table D. Shareholders of such a guarantee company will have a twofold liability, to pay for their shares and to honour their guarantee in the event of the company being wound up.

A guarantee company formed before 1981 could be either a public or a private company and could be formed with or without share capital. Since 1980 no company may be formed as, or become, a guarantee company with a share capital.

The provisions of the Act apply to guarantee companies unless specifically excluded.

(b) Unlimited companies

This type of company is defined as 'a company not having any limit on the liability of its members'. Every member is liable for the debts contracted by the company while a member but the liability will only arise if the company is wound up and is unable to meet its debts. It is possible for the members to restrict or even avoid liability through the company's issuing of a policy, or entering into a contract. The result is that the members' liability is restricted, or the company's funds alone are liable in respect of the policy or contract. All unlimited companies are private companies.

Unlimited companies are comparatively rare, but they are the only permitted forms of company for certain types of business organisations e.g. membership of the Stock Exchange.

An unlimited company:

(i) need not file its accounts, directors' and auditors' reports with the Registrar, so keeping its financial affairs private;
(ii) may purchase its own shares.

These two advantages are now of minor importance as the accounting provisions for small and medium-sized companies allow modified accounts to be filed and since 1981 all companies are allowed to purchase their own shares.

Unlimited companies may be formed with or without a share capital. If a company has a share capital it must submit an annual return. Its articles must correspond with Table E of the Act.

An unlimited company is not governed by the rules relating to the alteration of capital as are the other types of companies, so that it may reduce its capital (if it has a share capital) and pay back share capital to its members without restriction.

A share company or a guarantee company may be re-registered as an unlimited company. All the members must consent and the memorandum and articles must be altered. After all the formalities have been completed, a new certificate of incorporation will be issued by the Registrar, and a notice published in the *Gazette* (section 49).

The converse is allowed, and an unlimited company may re-register as either a company limited by guarantee, or limited by shares (see below). The steps to be taken are the same as for re-registration of limited to unlimited, except that the consent of all the members is not required, only that of 75 per cent of the membership (i.e. sufficient to pass a special resolution) (section 51). An unlimited company seeking to re-register as a public company must first re-register as a private limited company with a share capital and then re-register as a public company. Both steps may be undertaken in one process (sections 43–48).

(c) Companies limited by shares

A company limited by shares has 'the liability of its members limited by the memorandum to the amount, if any, unpaid on the shares held by them'. No further liability attaches to the holder of a fully paid share. Should the company become insolvent, he will not be required to contribute to the payment of its debts.

Public and private companies

The promoters of a company will have to decide whether a company should be formed as a private or a public company. A private company does not require a large amount of capital and is therefore suitable for small businesses and family concerns. It cannot seek public investment for its shares, but is not subject to the capital requirements of a public company.

Definitions

A *public company* must:

(i) state in its memorandum that it is a public company;
(ii) end its name with the designations 'public limited company' or 'plc', or their Welsh equivalents;
(iii) have a minimum share capital of £50 000 (section 1(3)).

A *private company* is any company that is not a public company (section 1(3)).

Since 22 December 1980, no company may be formed as a guarantee company with a share capital (section 1(4)). Therefore all public companies formed in the future will be companies limited by shares.

Re-registration of a private company as a public company

A private company may re-register as a public company, as may an unlimited company. It may do so by passing a special resolution to alter its memorandum and articles to conform with the requirements of a public company. An application for re-registration, signed by a director or the company secretary, is delivered to the registrar accompanied by the following documents:

(a) a printed copy of the altered memorandum and articles;
(b) a copy of a written statement by the company's auditors that in their opinion the balance sheet shows that at the balance sheet date the amount of the company's net assets was not less than the aggregate of its called up share capital and undistributable reserves;
(c) a copy of the balance sheet (prepared not more than seven months before the application) together with an unqualified report by the company's auditors;
(d) a copy of any report relating to the valuation of a non-cash asset accepted as payment or part payment for shares;
(e) a statutory declaration by a director or secretary that:
 (i) the special resolution has been passed,
 (ii) the nominal value of the company's allotted share capital is not less than the authorised minimum, i.e. £50 000,
 (iii) every allotted share has been paid up to at least one quarter of its nominal value,
 (iv) any required valuation of a non-cash asset has been properly carried out,
 (v) between the date of the balance sheet and the application for re-registration, there has been no change in the company's financial position which has resulted in the amount of its net assets falling below the aggregate of its called up share capital and undistributable reserves.

If the Registrar is satisfied that the application and declaration are in order he will then issue the company with a certificate of incorporation stating that it is a public company. The certificate is conclusive evidence that all requirements of the Act regarding re-registration have been complied with and that the company is a public company (section 47).

A similar procedure, with slight modifications, is followed for the re-registration of an unlimited company as a public company (section 48).

Re-registration of a public company as a private company

A public company may re-register as a private company by:

(a) passing a special resolution that it should be re-registered;
(b) delivering an application to the Registrar together with a printed copy of the memorandum and articles as altered by the resolution. The application must be signed by a director or the company secretary (section 53).

If the Registrar is satisfied that the application and the documents are in order he will issue the company with an appropriate certificate of incorporation which is conclusive evidence that the requirements of re-registration have been complied with and that the company is a private company (section 55).

Minority shareholders may apply to the court to cancel a resolution for the re-registration of a public company. The application must be made:

(i) within 28 days of the resolution being passed;
(ii) by shareholders holding five per cent of the company's issued share capital or any class of capital;
(iii) by not less than five per cent of the company's members if the company is not limited by shares;
(iv) by not less than 50 of the company's members.

A person who has voted in favour of, or consented to, the resolution may not make an application (section 54). The court may make an order confirming or cancelling the resolution or confirming it on such terms and conditions as it thinks fit. It may also provide for the purchase by the company of the shares of any member and for the resulting reduction of capital and the alteration of the memorandum and articles. If an application is made to the court by a minority opposing the re-registration of the company, the company must notify the Registrar. When the court order is made the company must then deliver, within 15 days, an office copy of the order to the Registrar (section 54).

Characteristics of public and private companies

Some of the characteristics of a *public company* are as follows.

(a) A public company may be registered with only two members.
(b) It must have a minimum capital of £50 000.
(c) It cannot commence business or borrow until section 117 is complied with, and the Registrar has issued a certificate.
(d) It must have a minimum of two directors, unless it was registered before 1 November 1929, in which case one director is sufficient.
(e) Directors, other than the first directors, have to be voted into office individually at a general meeting.
(f) Directors must, unless otherwise resolved, retire at the age of seventy.
(g) At a general meeting proxies are allowed to vote but, unless the articles provide otherwise, are not allowed to address the meeting.
(h) No distribution of the company assets may be made if it results in the value of the assets being below that of its liabilities and capital.
(i) Its secretary must have the requisite knowledge, experience and an appropriate qualification.
(j) If the net assets of the company fall to half of its called up share capital, an extraordinary general meeting must be summoned.

A *private company* must also have a minimum of two members. There is no upper limit on the number of members it may have.

(a) It needs only one director, and a director need not retire at the age of seventy unless the company is a subsidiary of a public company.
(b) At a general meeting, proxies may not only attend and vote but may also address the meeting.
(c) It cannot, however, offer its shares or debentures to the public and its articles will usually restrict the right to transfer its shares.
(d) It may provide financial assistance to a person to enable him to purchase its shares.

4 Oversea companies

These are companies incorporated outside Great Britain who establish a place of business within Great Britain (section 691). For the purpose of this section Great Britain is defined as England, Wales and Scotland, but not the Channel Islands or the Isle of Man. Certain provisions of the Act apply to these companies. An oversea company incorporated in the Channel Islands or Isle of Man is known as an *island company*.

Within one month of establishing a place of business within Great Britain, such a company must file with the Registrar:

(a) a certified copy of its charter or memorandum and articles;
(b) a list of directors and secretary;
(c) the name and address of at least one person resident in Great Britain authorised to accept service of process on behalf of the company.

If any alteration is made in any of the above particulars, the company must notify the Registrar. In every place where it carries on business, an oversea company must exhibit its name and the name of the country in which it is incorporated. If it is a limited company, it must also state this outside every place of business. This information must also appear on all the company's letters, notices and official publications.

An oversea company must prepare accounts. If the company is a holding company it must also prepare group accounts in such a form as if it were incorporated in Great Britain. Copies of these accounts must be delivered to the Registrar. This does not apply if the form of the company is such that it would be regarded as an unlimited company if it were incorporated in Great Britain.

5 Partnership companies

The Secretary of State for Trade and Industry may by regulations prescribe Table G, containing articles of association for a partnership company, i.e. a company limited by shares whose shares are intended to be held to a substantial extent by, or on behalf of, its employees.

Accounting classification

A company may be classified for accountancy purposes as a small or medium-sized company (section 246).

(a) A small company is a company which satisfies two of the following conditions:

(i) Its turnover must not exceed £2 000 000;
(ii) Its balance sheet total must not exceed £975 000;
(iii) The average number of employees, in a financial year, does not exceed 50.

It is not required to file a profit and loss account or directors' report, and only has to file an abbreviated version of its balance sheet (section 247).

(b) A medium-sized company is one which satisfies two of the following conditions:

(i) Its turnover must not exceed £8 000 000;
(ii) Its balance sheet total must not exceed £3 900 000;
(iii) The average number of employees, in a financial year, does not exceed 250.

It has to file a full balance sheet and directors' report, but is only required to file a modified profit and loss account, which does not disclose turnover and gross profit margin (section 247).

A private group which satisfies certain criteria does not have to prepare group accounts.

To qualify as a small group, it must meet two of the following requirements:

(i) Its aggregate turnover must not exceed £2 million net (or £2.4 million gross);
(ii) Its aggregate balance sheet total must not exceed £1 million net (or £1.2 million gross);
(iii) The aggregate number of employees must not exceed 50.

To qualify as a medium-sized group, it must meet two of the following requirements;

(i) Its aggregate turnover must not exceed £8 million net (or £9.6 million gross);
(ii) Its aggregate balance sheet total must not exceed £3.9 million net (or £4.7 million gross);
(iii) The aggregate number of employees does not exceed 250.

Dispensation will not be granted if any of the members of the group is a public, banking, insurance or investment company.

COMPANY CLASSIFICATION

(c) Companies which do not satisfy the small or medium-sized criteria, public companies, and insurance, banking and investment companies must prepare their accounts fully in accordance with the Act (section 246).

4
MEMORANDUM OF ASSOCIATION

A company's memorandum is a document which outlines a company's constitution and defines the scope of a company's powers. It is in effect a company's charter and regulates a company's relationship with the outside world. It is filed with the Registrar on a company's incorporation and may be inspected by any member of the public.

Form

The form and requirements of the memorandum are set out in sections 2 and 3 and consists of six basic clauses.

1   The company's name with 'limited' as the last word, if it is a private limited company or a company limited by guarantee. If it is a public limited company, the name must end with the words 'public limited company'. A company whose registered office is to be found in Wales may use the words 'cyfyngedig' for limited and 'cwmni cyfyngedig cyhoeddus' for public limited company. The permitted abbreviations are ltd, plc, cyf. and c.c.c.

MEMORANDUM OF ASSOCIATION

2 The country in which the registered office will be situated. This establishes a company's domicile.
3 The objects of the company.
4 In the case of a limited company, a declaration that the members' liability is limited.
5 The amount of the share capital and its division into shares of a fixed sum. This does not apply to unlimited companies and to companies not having a share capital.
6 The memorandum concludes with an association clause and must be signed by a minimum of two subscribers. Each states against his name the number of shares he takes.

Table F of the Companies (Tables A-F) Regulations 1985 illustrates the form of a memorandum of association of a public company limited by shares.

---

1 The company's name is 'Western Electronics Public Limited Company'.
2 The company is to be a public company.
3 The company's registered office is to be situated in England and Wales.
4 The company's objects are the manufacture and development of such descriptions of electronic equipment, instruments and appliances as the company may from time to time determine, and the doing of all such other things as are incidental or conducive to the attainment of that object.
5 The liability of the members is limited.
6 The company's share capital is £5 000 000 divided into 5 000 000 shares of £1 each.

We, the subscribers to this memorandum of association, wish to be formed into a company pursuant to this memorandum; and we agree to take the number of shares shown opposite our respective names.

Name and Addresses of Subscribers	**Number of shares taken by each Subscriber**
1 James White, 12 Broadmead, Birmingham.	1
2 Patrick Smith, 145A Huntley House, London Wall, London EC2.	1
Total shares taken	2

Dated   19//
Witness to the above signatures,
Anne Brown, 13 Hute Street, London WC2.

Content

Company name

A company's promoters are free to choose whatever name they please for a company, subject to certain statutory and common law limitations. The Registrar keeps an index of the names of existing companies (section 714) and a company may not be registered with a name which is similar to that of an existing company appearing on the index. The Registrar is also prohibited from registering a company by a name:

(a) which includes ltd, plc or unlimited other than at the end of the name;
(b) which is the same as a name already on the index;
(c) which is offensive;
(d) which would, by its use by a company, constitute a criminal offence (section 26).

Except with the approval of the Secretary of State, a company may not register a name which suggests a connection with the government or with a local authority. The Secretary of State may also specify that the use of certain words or expressions, as part of a company's name, requires his prior approval (section 29).

If the Secretary of State is of the opinion that a company has registered a name which is too like an existing name in the index, he may within twelve months direct the company to change its name. If a company has provided misleading information in order to register a particular name, the Secretary of State may, within five years of registration, direct the company to change its name. A company may also be directed to change its name when a name has been registered which gives so misleading an indication of the company's activities as to be likely to cause harm to the public (sections 28 and 32). The company may appeal to the court against such a decision.

Any person who is not a public company commits an offence if he carries on any trade business or profession under a name which includes, as its last part, 'public limited company' (or Welsh equivalent) (section 33(1)).

A public company commits an offence if, in circumstances in which the fact that it is a public company is likely to be material to any person, it uses a name which may reasonably be expected to give the impression that it is a private company (section 33(2)).

An action is also available at common law to an 'existing' company to seek an injunction to restrain another company from carrying on a business, or proposing to carry on a business, under a name which is likely to cause the public to believe that the business of the company is that of the 'existing' company.

In *Ewing v. Buttercup Margarine Co.*, a company was registered as the Buttercup Margarinc Co. Ltd to manufacture and deal in margarine. Unknown to the directors, another company had been registered as the Buttercup Dairy Co. Ltd. This company owned a chain of shops retailing dairy products in Scotland and Northern England. It was held that the names were so alike as to cause confusion, and the Buttercup Margarine Co. was restrained by injunction from carrying on its business under that name.

In *Exxon Corporation v. Exxon Insurance Consultants Ltd* the defendant company was restrained by an injunction from using the word Exxon as part of its name. The name had been invented by the Esso Petroleum Company who had a prior and exclusive claim to its use.

A company which carries on a business under a name which is not its corporate name is subject to the provisions of the Business Names Act 1985, e.g. Hops and Malt Ltd trading as the Cambrian Coast Brewery. It may not use any of the words listed in the schedule to the Business Names Act without the consent of the Secretary of State and the relevant bodies. It must state its registered name as well as its business name and address for the service of any documents, orders for goods or services, invoices and receipts and written demands for the payment of debts. The same information must be displayed, in a prominent position, in any business premises to which customers or suppliers have access. The company must supply its name and address to any person requesting the information.

A private guarantee company formed to promote commerce, art, science, education, religion, charity or any profession need not use the word 'limited' as long as it submits a statutory declaration that it fulfils the following conditions: The memorandum or the articles of association must state that the company intends to apply its income or profits solely for promoting its objects. It must also prohibit the payment of any dividend to its members and must provide that on its winding up it will transfer all its assets, otherwise available for distribution to its members, to another body with similar objects or to a body which has for its objects the promotion of charity (section 30).

A company may change its name at any time by special resolution. Its new name is subject to the same scrutiny as a first registration. The Registrar then issues a certificate of incorporation in the company's new name (section 28).

Every company is required to publish its full name outside its registered office and all places where it carries on business. The name must also be engraved on its common seal and be mentioned on its bills of exchange, cheques, promissory notes, invoices, receipts and business letters. The company and its officers may be fined for not complying with these provisions (sections 349 and 350).

An officer of the company may incur personal liability if the company's name is incorrectly mentioned on a bill, cheque, or order for goods, unless the debt is paid by the company. In *Atkins and Co. v. Wardle* it was held that the directors of the South Shields Salt Water Baths Co. Ltd, were personally liable when they accepted a bill of exchange on the company's behalf with the word 'Ltd' having been omitted. In *Bondina Ltd v. Rollaway Shower Blinds Ltd* two directors signed cheques, without directors after their signatures, on a bank cheque form. It was held that they were not personally liable on the cheques as the printed writing on the cheque clearly indicated that the cheque was drawn on the company's account.

A person who was a director (or shadow director) of a company within 12 months of that company going into insolvent liquidation, is prohibited for five years from becoming involved, say as a director and promoter, in any other company which uses the same or very similar name as the liquidated company, unless he first obtains the court's permission to do so (IA section 216). Contravention of this section is a criminal offence.

Registered office

The memorandum must state whether the registered office is to be situated in England, Wales or Scotland. This will determine a company's nationality and domicile. A company registered in England has British nationality, an English domicile and is subject to English law, whereas a company registered in Scotland has British nationality, a Scottish domicile and is governed by the laws of Scotland.

A company must have a registered office at all times, to which all communications and notices may be addressed. The location of the registered office can be altered at any time, by passing an ordinary resolution, or if there is authority in the articles, by a resolution of the board of directors. The location can be changed within the country of domicile, but it cannot be changed from England to Scotland and vice versa. Notice must be given to the Registrar and entered on the register. For 14 days after the date of registration documents may be served on the company at its previous address.

Documents, including notices and writs, are served on a company at its registered office.

A company must also keep certain registers and documents at its registered office. – If a person wishes to commence proceedings against a company in a county court he may serve a summons at a company's place of business (County Court (Amendment) Rules 1989). It is no longer necessary for a plaintiff to ascertain the address of a company's registered office. – These include a register of members, a register of directors and secretaries, a register of mortgages and charges, a register of debenture holders, a register of directors' interests in shares or debentures and a register of interests in shares, along with copies of directors' service contracts and the minute books of general meetings.

Objects clause

This clause sets out the objects for which the company is formed, which must be lawful. A company cannot enter into activities and contracts which are outside its objects clause as it would then be acting *ultra vires*, or beyond its powers. In *Ashbury Railway Carriage and Iron Co. v. Riche*, a company was formed to manufacture and repair railway carriages, and purchase, lease and work mines, minerals and land. The directors purchased a concession for building a railway in Belgium. It was held that the contract was *ultra vires* and void as it was beyond the objects of the company.

This clause offers protection to both shareholders and creditors. A company's shareholders are made aware of the purposes for which their investment can be applied, while any person contemplating dealing with the company is made aware of the limits of the company's contractual powers.

However, a party entering into a transaction with a company is not bound to inquire into the capacity of the company to enter into the transaction, or the powers of the board of directors to bind the company or authorise others to do so (section 35(6)).

A company's objects should be reasonably interpreted. Whatever is incidental to the objects set out in the memorandum should be regarded as *intra vires* (i.e. within the company powers), unless expressly forbidden. If a company's objects are as stated in the specimen memorandum – 'the conveyance of passengers and goods in ships or boats between such places as the company may determine' – a company would be given certain ancillary powers to achieve these objects. It could borrow money, have a bank account, contract for supplies, employ labour, bring and defend actions, pay pensions to its employees and lease premises. It must be shown that there is a connection between the power and the company's objects, and that the company will benefit from the exercise of the power.

An act which may be regarded as being reasonably incidental to a company attaining its objects will not be construed as being *ultra vires* the company if the company performs the act for purposes outside those set out in the memorandum (*Rolled Steel Product (Holdings) Ltd v. British Steel Corporation*).

Borrowing cannot exist as an independent activity, even though a company has been given borrowing powers in its object clause. It must be used to further an activity which is *intra vires* the company. In *Re Introductions Ltd*, a company was formed to provide entertainment and accommodation for overseas visitors. It had a power 'to borrow and raise money in such manner as the company' should think fit, and borrowed money from the bank to finance a pig breeding business. It was held that such borrowing was *ultra vires*.

Where a company's memorandum states that the company's objects are 'to carry on business as a general commercial company' (section 3A), the company may carry on any trade or business whatsoever and has the power to do all things that are incidental or conducive to the carrying on of any such trade or business.

These provisions will, in the case of a general commercial company, allow the company to reduce the number of paragraphs in its memorandum. Non-commercial companies will probably retain a large number of paragraphs in their object clauses to give them a wide range of powers. A company will still need to state expressly powers that might not be regarded as incidental or conducive to its business, e.g. the power to make gratuitous dispositions; to acquire shares in other companies (otherwise it could not be a holding company); to dispose of property other than for the purposes of its business; to provide loans, securities, guarantees, etc.

The Courts have evolved certain rules in interpreting the object clause, the most important of which is the main object rule.

According to the Courts, the first paragraph sets out the company's main object. Such a paragraph controls and limits the operation of the succeeding paragraphs. Should the main object fail, then the substratum of the company is destroyed and the company may be wound up. In *Re German Date Coffee Co.* a company was formed to extract coffee from dates by the use of a German patent. The patent was not obtained, but the company successfully used a Swedish patent. It was held that the company should be wound up. Its main object had failed as it envisaged the use of a German patent.

Companies have sought to exclude this rule by various means.

In *Cotman v. Brougham*, a rubber company's objects clause concluded with a statement that each of its thirty sub-clauses should be considered as a separate and independent main object. One clause authorised the company to deal in shares in other companies, and it underwrote shares in an oil company. It was held that the underwriting was valid.

In *Bell Houses v. City Wall Properties* the memorandum of a property company contained a clause which authorised the company, 'to carry on any trade or business whatsoever, which can in the opinion of the board of directors be advantageously carried on by the company in connection . . . with the general business of the company'. The directors entered into a contract to introduce another company to a financier in return for a commission. It was held that such a contract was valid.

In *Re New Finance and Mortgage Co Ltd*, a clause in the objects clause allowed the company to act as 'financiers, capitalists, concessionaires, bankers, commercial agents, mortgage brokers, financial agents and advisers, exporters and importers of goods and merchandise of all kinds and merchants generally'. It was held that the phrase 'merchants generally' gave the company authority to operate garages, selling petrol, cars and car accessories.

The power to make gratuitous payments

A company's object clause may include express powers to make gifts, provide gratuities and pensions for present and former employees, provide for employees on the cessation of a business and give guarantees in respect of the liabilities of third parties. It would appear that the exercise of these powers in a proper manner by the directors is valid.

In the absence of an express power a company's entitlement to make gifts and provide gratuities must be considered in relation to its activities.

Political, educational and charitable donations are usually permitted as long as the donation is incidental or beneficial to the company's business. In *Evans v. Brunner, Mond and Co. Ltd* a chemical manufacturing company made gifts of £100 000 to universities and other research bodies for 'the furtherance of scientific education and research'. Although the company's object clause did not contain an express power to make gifts, it authorised activities that were incidental or conducive to the attainment of the objects. It was held that as the company would benefit generally from scientific research, the gift was valid.

In *Simmonds v. Heffer*, the League against Cruel Sports (a guarantee company) donated £80 000 to the Labour Party which had pledged to ban hare coursing and deer hunting if elected. £50 000 was given without any conditions attached to the gift while £30 000 was to be used for publicising the manifesto pledge. It was held that the gift of £50 000 was *ultra vires* as it was not restricted to the League's aims.

A gift to former directors or their dependants may not be valid, unless the payment is considered to be for the benefit of the company. *Re Roith (W & M) Ltd* (see page 165). If, however, a payment of a pension is authorised by the memorandum it would appear that the payment is valid and does not have to be exercised for the benefit of the company. In *Re Horsley and Weight* a company's objects empowered the company to grant pensions to its present and past employees and to its directors. The company granted a pension to a retiring director. The company was later wound up and the liquidator sought a declaration that the payment was *ultra vires*. It was held that as the power to grant pensions was a main object of the company it was valid.

A company may make provision for its employees and former employees under Section 719 which provides that a company's powers include the power to provide for its employees on the cessation or transfer of the whole or part of its undertaking (see page 169). This overrules *Parke v. Daily News Ltd* (see page 170) where it was held that such a payment was *ultra vires*.

The ultra vires *doctrine*

The *ultra vires* doctrine is abolished as between a company and third parties. Section 35(1) provides that 'the validity of an act done by a company shall not be called into question on the ground of lack of capacity by reason of anything in the company's memorandum'.

A third party who does not act in good faith, that is was aware of the *ultra vires* nature of the transaction, or was put on inquiry by unusual circumstances, can no longer rely on the *ultra vires* rule as a defence to avoid a disadvantageous contract that was not sanctioned by the company's objects.

The *ultra vires* doctrine still remains effective as between a company and its members. Any member may apply to the court to restrain a company from undertaking an *ultra vires* act and the directors remain liable for *ultra vires* acts entered into by them, unless the company sanctions their release from liability by special resolution. A company may also ratify an *ultra vires* transaction entered into by the directors by special resolution (section 35(2)(3)).

Special provisions apply to charitable companies. An *ultra vires* act cannot be enforced against a charitable company by a person who is aware of its charitable status. A charitable company that does not include the words 'charity' or 'charitable' in its name must now state that it is a charity on all its letters, notices and other business stationery (sections 30B, 30C).

Alterations of objects

A company may change its objects, by special resolution, in order to enable it to meet changed circumstances (section 4).

Minority dissenting shareholders may petition the court to cancel the alteration. If this is done within twenty-one days of passing the resolution the Court will suspend the alterations. The dissenting shareholders must hold at least 15 per cent of the issued capital of the company, or 15 per cent of the issued shares of any class (if the company has two or more classes of shares). An application may also be made by the holders of 15 per cent of any debentures issued before 1 December 1947 and secured by a floating charge. Accordingly notice of a special resolution to alter the objects clause must also be given to such debenture holders. Only those individuals who voted against the resolution, or abstained, or who were not at the meeting, can object.

The Court may confirm or cancel the alteration, or confirm it subject to conditions, or alternatively adjourn the proceedings so that agreement may be reached for the purchase of the shares of the dissenting shareholders (section 5).

If no application opposing the alteration is made within the twenty-one days, the company must, within a further fifteen days, deliver to the Registrar a printed copy of its memorandum as altered.

If an application is made, the company must notify the Registrar immediately, and when the Court order is made the company must within fifteen days file a copy of the order together with a printed copy of the memorandum, if it has been altered (section 6).

Limited liability clause

This clause provides that 'the liability of the members is limited'. Similar words are used in a memorandum of a company limited by shares, as in a company limited by guarantee.

In the case of a company limited by shares, its effect is that a member shall only be liable to contribute the amount unpaid on his shares. In the case of a company limited by guarantee, a member's liability must not exceed the amount of his guarantee. If the guarantee company has a share capital a member's liability must not exceed the amount of his guarantee, plus any amount which remains unpaid on his shares. A typical guarantee clause is found in Table C:

> Every member of the company undertakes to contribute such amount as may be required (not exceeding £100) to the company's assets if it should be wound up while he is a member of within one year after he ceases to be a member, for payment of the company's debts and liabilities contracted before he ceases to be a member, and of the costs, charges and expenses of winding up, and for the adjustment of the rights of the contributories among themselves.

The effect of the limited liability clause is that a member's liability cannot be altered without his consent. He cannot be compelled to take more shares, or to increase his liability to contribute more money, unless he agrees to this in writing.

If a limited company wishes to re-register as an unlimited company, it may only do so with the written consent of all its members, as their liability will be dramatically altered. A member's liability will also be altered if a company carries on business without having at least two members for more than six months. The surviving member who is aware of the fact is liable (jointly and severally with the company) for the debts of the company contracted after the six month period (section 24).

A company's memorandum may state that the liability of its directors is unlimited. Any person who is invited to join the board of directors of such a company must be informed in writing of the existence of this clause (section 306).

The capital clause

The capital clause sets out the amount of the nominal capital and its division into shares of fixed amounts (e.g. the share capital of the company is £40 000 divided into 40 000 shares of £1 each).

If the shares are divided into various classes (e.g. 20 000 £1 ordinary shares, 20 000 £1 preference shares) it is unnecessary to specify this in the memorandum as reference to the types of shares and their respective rights is found in the articles.

It is comparatively easy for the company to increase its authorised capital at a later date. All that is required is an ordinary resolution (section 121), but if a company wishes to reduce its capital it requires a special resolution and the Court's approval (section 135).

The association clause

The memorandum concludes with an association clause by which the subscribers declare that they desire to be formed into a company. There must be at least two subscribers. Each signs in the presence of a witness for a minimum of one share. The witness attests each signature, and one person may witness all the signatures.

Other clauses

Clauses are sometimes inserted in the memorandum which are normally found in the articles. Such clauses may define the rights which attach to different classes of shares with regard to dividend, voting, and participation in the company's assets on a winding up. These can be altered in the same manner as the objects clause (i.e. a special resolution, and a provision allowing for minority dissent – section 17).

If the memorandum provides a procedure for the alteration of these clauses, this must be followed, rather than the procedure mentioned above. A company may render these clauses unalterable by inserting a provision in the memorandum prohibiting their alteration.

5
ARTICLES OF ASSOCIATION

The articles contain the internal regulations for the management of the company's affairs. They govern the rights of the members among themselves and set out the manner in which a company must conduct its affairs. As the articles are subsidiary to the memorandum, any article which is inconsistent with the provisions in the memorandum is invalid. An article may not contain anything illegal or authorise anything impliedly or expressly forbidden by the Act, for example, the payment of a dividend out of capital, or the issue of shares at a discount.

A set of model articles is found in The Companies (Tables A–F) Regulations 1985. (The articles mentioned in the text are the articles found in Table A.) A share company may adopt Table A instead of registering its own articles, or it may specifically exclude Table A and set out its own articles. The third alternative is for a company to set out its own articles and adopt part of Table A.

If a company's own articles are silent on a particular point the appropriate provisions of Table A will apply, unless it is stated that Table A has been specifically excluded. In practice some modification of Table A is invariably found to be necessary. Companies often modify provisions as to class rights, directors' rights and quorums to suit their own circumstances.

All the major Companies Acts since 1862 have contained a model set of articles in the form of Table A and each has differed in some respects from the previous model. The Table A which applies to a company is the Table A in force at the date of a company's incorporation; for example, a company formed in 1906 is subject to Table A of the Companies Act 1862, a company formed in 1945 is subject to Table A of the Companies Act 1929, a company formed in 1979 is subject to Table A of the 1948 Companies Act.

Model forms of memoranda and articles for guarantee companies are set out in Tables C and D, and for an unlimited company having share capital in Table E of the Act.

If articles are registered they must be printed, divided into separate consecutive paragraphs, and signed by the subscribers to the memorandum in the presence of a witness who must attest the signature (section 7).

The contents of the articles

The articles usually include provisions dealing with the following:

the allotment of shares;
share capital and variation of class rights;
lien and calls on shares;
forfeiture, transfer and transmission of shares;
conversion of shares into stock;
increase and reduction of capital;
borrowing powers;
general meetings;
voting at meetings;
appointment; duties and powers of directors and managing directors;
appointment and remuneration of the secretary;
the company seal;
accounts and audit;
dividends, reserves and capitalisation of profits;
serving of notices;
special provisions relating to winding up.

Alteration of the articles

A company is given power to alter or to add to its articles by special resolution (section 9). A company cannot deprive itself of this power, and any article may be altered as long as the alteration is not inconsistent with the Act and the company's memorandum.

The articles of a private company may also be altered by written resolution, as long as the written agreement of all the shareholders is obtained (section 381A).

The alteration is invalid if it amounts to an oppression of, or fraud upon, a minority. If an alteration of an article is beneficial to a company, but prejudices a minority, the alteration will be upheld. In *Allen v. Gold Reefs of West Africa*, the company had a lien on partly paid shares only. A shareholder, the only holder of fully paid shares, died indebted to the company. The company altered its articles to impose a lien on all shares, thus giving it a lien over the deceased shareholder's shares. It was held that such an alteration was valid. In *Sidebottom v. Kershaw, Leese and Co.* the company's articles were altered to allow the company to require any member who carried on a business competing with the company to sell his shares at a fair price to nominees of the directors. Sidebottom, a shareholder, operated mills in competition with the company. It was held that the alteration was valid as a shareholder who was also a business competitor might cause loss to the company.

In *Greenhalgh v. Arderne Cinemas Ltd* the majority shareholders wished to sell their shares to a third party. The articles contained a clause which stipulated that any member who wished to sell his shares to a non-member must first offer his shares, at a fair price, to his fellow members. The company altered its articles so that any shareholder could sell his shares to a third party, if permitted to do so by an ordinary resolution. This was held valid and for the benefit of the company as a whole, despite the fact that a minority shareholder would firstly have to offer his shares to the majority under the existing clause.

In *Brown v. British Abrasive Wheel Co. Ltd*, the company required further capital. The holders of 98 per cent of the company's share capital were prepared to advance additional capital if they could acquire the remaining 2 per cent shareholding. The minority shareholders refused to sell and the company passed a resolution enabling a 90 per cent majority to acquire the shares of any dissenting minority. This was held to be invalid as it was solely for the benefit of the majority shareholders and not for the company's benefit.

If a company is in breach of contract as a result of altering its articles such an alteration is nevertheless valid and the other party cannot obtain an injunction to prevent the alteration; the remedy lies in damages. In *Southern Foundries (1926) Ltd v. Shirlaw*, Shirlaw was appointed by contract to be managing director for ten years. As a result of a merger, the articles were altered so that Shirlaw could be removed from office before the end of the ten-year period. It was held that he was entitled to damages for wrongful dismissal.

An alteration that increases the liability of a member to contribute to the company, for example by increasing his shareholding, or his liability to pay money to the company, is not binding unless he agrees to this in writing (section 16).

The memorandum and articles filed with the Registrar may be inspected by any person and the company must supply a copy of the memorandum and articles on payment of not more than five pence per copy.

The effect of the memorandum and articles

The Act provides that the memorandum and articles shall, when registered, bind the company and its members as if they had been signed and sealed by each member and contained agreements on the part of each member to observe all their provisions (section 14).

The result is that the articles and memorandum form a contract between the company and each member, and each member in his capacity as member is bound to the company by the provisions found in the articles. A member is bound by contract to pay the amounts outstanding on his share and a member of a guarantee company is similarly bound to contribute the amount of his guarantee on the winding up of the company. The Act provides that these are specialty debts which may be recovered by the company within twelve years. In *Hickman v. Kent or Romney Sheep Breeders Association*, a dispute arose between Hickman, a member, and the company, relating to the company's refusal to register certain of his flock in the Association's stud book. One of the company's articles specified that any dispute between the company and its members should be submitted to arbitration. Hickman nevertheless brought an action in the High Court against the company. It was held that the company was entitled to have the court action stayed and the dispute referred to arbitration.

In *Beattie v. E & F Beattie* the articles of a company provided that any dispute between a company and its members should be submitted to arbitration. A dispute arose as to the payment of fees to a director and the director concerned sought to have the matter submitted to arbitration. It was held that as the dispute concerned his capacity as a director the matter should be heard by the court.

A member may sue a company if it denies him those rights accorded to him in the articles or the memorandum. A member has compelled a company to restore his name to the register when it was wrongfully removed; to pay dividends; return capital on a winding up. In *Pender v. Lushington*, the articles of a company provided that a member should not be entitled to more than 100 votes. Certain shareholders who held more than 100 shares transferred certain shares to nominees in order to exercise greater voting power. The company refused to recognise the votes of the nominees. It was held that the company was contractually bound by the articles to allow those votes to be recorded. A similar principle was applied in *Wood v. Odessa Waterworks Co.* (see page 130).

The memorandum and articles also have effect as a contract between the members themselves, which may be enforced directly by one member against another without the aid of the company. In *Rayfield v. Hands*, the articles of a private company provided that if a member intended to transfer shares he should inform the directors 'who will take the said shares equally between them at a fair value'. The directors refused to buy Rayfield's shares. It was held that the articles bound the directors, as members, to purchase the shares.

In *Borland's Trustee v. Steel Brothers and Co. Ltd*, the articles provided that the shares of any member who was adjudged bankrupt should be sold to certain persons at a fair price, not exceeding par. Borland became bankrupt and it was held that his trustee must sell his shares in accordance with the articles.

The memorandum and the articles do not bind the company to an outsider, nor do they form a contract with a member other than in his capacity as a member. In *Eley v. Positive Government Security Life Assurance Co.*, the articles provided that Eley should be employed for life as a solicitor to the company and should not be removed except for misconduct. He became the company's solicitor and later became a shareholder. The company ceased to employ him as its solicitor and he sued for breach of contract. It was held that he could not succeed, as the contract which he sought to enforce was not conferred upon him in his capacity as a shareholder.

However a provision in the memorandum or articles can be evidence of the existence of a contract. In *Re New British Iron Co. (Ex Parte Beckwith)*, the articles of a company provided that the directors should have a share qualification and should be paid fees of £1 000 a year. The company was wound up and a director claimed for his fees. It was held that, although the articles did not constitute a contract, they were evidence that the director had accepted office on the basis of the articles, and the company was liable to pay his fees.

6
THE PROMOTER

A promoter has been defined as 'one who undertakes to form a company . . . and to set it going, and who takes the necessary steps to accomplish that purpose' (*Twycross v. Grant*). Any person who takes part in forming a company or in raising capital for a proposed or newly formed company is *prima facie* a promoter. A person may take a relatively minor part in promoting a company and yet find himself a promoter of that company. Individuals who have issued a prospectus, negotiated contracts for the purchase of property, obtained directors, and placed shares have been held to be promoters of companies.

A person who acts in a professional or technical capacity for a promoter – a solicitor who undertakes legal work for a company's formation, or an accountant or valuer who prepares accounts or valuations for a promoter – will not be regarded as a promoter.

Duties of a promoter

Theoretically a promoter is allowed to make a profit from promoting the company, as he is not a trustee or an agent for the company, as it is not yet in existence. In practice, the courts have ruled that as the promoter stands in a fiduciary relationship to the company he must not make, either directly or indirectly, any profit from the promotion unless the company assents.

A promoter must disclose any profit which he is making by promoting the company, either to an independent board of directors or to the existing and intended shareholders, for example by means of a prospectus. Disclosure to an independent board is rarely possible as the promoters are usually the first directors of the company.

In *Erlanger v. New Sombrero Phosphate Co.*, a syndicate managed by Erlanger purchased for £55 000 an island reputed to contain large quantities of phosphate. Erlanger formed a company to purchase the island from the syndicate for £110 000. The company's directors were nominated by him. The profit made by the promoters was not disclosed to the shareholders or to an independent board. The original directors were later removed from office, and the company successfully sued for rescission of the contract and for the recovery of the purchase money from the syndicate.

Remedies against a promoter

The following remedies may be available to a company if a promoter has failed to make full disclosure of any profit made by him.

Firstly, rescission of any contract made with the promoter. This was possible in the case of *Erlanger v. New Sombrero Phosphate Co.* This remedy is not available if it is not possible to restore the promoter and the company to their former positions, for example where the company has resold the property to a third party.

Secondly, the company may compel the promoter to account for any secret profit made by him. If a company succeeds in an action for rescission any secret profit is normally recovered as a result of the action, but such a profit may be recovered even though the company does not sue for rescission of the contract. In *Gluckstein v. Barnes*, a syndicate purchased Olympia for £140 000, and formed a company which purchased the property from the syndicate for £180 000. The directors, who were members of the syndicate, disclosed this profit. The syndicate had also purchased debentures in Olympia at a very low price. As a result of the sale to the company, the debentures were repaid in full and the syndicate made an additional profit of £20 000, which they did not disclose. It was held that the directors must account for this sum to the company.

Thirdly, the company can sue for damages for breach of a fiduciary duty on the basis that the promoter is negligent in not disclosing his interest. In *Re Leeds and Hanley Theatre of Varieties Ltd*, a company purchased two music halls for £24 000 and conveyed these properties to its nominee. The company promoted another company and instructed their nominee to sell the properties to the second company for £75 000. No mention was made of the first company's interest in the transaction in the prospectus or elsewhere. The promoters were held liable in damages.

A dishonest promoter may find himself liable at a later date. If the company is wound up, a promoter may be sued for misfeasance and may be ordered by the Court to make restitution to the company.

Payment of a promoter

As a company does not have legal capacity before its formation, a promoter is not able to make a contract with the company to be paid for promotion services, or to be indemnified for any expenses incurred by him. The articles usually give authority to the director to pay the promoter for his services. A company's articles usually provide that the directors may pay all the expenses incurred in the promotion and registration of a company. There is usually no problem in practice as the promoters or their nominees are usually the first directors of a company.

Payment can be made to a promoter in various ways. He may be paid a commission for promoting a company. Alternatively, he may be allotted shares as payment for his services. These are usually ordinary shares, but sometimes promoters are given deferred or founders' shares. In other cases promoters are given the option to subscribe for shares at par. This can be a valuable form of payment if the shares are likely to go to a premium. Promoters can also be given debentures as payment.

Any amount paid or benefit given must be disclosed by the promoter to the company, and also by the company in any prospectus issued within two years.

Pre-incorporation contracts

A promoter who enters into a contract on behalf of a company before its incorporation (i.e. a pre-incorporation contract) may face certain problems. As the company is not in existence at the time of making the contract it cannot ratify such a contract after its formation. Any person who acts as an agent for such a company is personally liable on the contract. Section 36 states that 'where a contract purports to be made by a company, or by a person as agent for a company, at a time when the company has not been formed, then subject to any agreement to the contrary the contract has effect as one entered into by the person purporting to act for the company or as agent for it, and he is personally liable'.

In *Kelner v. Baxter,* three individuals entered into a contract for the supply of wines and spirits on behalf of the Gravesend Royal Alexandria Hotel Company, which had not at that time been incorporated. The company was incorporated, experienced financial difficulties and was wound up. It was held that the promoters were liable for its pre-incorporation contracts.

A recent decision (*Phonogram Ltd v. Lane*) illustrates the operation of section 36. A contract was made by Lane 'for and on behalf of' a company to be formed, with Phonogram Ltd. The company was never incorporated, although incorporation was originally intended. Phonogram Ltd sued Lane for the sum advanced under the contract, which was returnable under the terms of the contract. It was held that Lane was personally liable for repayment of this sum.

A promoter may avoid this liability by providing in the contract that his liability shall cease if the company enters into a new contract on similar terms, or by inserting a clause that either party may rescind the contract if it is not adopted by the company within a specified time (e.g. three months). Alternatively, a contract may be prepared in draft form to be entered into by the company and the other party, after incorporation.

A company is not bound by a pre-incorporation contract. In *Re English and Colonial Produce Company Ltd*, it was held that a solicitor, who had drafted documents for a company before it was incorporated, was unable to recover his fees from the company.

A company cannot enforce a pre-incorporation contract against the other party. In *Natal Land & Colonisation Co. v. Pauline Colliery and Development Syndicate*, the Pauline Colliery Syndicate had, before its incorporation, taken an option on some lands. When the syndicate sought to exercise the option, the other party refused to grant a lease. It was held that the contract could not be enforced.

If a public company enters into a contract before it receives its section 117 certificate from the Registrar, the contract will be binding. Should the company fail to meet its obligations under the contract, its directors will be jointly and severally (individually and collectively) liable to indemnify the other party to the contract.

7
RAISING CAPITAL

Companies raise money and finance their activities in various ways. The method chosen will depend on a number of factors, including the cost of raising the required capital and the amount of interest or dividend to be paid to investors or shareholders. A public issue of shares is unsuitable for a small company, as this is a costly exercise which could not be justified in terms of the amount that could be raised.

Small companies generally finance their activities in other ways. It may be cheaper to lease machinery and equipment, rather than purchase these items. Alternatively, a company may acquire such items on hire purchase or under a credit sale agreement, thus spreading the cost over a longer period of time.

It may be possible for a company to negotiate a private loan from a bank, or a merchant bank, or an insurance company.

A company may also negotiate privately with individuals to invest in its shares or debentures. In the case of a small company the negotiations are usually conducted by its directors, but a large company seeking to obtain a substantial investment will usually employ an intermediary, such as a bank or an issuing house, to act on its behalf. This is known as a private placing.

A company is under no obligation to distribute the whole of its profits as a dividend. A prudent company makes provision for the depreciation of its fixed assets, such as plant and machinery, by allocating a fraction of its profits to a fund to finance purchases of equipment. It may also allocate part of its profits to finance the future expansion of its business. The articles usually give the directors authority to create a reserve out of the company's profits.

As shareholders expect to be paid a dividend, a company may have to find a method of satisfying members whilst retaining profits. This can be achieved by capitalising profits and issuing fully paid bonus shares or debentures to its shareholders. The shareholders may then, if they so wish, sell their bonus shares and debentures to compensate them for their loss of dividend. Two statutory provisions apply to a private company.

(a) It must not apply for its shares to be listed on the Stock Exchange (FSA section 143).
(b) In general it may not issue an advertisement offering its shares for a sale. It may only do so if an advertisement is covered by an order made by the Secretary of State (FSA section 170).

A company may raise additional capital by a rights issue. It sends to each existing shareholder or debenture holder a circular, known as a letter of rights, inviting him to subscribe for additional shares or debentures in proportion to his original holding. The letter of rights is usually renounceable, so that the recipient can sign the renunciation and sell his right to subscribe to some other person. The modern practice is to send the shareholder or debenture holder a provisional letter of allotment by which these new shares or debentures are actually allotted, subject to his right to reject them if he does not wish to subscribe.

A public company may 'place' its shares or debentures with an issuing house, or a firm of stockbrokers at an agreed price. The issuing house will place the securities with its clients or associates, at a price above that paid to the company. An issuing house, a bank or a stockbroker may also act as an agent for the company and invite its clients to purchase shares from the company. Payment of a commission for this service is known as brokerage.

A public company may invite the public to subscribe for its shares or debentures, by issuing a prospectus. A company will make a direct public issue only if it is confident that due to its reputation, or the price of its shares, all the issue will be taken up. A prudent company will, nevertheless, arrange for such an issue to be underwritten. Most companies offer their shares or debentures to the public by an offer for sale. An issuing house subscribes for an issue of shares or debentures and invites the public to purchase those securities from it at a higher price.

8
SHARE OFFERS

Offers of listed securities

A public company which seeks a Stock Exchange quotation must apply to the Stock Exchange for admission to the Official List. If the application is successful, the shares will be listed, which makes them freely marketable. Part IV of the Financial Services Act deals with the official listing of securities, which include shares, debentures, stock, etc. For convenience this chapter will refer only to shares.

An application for listing must be made by the issuer (or with the issuer's consent) to the Stock Exchange (FSA section 143) and must contain such information as may be specified in the listing rules. An application may be refused if the Stock Exchange considers that a listing would be detrimental to investors' interests, or that the shares are officially listed in another EC member state and those listing regulations have not been complied with (FSA section 144).

The listing regulations usually require the submission and publication of listing particulars which must contain all such information as investors and their professional advisers would expect to find in order to make an informed assessment of:

1 the assets, liabilities, financial position, profits, losses and prospects of the issuer of the shares; and
2 the rights attaching to those shares.

The duty of disclosure is restricted to information which is known to the person compiling the particulars or which it would be reasonable for him to have obtained by making enquiries.

In deciding what information should be disclosed, attention must be paid to the following:

(a) the nature of the shares and the issuer;
(b) the nature of the prospective purchasers;
(c) the fact that certain matters will be known to professional advisers who would reasonably be expected to be consulted by potential investors;
(d) any information already available to investors or their professional advisers (FSA section 146).

If a significant change has occurred, or any significant new matter has arisen between the time of preparing the listing particulars and the commencement of dealings in the shares the issuer must submit *supplementary listing particulars* of the changes to the Stock Exchange for approval and publication (FSA section 147). If the issuer is unaware of the change, or new matter, he is not under a duty to submit supplementary listing particulars, unless he is notified of the change or new matter by the person having responsibility for the listing particulars, who is under a duty to inform the issuer (FSA section 147).

The Stock Exchange may give exemption from the duty to disclose on either of the following grounds:

(i) that disclosure would be contrary to the public interest.
(ii) that disclosure would be seriously detrimental to the issuer of the shares.

The Secretary of State or the Treasury may certify that the disclosure of information would be contrary to the public interest.

Information which is detrimental to the issuer must nevertheless be published if its non-disclosure would be likely to mislead a potential purchaser as to any facts which he should know in order to make an informed assessment (FSA section 148).

A copy of the listing particulars or supplementary listing particulars must be registered with the Registrar on or before the date of publication (FSA section 149).

Offers of unlisted securities

Offers of unlisted securities are dealt with in Part V of the Financial Services Act. (As before the references in this part of the chapter are to the offers of shares).

The following definitions are found in Part V:

Advertisement offering shares

An advertisement offers shares if:

(a) it invites a person to enter into an agreement for or with a view to subscribing for or otherwise acquiring or underwriting any shares; or
(b) it contains information calculated to lead directly or indirectly into such an agreement.

Approved exchange

An approved exchange is a recognised investment exchange approved by the Secretary of State, either generally or in relation to specified dealings.

Prospectus

A document containing information about shares on their admission to dealings on an approved exchange.

Offers of shares on admission to an approved exchange

Any advertisement offering shares which are to be admitted to dealings on an approved exchange is prohibited unless:

(a) a prospectus containing information about the securities has been approved by the exchange and delivered to the Registrar; *or*

(b) the prospectus has to be submitted, approved and delivered before there can be an acceptance of the offer (FSA section 159).

A prospectus is *not* required:

(i) if a prospectus relating to the shares has been registered in the previous 12 months and the approved exchange certifies that potential investors have sufficient information to enable them to decide whether to invest, from that prospectus and other published information (FSA section 159).

(ii) if the offer is conditional on the listing of the shares, or if they have been listed in the previous 12 months and the approved exchange certifies that there is sufficient information already available for investors (FSA section 161).

(iii) if the advertisement consists of a registered prospectus under FSA section 159, or containing only the following information: the name and address of the issuer; the nature, number, nominal value and price of the investments; a statement that a prospectus is or will be available and instructions for obtaining a copy of the prospectus (FSA section 161).

(iv) if other shares issued by the same person are already dealt with on the approved exchange which certifies that potential investors have sufficient information to decide whether to invest. The shares need not be the same class as those in the present offer (FSA section 161).

(v) if the shares are dealt in an overseas exchange and the Secretary of State considers that the law of that country provides UK investors with protection at least equivalent to that contained in the Financial Services Act (FSA section 161).

Other offers of shares

Advertisements offering shares which are not to be admitted to dealings on an approved exchange are divided into primary offers and secondary offers.

1 A *primary offer* is an advertisement that is not issued in connection

SHARE OFFERS

with dealings on an approved exchange which invites persons, either directly or indirectly, *to subscribe for or underwrite* the shares to which the advertisement relates.

2   A *secondary offer* is an advertisement which is not issued in connection with dealings on an approved exchange and which invites persons, either directly or indirectly, to *acquire* the shares to which the advertisement relates. The advertisement must be issued by:

(a)   a person who has acquired the shares from the issuer with a view to making such an offer; *or*

(b)   a person who has acquired the shares from a person other than the issuer with a view to making an offer, provided that the shares have not been dealt with on an exchange or held by a person as an investment; *or*

(c)   a person who is a controller of the issuer and is acting with the issuer's consent or participation in making the offer (FSA section 160).

A person may *not* issue an advertisement offering shares which amounts to a primary or secondary offer unless:

(a)   he has delivered a prospectus to the Registrar for registration; *or*

(b)   the advertisement is such that no agreement may be entered into as a result of it until a prospectus has been delivered to the Registrar (FSA section 160).

A prospectus is *not* required:

(i)   for a secondary offer if a prospectus has been delivered for registration in the previous 6 months in respect of a previous offer of the same shares by a primary or secondary offer (FSA section 160).

(ii)   if the Secretary of State makes an exemption order in respect of primary and secondary offers in the following categories:

- advertisements of a private character e.g. by reason of a connection between the issuer and the potential investors;
- advertisements dealing with investments only incidentally;
- advertisements issued only to expert investors who can understand any risks involved;
- any other classes of advertisement as he thinks fit;

(iii) for shares listed or to be listed on the Stock Exchange (FSA section 161).
(iv) for any advertisement which consists of a registered prospectus or which is limited in content.
(v) for shares issued by the same person which are already dealt with on an approved exchange.
(vi) for shares already dealt in an overseas exchange if the Secretary of State considers that the law of that country provides UK investors with protection at least equivalent to that contained in the Financial Services Act.

Contents of prospectus

A prospectus must contain such information and comply with any requirements laid down by the Secretary of State. (These are similar to the listing particulars for listed shares.)

If it appears to the Secretary of State that an approved exchange has prospectus rules which provide investors with protection at least equivalent to the rules made by him he may direct that the prospectus complies with the rules of the exchange (FSA section 162).

A prospectus must contain such information as investors and their professional investors would reasonably require to enable them to make an informed assessment of:

1 the assets and liabilities, financial position, profits and losses and prospects of the issuer; and
2 the rights attaching to the shares.

This duty of disclosure is limited to information which is known to the person compiling the prospectus or which it would be reasonable for him to obtain by making enquiries.

In deciding what information should be included in a prospectus, regard must be had to:

(a) the nature of the shares and the issuer;
(b) the nature of the prospective purchaser;
(c) the fact that certain matters will be known to professional advisers who would reasonably be expected to be consulted by those prospective purchasers;

(d) any information already available to investors or their professional advisers as a result of statutory disclosure requirements.

If a significant change occurs or a significant new matter arises after a prospectus has been registered, a *supplementary* prospectus must then be registered.

An approved exchange may, if so directed by the Secretary of State, authorise the omission from a prospectus or supplementary prospectus of any required information on the grounds that its disclosure:

(i) would be contrary to the public interest; or
(ii) would be seriously detrimental to the issuer of the securities.

Information must be published if its non-disclosure would be likely to mislead a potential purchaser as to any facts which he must know in order to make an informed assessment (FSA section 165).

Underwriting

Before a company offers shares or debentures to the public it will usually enter into a contract to have the issue underwritten. This is an agreement with an underwriter, that in the event of the public not taking up the whole of the issue or the number specified in the agreement he will, for a commission, take an allotment of those shares that are not taken up by the public. The underwriting agreement may be made with a broker, an issuing house, an insurance company, a syndicate or a bank.

The underwriting commission is calculated on the number of shares underwritten, and is payable whether or not the underwriter is called upon to take up any shares. The commission may be a payment of newly issued shares, or money received for them, but it is also permissible to give underwriters an option to subscribe for shares at a specified price, within a specified time.

The terms of the agreement may be contained in an underwriting letter, but are usually found in an underwriting agreement concluded between the company and the underwriters.

The underwriters will usually enter into a subsidiary contract with sub-underwriters to relieve them of some of their liability. A commission will be paid by the underwriters to the sub-underwriters, and this is known as an over-riding commission.

The Act allows payment of underwriting commission as long as certain requirements are fulfilled. Section 97 states that a company may pay a commission to any person in consideration of his subscribing or agreeing to subscribe for, or procure subscriptions for any shares in a company if:

(a) payment of the commission is authorised by the articles;
(b) the commission does not exceed 10 per cent of the issue price of the shares, or the amount or rate authorised by the articles, whichever is the lower.

Section 97 does not apply to the underwriting of debentures, which may be issued at a discount.

Brokerage

This is a payment made to an issuing house or brokers in return for their placing the company's shares or debentures. The distinction between brokerage and underwriting is that brokerage does not involve the brokers in any risk of having to take up the shares and they are not personally involved in the issue.

Payment of brokerage is allowed if authorised by the articles. The amount or rate must be reasonable in the ordinary course of business (¼ per cent is regarded as reasonable).

9
LIABILITY FOR FALSE STATEMENTS IN A PUBLIC OFFER OF SHARES

Civil liability

It is essential for a person seeking redress to show that he has been induced to subscribe on the strength of a false or misleading statement in a prospectus or listing particulars.

Rights against the company

The main remedy against the company is for rescission of the contract, that is the cancellation of the contract, removal of the plaintiff's name from the register, and repayment of any money paid to the company.

The plaintiff must prove that the statement complained of was a statement of fact, not of opinion. If a prospectus gives an opinion regarding the company's prospectus and future profits and these are not fulfilled, a subscriber will have no remedy. In *Aaron's Reefs v. Twiss* a statement in a prospectus that a gold mine had been proved rich, when in fact three companies had unsuccessfully attempted to work the mine, was held to be a misrepresentation, and entitled Twiss to a rescission of his contract to purchase 100 shares.

A statement is deemed to be untrue if it is misleading in its context, even though the statement is literally true. In *R v. Kylsant*, a prospectus issued by the Royal Mail Company stated that 'the dividends on the ordinary stock during the last seventeen years have been as follows', and set out the dividends from 1911 to 1927. The company had suffered trading losses from 1921 to 1927, and was only able to declare a dividend by using accumulated reserves and tax rebates from excess profits paid by the company during the 1914–18 war. It was held that the prospectus was 'false in a material particular'.

An omission can be a material misrepresentation of fact, if the omission makes that which is stated misleading. In *Coles v. White City (Manchester) Greyhound Association Ltd*, a piece of land was described in the prospectus as 'eminently suitable', although the land was subject to a planning resolution by the local authority. No compensation would be paid for any buildings that had to be demolished, unless the local authority had given permission for their erection. Consent to build a greyhound stadium was refused. It was held that the description of 'eminently suitable' was misleading in view of the omission of these facts, and the shareholders who applied for shares on the basis of the prospectus were entitled to rescind their contracts.

Rescission is only available to the allottee, so that a person who buys shares on the market on the basis of statements in the prospectus has no remedy against the company. In *Peek v. Gurney*, Colonel Peek purchased 2000 shares from the original purchaser after reading the company's prospectus. The statements were false, the company went into liquidation, and Colonel Peek had to pay as a contributor for £100 000 in respect of the shares. It was held that he had no rights against the company as the prospectus was directed at the original allottee only.

Any such contract is valid, though voidable, until rescinded. Even a short delay after the discovery of the mis-statement may be disastrous and deprive the individual of his right to set aside the contract. This right will be lost if there is an implied ratification, for example where individuals, being aware of the mis-statement, have endeavoured to sell their shares, have attended and voted at meetings, executed transfers of shares or have simply treated the contract as subsisting by accepting dividends. The right to rescind will be lost where it is impossible to restore the parties to their former position, as when the shares are sold.

The deceived shareholder may sue the company for damages if the company has fraudulently misrepresented material facts. The action is for the tort of deceit. The shareholder must prove that the misrepresentation was one of fact, that it was material and that as a result of acting upon it he has suffered loss or damage. A plaintiff who sues a company for fraud need no longer rescind his contract to take the shares. Most plaintiffs will opt for an action for compensation under sections 150 or 166 FSA, as fraud need not be proved and the mere untruth of the statement is sufficient.

If the misrepresentation was made innocently (i.e. the company was unaware that it was untrue) the company may be liable in damages. The company may be able to avoid liability if it can prove that it had reasonable grounds to believe, and did believe up to the time the shares were issued, that the facts represented were true.

Rights against directors or promoters

If the directors have been fraudulent in misrepresenting facts stated in the prospectus, they will be liable in damages for the tort of deceit. In order to prove fraud, the plaintiff must show that the defendant 'makes a statement to be acted upon by others, which is false and which is known by him to be false, or is made recklessly or without care whether it is true or false'.

A director will not be liable for deceit for a false statement made in a prospectus if he honestly believes the statement to be true, even if there are no reasonable grounds for his belief. In *Derry v. Peek*, a prospectus stated that the Plymouth and District Tramways Co. had the right to work its trams by steam instead of horses, by virtue of a special Act of Parliament. The consent of the Board of Trade had to be obtained for such a change. It refused to give its consent and the company had to be wound up. Peek, who had taken shares on the strength of the prospectus, sued the directors for fraud. It was held that they were not liable as they honestly believed the statement as to steam power to be true.

An individual who buys shares in the market on the strength of a prospectus has no right against the directors if the prospectus contained a misrepresentation (as in *Peek v. Gurney*), unless the directors intended by issuing the prospectus to encourage and induce purchases in the market. In *Andrews v. Mockford*, a father and son concocted a prospectus for the Sutherland Reef Company, a gold mining company which never existed. A copy of the prospectus was sent to Andrews, amongst others. He decided not to purchase any shares but kept the prospectus. A few months later he read that the company had made a rich discovery on its property and that the main shaft was down fifty feet. The newspaper report was based on a bogus telegram and Andrews bought shares on the stock market. The company was wound up, and Andrews sued Mockford for damages on the basis that there was one continuous fraud which had induced him to purchase the shares. It was held that the action succeeded.

Statutory remedies providing compensation

The Financial Services Act provides statutory remedies for misrepresentation and omissions in listing particulars (sections 150–152) and prospectuses (sections 166–8). The provisions are almost identical and, unless the contrary is stated, similar provisions apply to both. These provisions also apply to supplementary listing particulars and supplementary prospectuses.

(a) Any person responsible for listing particulars (supplementary listing particulars) or a prospectus (a supplementary prospectus) is liable to compensate any person who has acquired any of the shares in question and suffered loss as a result of

  (i) any untrue or misleading statement in the particulars or prospectus; *or*
  (ii) the omission of any matter required to be included.

(b) Any person who fails to comply with the provisions relating to the issue of supplementary listing particulars, or a supplementary prospectus, is also liable to compensate any person who has suffered loss (as in *(a)*).

Persons responsible for listing particulars or a prospectus

1 The issuer of the shares.
2 Directors of the issuer.

3   Any person named in the particulars or prospectus as having agreed to become a director.
4   Any person stated in the particulars or prospectus as having accepted responsibility for any part of the document.
5   Any other person who has authorised the contents of any part of the particulars or prospectus.

Neither the issuer, nor a director, nor a person who has agreed to become a director, is responsible for the contents of the prospectus if he has not made or authorised the offer to which the prospectus relates. (This does not apply to listing provisions as the issuer's consent must be given before an application for listing can be made.)

Neither a director nor a person who has agreed to become a director is responsible for any particulars or prospectus published without his knowledge or consent if on becoming aware of publication he immediately gave reasonable public notice of that fact.

A person who has accepted responsibility for part only of the particulars or prospectus, or who has authorised the contents of the document is only responsible for that part and only if it is included in substantially the form and context to which he has agreed.

Exemptions from liability to pay compensation

The following defences are available to a person sued for compensation under FSA, sections 150, 166.

1 Reasonable belief in the truth of the statement

He must satisfy the court that at the time of submitting the particulars or prospectus for registration he reasonably believed, having made reasonable enquiries, that the statement was true and not misleading, or the omission was proper and:

(a)   that he continued in that belief until the time when the shares were acquired; *or*

(b) that they were acquired before it was reasonably practical to bring a correction to the attention of potential investors; *or*
(c) that before the shares were acquired he had taken all reasonable steps to ensure that a correction was brought to the attention of potential investors; *or*
(d) that he continued in that belief until after dealing in the shares had commenced and the shares were acquired after such a lapse of time that he ought reasonably to be excused.

2 Expert's statements

The statement was made by or on the authority of an expert with the expert's consent and at the time he believed, on reasonable grounds, that the expert was competent to make or authorise the statement and had given his consent to its inclusion in the form and context in which it was included. This belief must exist both at the time of submission of the particulars or registration of the prospectus and when the shares were acquired unless:

(a) they were acquired before it was reasonably practicable to bring the fact that the expert was not competent or had not given his consent to the attention of persons likely to acquire the shares; or
(b) that he took reasonable steps to bring that fact to the attention of those investors before the shares were acquired; or
(c) that he held that belief until after dealing had commenced in those shares and they were acquired after such a lapse of time that he ought in the circumstances to be reasonably excused.

3 Publication of correction

That before the shares were acquired a correction, or the fact that an expert was not competent, or had not given his consent was published to bring it to the attention of potential investors; or he took reasonable steps to secure its publication and reasonably believed it to have been published.

An expert includes any engineer, valuer, accountant or other person whose professional, qualifications or experience give authority to a statement made by him.

4 Official statement

The statement was made by an official person or contained in a public official document and fairly and accurately reproduced in the particulars or prospectus.

5 Knowledge of defect

The person suffering the loss acquired the shares with the knowledge that the statement was false or misleading, or knew of the omitted matter, or of the change or new matter.

6 Reasonable belief

The failure to submit supplementary listing particulars or a supplementary prospectus was a reasonable belief that the change or new matter did not call for supplementary listing particulars or a supplementary prospectus (FSA sections 151, 167).

Negligence

It may be possible to claim damages for negligent misrepresentation under the principle in *Hedley Byrne Co v. Heller and Partners*. This provides that if a person negligently makes a false statement in circumstances where he should have foreseen that another party would act upon that statement to his detriment he is liable for any financial loss suffered by that other party. It was held in *Diamond Manufacturing Co Ltd v. Hamilton* that a company's auditors were liable to a purchaser of shares to whom they had handed an audited copy of the company's balance sheet, which was later found to be incorrect. The purchaser had entered into the contract on the basis of a representation as to the accuracy of the balance sheet.

Criminal liability

Section 19 of the Theft Act 1968 provides that where an officer of a company, with intent to deceive its members or creditors about its affairs, publishes or concurs in publishing a written statement or account which to his knowledge is or may be misleading, false or deceptive in a material particular, is liable to imprisonment for a term not exceeding seven years. It was under a forerunner of this section in the Larceny Act that Lord Kylsant was convicted (*R v. Kylsant*). It is an offence for a person to make a statement, promise or forecast, which he knows to be misleading, false or deceptive; or dishonestly conceal any material facts, or recklessly make a statement, promise or forecast (dishonestly or otherwise) which is misleading, false or deceptive to induce a person to enter or refrain from entering into an investment agreement (FSA section 47).

It is also an offence under FSA section 47 for a person to do any act or engage in any course of conduct which creates a false or misleading impression as to the market in or the value of any investment, in order to induce a person to subscribe or to refrain from subscribing for those investments, unless he can show that he reasonably believed that he would not create such an impression.

Both offences under FSA section 47 carry a maximum of seven years imprisonment.

10
MEMBERSHIP OF A COMPANY

How persons become members

A person becomes a member of a company when he agrees to become a member and his name is entered in the register of members (section 22). In the case of a share company its shareholders are its members.

A person becomes a member in one of the following ways:

(a) by purchasing shares from a previous member, e.g. on a stock exchange. The company registers the transfer and enters his name on the register of members.

(b) by applying to the company for an allotment of shares. When shares are allotted to him, the company will enter his name on the register.

(c) by subscribing to the company's memorandum. As soon as the company is registered, the subscriber's name is entered on the register.

(d) by signing and filing an undertaking, as a director, to take and pay for qualification shares.

(e) by succeeding to shares on the death or bankruptcy of a member.
(f) by estoppel where a person's name is placed on the register in error or is not deleted when he transfers his shares. If he is aware of the error and fails to take steps to rectify the error he may be estopped from denying that he is a member.

Any person not under a disability may become a member, unless the company's articles impose a restriction as they often do, in the case of minors and aliens. Articles often give a power to the directors to refuse a transfer to persons of whom they do not approve.

Who may become members?

Companies

A company may become a member of another company if its memorandum contains a power to hold shares, or if it takes shares in payment of a debt by way of compromise. It attends meetings by appointing a duly authorised representative to attend and vote on its behalf.

A company may only acquire its *own* shares in one of the following ways:

(a) The acquisition by a company of any of its fully paid shares, other than for a valuable consideration (e.g. a gift of its own shares to a company in a bequest).
(b) The acquisition of its shares in a reduction of capital.
(c) The redemption or purchase of any shares in accordance with the Act.
(d) The purchase of its shares as a result of a Court Order under section 459 when the minority complain of unfair prejudice, or as a result of an alteration of the company's objects.
(e) The forfeiture or surrender of shares.

In situations *(b)*, *(c)* and *(d)* the company must immediately cancel the shares; in situations *(a)* and *(e)* the shares must either be disposed of or cancelled within three years (section 146).

If a person acquires shares in a limited company as a nominee of that company he is deemed to hold the shares on his own account, with the company having no interest in the shares. If the nominee does not pay the company the sums due on the shares, the directors shall be jointly and severally liable with the nominee for payment of any outstanding sums.

The general prohibition on a company and its subsidiaries giving financial assistance (by means of a gift, loan, guarantee or otherwise) for the purchase of its own shares does not apply if the company's principal purpose in giving financial assistance is incidental to some larger purpose, and the assistance was given in good faith in the interests of the company (sections 151, 153).

A company may provide financial assistance in the following circumstances:

(i) for a loan made in the ordinary course of business by a company whose ordinary business is lending money.
(ii) for an employee share scheme, if the assistance is given in good faith in the company's interests.
An employee share scheme is a scheme for encouraging or facilitating the holding of shares or debentures in a company (or its holding company) for the benefit of its employees or former employees, or the wives, husbands, widows, widowers and infant children of such employees.
(iii) Loans to employees, other than directors, to purchase fully paid shares in the company.

A public company may only provide financial assistance in these circumstances, if the company has net assets which are not thereby reduced or, to the extent that those assets are thereby reduced, if the assistance is provided out of distributable profits (section 154(1)).

The prohibitions are relaxed in the case of private companies. In general a private company may provide financial assistance to any person, including a director, for the acquisition of its own shares. Such financial assistance may only be provided from the company's distributable profits. A subsidiary may not provide financial assistance for the acquisition of shares in its holding company, if it is also a subsidiary of a public company, which is itself a subsidiary of that holding company (section 155).

A special resolution must sanction the financial assistance to be given, unless the company proposing to give the financial assistance is a wholly owned subsidiary.

The directors of the company proposing to give the financial assistance must make a statutory declaration that they have formed the opinion that after giving this financial assistance the company will be able to pay its debts in full over the following year. The auditors must also append a report to the effect that they are not aware of anything to indicate that the directors' declaration is unreasonable in the circumstances (section 156).

The holders of 10 per cent of the issued shares or capital of the company or 10 per cent of the membership who did not vote in favour of the resolution may apply to the Court for the resolution to be cancelled. The Court may confirm the resolution, cancel the resolution or make an order for the purchase of the interests of dissentient members and may make these orders on such terms and conditions as it thinks fit (section 157).

The relaxation of this prohibition will make it easier to carry out a 'management buy-out'. Managers of private companies who wish to buy up the shares of their company from the existing owners will be allowed to secure loans on the company's assets.

Subsidiary companies

As a general rule a subsidiary company may not hold shares in its holding company (section 23) unless:

(a) The subsidiary was a member of its holding company before 1 July 1948 or held shares in the parent company before it became a subsidiary. It may continue to be a member, but it cannot vote at the meetings of its holding company.
(b) The subsidiary holds the shares as a personal representative or trustee and neither company has any beneficial interest under the trust, other than in the ordinary course of business (e.g. a bank's subsidiary company, dealing with executorship and trustee matters may hold the bank's shares as a result of being appointed an executor or trustee).
(c) The subsidiary is a market maker on a recognised investment exchange. It may hold shares in its holding company for the purpose of making a market in those shares.

Joint holders

Shares may be allotted to two or more persons jointly, and will be registered in their names. The articles usually state that the company shall not be bound to issue more than one share certificate, and that only the first named in the register is entitled to a share certificate, to a dividend, to notice of meetings, and to a vote. When such a share is transferred, the joint holders must join in the transfer, and on the death of one joint holder the shares are vested in the survivor.

Minors

A minor (i.e. a person under the age of eighteen) may become a member unless forbidden in the articles. A minor may repudiate a contract to take shares before or within a reasonable time of becoming eighteen (i.e. the contract is voidable). If he does repudiate, he cannot recover any money paid for the shares unless there has been a total failure of consideration. In *Steinberg v. Scala (Leeds) Ltd*, an infant agreed to take 500 £1 shares in a company and paid 10s (50p) on each share. She did not receive a dividend on the shares and whilst an infant sued to recover the money she had paid, and sought a declaration that she was not liable for future calls. It was held that she was not liable for future calls, but as the shares had at one time had a market value she could not recover the money she had already paid.

Bankrupts

A bankrupt may be a member of a company and, unless the articles provide otherwise, a shareholder does not cease to be a member if he becomes bankrupt. As a member he is entitled to vote at meetings, but the articles usually provide that notice of meetings is to be sent to the trustee in bankruptcy, and so the bankrupt will vote in accordance with the dictates of the trustee. However, an undischarged bankrupt may not become a director without the leave of the Court by which he was adjudged bankrupt (CDDA section 11).

A company may prove in a member's bankruptcy for any unpaid

calls. The trustee may however disclaim partly paid shares as onerous property (1.A section 315), in that the shares have little value and are a potential liability.

Personal representatives

A member's personal representatives, i.e. his executor (if a will has been made) or an administrator (if no will was made), will succeed to his shares on a member's death. A company will recognise the rights of personal representatives on production by an executor of evidence of probrate of a will or on production by an administrator of letters of administration of an estate.

A deceased member's estate remains liable for calls if the shares are not fully paid.

A personal representative is entitled to transfer the shares and receives all dividends, bonuses or other benefits from the shares without being registered as a member, but the articles usually preclude him from voting (Article 31).

The articles usually provide that a personal representative may choose to be registered as a member (Article 30), or he may be required by the directors either to register as a member or to transfer the shares.

If he chooses to be registered as a member he becomes personally liable for calls, although he is entitled to an indemnity from the estate of the deceased member.

Firms

As a firm is not a legal entity it should be registered as a member and the partners should be asked for their consent to registration as joint holders.

Lenders

A person who lends money to the company on a mortgage of its shares may become liable as a member if the shares are registered in his name.

In *Re Paper Patent Manufacturing Co. Addison's Case,* Addison lent the company £500 and took 100 £5 shares as security for the loan, with a proviso that the money was to be repaid on a month's notice and that the shares should then be cancelled. Notice was given and the money was repaid, but it was later held that Addison was liable to pay £500 for the shares.

— Rights and liabilities of members —

In a share company, the member's liability is to pay for his shares in full, that is for the whole nominal amount of his shares. If he was allotted shares as a result of a prospectus application, he is liable for the amounts due on application and allotment, and for any instalments specified in the terms of issue. Any further amounts outstanding on the shares may be called up by the directors at some future date. Should any amount remain unpaid and the company is wound up, the liquidator will call upon the shareholder to pay the outstanding amount.

If a shareholder transfers partly paid shares he may incur liability in the event of the company being wound up within one year. Should the existing shareholders be unable to pay their contributions, previous shareholders may be placed on the 'B' list of contributories.

If the company carries on business for more than six months with less than two members, the remaining member may become liable for the company's debts contracted after the six month period, without limit of liability.

A member has major rights in that he is entitled to a dividend, when a dividend has been duly declared. He has a right to vote at meetings and can appoint anyone as his proxy to attend and vote in his place. He has a right in the winding up of the company to receive a proportionate part of the capital (after the payment of the company's debts), or to participate in the distribution of the company's assets.

He has the right to transfer his shares to whomsoever he wishes, unless he is forbidden to do so or is restricted by the articles.

A member is entitled to a share certificate, to a copy of the memorandum and articles and, unless provided otherwise by the articles, to receive a notice of general meetings. He is entitled to receive a copy of every balance sheet laid before a general meeting, and has the right to inspect copies of directors' service contracts, various registers, and the minutes of general meetings.

He may, on his own or with other members, requisition a general meeting, circulate resolutions and petition the Court for the winding up of the company, or for relief where the members are unfairly prejudiced.

Termination of membership

A person ceases to be a member when his name is removed from the register on the occurrence of any of these events:

- A transfer of all his shares.
- The forfeiture or surrender of all his shares.
- The sale of all his shares by a company to enforce a lien.
- The death of the member and the transfer of his shares to his personal representative.
- The expulsion of the member from a company.
- The bankruptcy of the member and the registration of the shares in the name of his trustee in bankruptcy, or their disclaimer by the trustee.
- The issue of share warrants.
- The redemption of redeemable shares.
- The winding up of a company.
- A court order for the purchase of shares by a company under sections 5, 54, 459–461 and the purchase by members under sections 459–461.
- The purchase by an offerer of the shares of a dissentient member in a takeover bid (section 428).

Register of members

A company must keep a register of its members containing:

(a) the name and address of each member.
(b) a statement of the shares held by each member. If the shares are of different classes, each class must be distinguished.

(c) the amount paid or agreed to be considered as paid upon the shares.
(d) the date on which each person became a member.
(e) the date on which each person ceased to be a member (section 352).

A company with more than fifty members must keep an index of its members, and the register and index must be open to inspection during business hours, free of charge, to members (sections 354, 356). The register may be a bound book or the entries may be made by recording the information in any other manner e.g. computerised, as long as adequate precautions are taken to prevent falsification (section 722). Non-members may be charged 5 pence (or less), if the company so prescribes, for inspecting the register. Any member or any other person may require the company to provide a copy of the register on payment of 10 pence per 100 words. The company must provide this copy within ten days of its being requested (section 356).

The Court has power to rectify the register if a person's name is entered or omitted from the register, without sufficient cause; or default is made; or unnecessary delay takes place in entering the fact that a person has ceased to be a member.

As well as rectification, the Court may order the payment by the company of any damages sustained by the aggrieved party (section 359).

A company may, on giving notice in a newspaper circulating in the district in which its registered office is situated, close the register of members for up to 30 days a year (section 358).

Notice of trusts

Notice of a trust cannot be entered on the register, even if the company has constructive notice of the existence of a trust. In *Simpson v. Molson's Bank*, the executors of a will transferred shares to a third party in breach of the terms of the will, and he was registered by the company as the holder of the shares. Not only did the company have a copy of the will, but one of its directors was an executor of the will. It was held that the company's sole responsibility was to satisfy itself that the executors were properly appointed and had authority; it was not concerned with the contents of the will.

As far as a company is concerned the person whose name is entered on the register is the beneficial owner of the shares. If the shares are held by a trustee the company is not liable to any beneficiary for any breach of trust, or for any fraudulent transfer of the shares by the trustee. The trustee is liable for any calls on the shares, even though the calls exceed the value of the trust property in his hands.

A beneficiary can protect his interest by serving a 'Stop Notice' on a company. He makes an application to the Court, with a supporting affidavit, giving particulars of his interest and this is served on the company. If a company receives any request to transfer the shares or pay a dividend on them, it must inform the person who lodged the notice, and must not accept the transfer, or pay a dividend until eight days have expired after giving such notice. This enables the person lodging the notice to obtain an injunction within the eight days and so prevent the company from transferring the shares or paying a dividend.

Register of interest in shares

If a company's shares are listed on a stock exchange it must also keep a register of any person who becomes interested in 3 per cent or more of its issued shares which carry an unrestricted right to vote at general meetings (section 211). A person must notify the company of such an interest within two days.

A person has a notifiable interest if:

(a) he enters into a contract to buy shares;
(b) not being the registered holder, he is entitled to exercise or control the exercise of any right conferred by holding shares;
(c) he has a right to call for delivery of shares to himself or to his order; or
(d) he has a right to acquire an interest in shares or is under an obligation, whether absolute or conditional to take an interest in shares (section 208).

An interest may also be notifiable if held by a person's spouse, infant child, step child or by a company which he controls (section 203).

If a person already has a 3 per cent holding and either increases or diminishes his holding by 1 per cent without reducing his holding to below 3 per cent, he must also inform the company within two days, as must a person whose holding falls below 3 per cent (sections 198, 202).

Sections 204–206 impose obligations on members of a 'concert party' to notify a public company (the target company) of interests in voting shares. A concert party agreement is any agreement to acquire an interest in the shares of a public company. Each party to the agreement relies on the other party to retain the shares acquired, as a result of obtaining this interest. They must inform the target company of their collective holding. They may appoint an agent for this purpose, but if they do not, they must notify the company individually. Each party is under a duty to inform the other parties of their holding, so that they may comply with their obligation to notify the company when (or if) it arises.

A public company may require any person who, during the last three years, has been interested (or who it believes has been interested) in its voting shares to provide information to the company as to the extent of his interest. In the event of obtaining unsatisfactory replies, or no replies, the company may apply to the Court for restrictions (e.g. non-payment of dividends, no votes to be exercised) to apply to its shares. Members holding 10 per cent or more of the company's shares may require the company to use this power to investigate the ownership of shares.

A register of the results of the enquiries undertaken in connection with such interests must be kept and made available for inspection by the members and the public.

The annual return

Every company having a share capital is required to make an annual return to the Registrar (section 363) stating:
(a) the address of its registered office.
(b) the type of company it is and its principal business activity.
(c) the address where the registers of members and debenture holders are kept (if not kept at the registered office).
(d) the amount of share capital and the number of shares authorised and issued.

(e) the nature of each class of share and the total number and aggregate nominal value of the issued shares of that class.
(f) a list of names and addresses of members and those ceasing to be members since the last return, stating the number of shares held and the number transferred.
(g) particulars of the directors and secretary.
(h) if the company has elected to dispense with the laying of accounts and reports before the company in general meeting, or to dispense with the holding of annual general meetings, a statement to that effect.

A company must deliver successive annual returns, each of which is made up to a date not later than its return date, i.e. either the anniversary of its incorporation or, if the last return was made up to a different date, the anniversary of that date. The return must be delivered to the Registrar within 28 days after the date to which it is made up. Late delivery may be penalised by a default fine and a daily default fine (sections 363, 364 and 364A).

11
SHARE CAPITAL

Various terms are used in respect of share capital.

(a) Nominal or authorised capital is the nominal value of shares which a company may issue. This amount is stated in the memorandum of association and may be increased or reduced.

(b) Issued capital is the nominal value of the shares which have actually been allotted by the company, whether for cash or some other consideration.

(c) Paid up capital is the total amount paid up or credited as paid up on the shares issued.

(d) Uncalled capital is the total amount not called up on the shares issued.

(e) Reserve capital is that part of the uncalled capital which may only be called up in the event of the company being wound up.

(f) Equity share capital is that part of the issued capital which gives its holders an unrestricted right to participate in dividends and distribution of capital. It normally consists of the ordinary shares or the ordinary and deferred shares.

Classes of share capital

A company may confer different rights on different classes of shares. Table A provides that 'any share may be issued with such rights or restrictions as the Company may by ordinary resolution determine' (Article 2). The various rights attaching to the various classes of shares are usually set out in the company's articles, or in the terms of issue of the shares. Different classes of shares attract different types of investors. While the ordinary shares offer the promise of greater financial rewards, the preference shares promise a more secure if less spectacular return on investment. If additional capital is only required for a limited time, a company may issue redeemable shares.

The main classes of shares are: ordinary shares; founders' or deferred shares; and preference shares.

(a) Ordinary shares

Ordinary shares are often referred to as the equity capital of the company. The holders of these shares are entitled, in the absence of any deferred shares, to the balance of the distributed profit and in a winding up to the balance of the assets.

Companies are allowed to issue non-voting shares, but such shares are frowned upon by the Stock Exchange. Non-voting ordinary shares are a separate class of shares from the ordinary voting shares.

(b) Founders' or deferred shares

The holders of these shares are only entitled to a dividend if the dividend on the ordinary shares reaches a fixed amount, for example, the deferred shareholders may be entitled to 25 per cent of the profits, after a dividend of 10 per cent has been paid on the ordinary shares.

These shares are rarely issued today, but at one time they were fairly common. They are sometimes referred to as founders or management shares as they were often issued to the promoters who were prepared to wait until the very last moment for their share of the profits, thus showing their confidence in the company. Unfortunately, many of these shares were issued by unscrupulous promoters who perpetrated frauds on the public and this type of share became very unpopular with investors. Most deferred shares have now been converted into ordinary shares.

(c) Preference shares

These are shares which are given certain preferential rights over the other shares in a company. There are different types of preference shares and their rights vary accordingly, but the two principal rights usually enjoyed by those shares are:

(i) a right to preference in the payment of a dividend; and
(ii) a right to preference in the repayment of capital in a winding up.

Preference shareholders are entitled to receive a dividend which is expressed as a percentage of the nominal amount of the share (e.g. 6 per cent preference share) when a dividend is declared. A preference shareholder is not entitled to 6 per cent per annum but to preferential treatment on the declaration of a dividend.

Unless stated otherwise a preference share is cumulative, that is, if no dividend is declared on the preference share in any year, the arrears of dividend are carried forward and must be paid before any dividend is paid on the ordinary shares. For example, if no dividend is declared on 6 per cent preference shares in 1985, 1986 and 1987 they would be entitled in 1988 to arrears of 24 per cent before the ordinary shareholders were paid any dividend.

The articles may provide that the shares are participating in that after the preferences and ordinary shares have received specified dividends, the preference shareholders will be entitled to participate in the surplus profits of the company.

The general rule in a winding up is that all shareholders should be treated equally, so that if any group of shareholders is to receive preferential treatment this must be expressly stated in the articles or the terms of issue of the shares. Most articles give preference shareholders priority to repayment of capital in a winding up, and if no other rights are given it is assumed that they are not entitled to share in any assets which remain after the repayment of the capital.

If the articles or terms of issue of the shares do not grant preference shareholders any priority in winding up, they will be entitled to share equally with the ordinary shareholders in the repayment of capital and in the division of any surplus assets.

In a winding up preference shareholders have no rights to any outstanding arrears of dividend unless the articles specifically give that right.

Redeemable shares

A company limited by shares may, if authorised by its articles, issue redeemable shares which may be redeemed at the option of the company or the shareholder. These shares are issued when the company requires additional capital for a limited time only.

(i) The shares may only be redeemed if they are fully paid.
(ii) The shares may only be redeemed out of the distributable profits available for dividend, or out of the proceeds of a fresh issue of shares made for the purpose.
(iii) If the shares are redeemed from profits, profits equal to the nominal amount of the shares redeemed must be transferred to a capital redemption reserve fund.
(iv) The capital redemption reserve fund may be used to pay up unissued bonus shares to be issued as fully paid to members.
(v) Any premium payable on redemption must be provided out of distributable profits or out of a fresh issue of shares made for the purposes of redemption.
(vi) When a company is redeeming shares, it may issue shares to an equivalent nominal amount of the redeemed shares, without being regarded as having increased its share capital, as long as the old shares are redeemed within one month of the issue of the new shares (sections 159, 160).

Notice of the redemption must be given to the Registrar within one month.

The redemption of shares does not amount to a reduction of capital as the redeemed shares remain part of the nominal capital of the company and must be shown in the balance sheet.

Share warrants

A company may, if its shares are fully paid up and it is given authority by its articles, issue share warrants stating that the bearer is entitled to the shares specified therein. They are negotiable instruments and may be transferred by delivery of the warrant.

When a share warrant is issued, the member's name must be struck off the register. Certain particulars must then be entered in the register, namely that a warrant has been issued, a statement of the shares included in the warrant, and the date of issue of the warrant.

The payment of a dividend is usually made by means of a coupon attached to the warrant, which is sent to the company when a dividend is advertised. The holder of a warrant may at any time surrender his warrant, be entered in the register, and issued with a share certificate.

If the articles so provide, he may be deemed to be a member of the company for certain purposes. The articles usually provide that the holder of a warrant may not requisition a meeting, give notice of resolutions, or vote unless he first deposits his warrant with the company before a general meeting. At the conclusion of the meeting the warrant is returned to him.

A share warrant is unsuitable as a qualification share for a director, as a company would be unable to ensure that he continued to hold the warrant.

Increase and alteration of share capital

A share company or a guarantee company having share capital may alter its share capital so as to:

(a) increase its share capital by creating new shares;
(b) consolidate and divide its shares into shares of larger amount;
(c) sub-divide its shares or any part of them into shares of a smaller amount. When the shares are not fully paid the proportions paid up and unpaid will remain unaltered;
(d) convert its paid up shares or re-convert its stock into paid up shares;
(e) cancel any unissued shares.

The articles must authorise any of these alterations which must be made by the company at a general meeting. An ordinary resolution is sufficient, unless the articles provide otherwise (section 121).

The Registrar must be informed of any alteration in the share capital. Notice of an increase in share capital must be forwarded to him within fifteen days, with a copy of the resolution authorising the increase. Notice of any of the other alterations listed above must be given to the Registrar within one month.

(i) The articles normally give authority to increase capital. Article 32 provides that a company may by ordinary resolution increase its share capital by new shares of such amount as the resolution prescribes. If the articles do not give this power they must be altered by a special resolution before a resolution to increase the capital can be passed.

(ii) A company may consolidate and divide its shares and if the shares are found to be divided into unwieldy or inconvenient amounts, for example 50 000 shares of 35p each might be consolidated in 17 500 shares of £1 each.

(iii) A company may sub-divide its shares if the nominal or market value of the share is so high that it restricts dealings in the shares, for example £100 shares might be sub-divided into ten £10 shares.

(iv) The conversion of fully paid shares into stock offers certain advantages: e.g. stock need not be numbered; may be divided into any fraction and may be transferred in any amounts subject to any restriction in the articles.

(v) Only unissued shares can be cancelled; that is, it is possible to cancel authorised capital, not issued capital. This is sometimes known as diminution of capital, to distinguish it from a reduction of capital. It is rarely invoked, but it has been used when the capital structure of a company has been altered in an amalgamation or reconstruction, or when a company has wished to rid itself of unissued shares carrying burdensome rights.

Reduction of capital

The capital of a company may not be reduced except as permitted by the Act which provides that a limited company may, if authorised by its articles, reduce its share capital. The method is by special resolution and the Court must confirm the reduction (section 135).

If the articles do not contain the power to allow a reduction of capital, the articles must be altered so as to allow this power by special resolution, and a further special resolution must be passed to sanction the

SHARE CAPITAL

reduction. These resolutions may be passed successively at the same meeting.

Companies reduce their capital for a variety of reasons, for example:

1 A company having partly paid up shares may have surplus capital and may wish to relieve its members of their liability in respect of the amount not paid up (e.g. a company having a share capital of 10 000 £1 shares with 50p paid on each share may wish to reduce its capital to 10 000 fully paid shares of 50p each).
2 A company may have capital in excess of its requirements and may wish to return some of it to its shareholders. This often happens when a company sells part of its undertaking and decides to confine its activities to the remaining section of the business (e.g. a company with a share capital of 10 000 fully paid £1 shares wishes to reduce its capital to 10 000 fully paid 50p shares, the remaining 50p per share to be returned in cash, to each member).
3 A company may wish to cancel paid up share capital which has been lost or is not represented by available assets (e.g. a company with a share capital of 10 000 fully paid £1 shares may only have assets amounting to £5 000, and may seek to reduce its capital to 10 000 fully paid shares of 50p each).

Where the proposed reduction involves either a diminution of the liability of shareholders, or the return of paid up capital to shareholders, the company's creditors are entitled to object. The Court then settles a list of creditors, who either consent to the reduction or are paid off by the company (section 136).

A public company may not reduce its capital below the statutory minimum under section 135, unless it first re-registers as a private company (section 139).

The Court may make the order on such terms and conditions as it thinks fit. It may also require the company to add the words 'and reduced' to its name for a period of time, and for the company to publish the reasons for the reduction and the causes which led to the reduction. (section 137).

The order confirming the reduction must be produced to the Registrar and a copy of the order and a minute showing details of the company's new capital structure must be delivered to him. The order and the minute are then registered. The minute is deemed to be substituted for the corresponding part of the memorandum and is valid and alterable as if it had been originally contained in the memorandum. The Registrar then issues a certificate which is conclusive evidence that all the requirements of the Act in respect of the reduction of the share capital have been complied with and that the share capital is as stated in the minute. (section 138)

Purchase of shares

A limited company having a share capital may purchase its own shares, if so authorised by its articles (Article 35), (section 162). It may purchase its shares in both off-market and market transactions (section 163).

An off-market purchase is a purchase other than on a recognised stock exchange, or is a purchase on a recognised stock exchange which is not subject to a marketing arrangement on that stock exchange (section 163(1)). The terms of the proposed contract of purchase must be authorised by a special resolution of the company, before it enters into such a contract. In the case of a public company, the authority must specify a date, no later than 18 months after passing the resolution, on which the authority is to expire. A purchase is invalid if a member, holding shares to which the resolution relates, votes in favour of the resolution, and the resolution would not have been passed without his votes (section 164).

A market purchase is a purchase on a recognised stock exchange (section 163(2)). The purchase must be authorised by the company in general meeting. The authority may be unconditional or subject to conditions, and must specify the maximum number of shares authorised to be acquired, the minimum and maximum prices which may be paid for the shares, and the date on which the authority expires (section 166). A contract under which the company becomes entitled or obliged to purchase its shares (e.g. options) is termed a contingent purchase contract. The purchase of its shares by a company in these circumstances must be approved in advance by special resolution (section 165).

Payment of the purchase price must normally be made from a company's distributable profit, and an amount equal to the nominal value of the shares purchased must be transferred to a capital redemption reserve. The reserve may be applied by the company in paying up unissued shares to be allotted to members as fully paid bonus shares (section 162).

A company may not assign rights, which it has acquired under contract, for the purchase of its own shares (section 167). It may, however, release its rights under a contract for an off market purchase or a contingent purchase provided the release is authorised in advance by special resolution (section 167).

Any payment made by a company in consideration of acquiring an option to purchase its own shares under a contingent purchase contract, or any variation of an off-market purchase contract or contingent purchase contract or the release from any of its obligations under a contract for an off-market purchase, a contingent purchase contract, or a contract for a market purchase, must be funded from the company's distributable profits (section 168).

A company must file a return with the Registrar of shares purchased, within 28 days of the delivery of the shares. A company must also keep, for 10 years, a contract of purchase at its registered office, which must be open to inspection to any member of the company, and in the case of a public company, to the public (section 169).

A private company may, if authorised by its articles, make a purchase of its own shares out of capital, after exhausting any available profits and/or the proceeds of any fresh issue of shares made for the purposes of purchase. Such a payment must be approved by special resolution (sections 171, 173). The directors must also make a statutory declaration that having made a full inquiry into the company's affairs and prospects they have formed the opinion that the company will be able to meet its debts initially on purchasing its shares, and in the following year. The auditors must also append a report to the same effect (section 173).

Within the week following the resolution, the company must publish in the *Gazette* a notice stating that it has approved the payment out of capital; the amount of capital involved; the availability for inspection of the directors' and auditors' report; and that any creditor may apply to the Court within five weeks for an order prohibiting the payment. It must also publish a notice to the same effect in an appropriate national newspaper, or give notice in writing to each of its creditors (section 175).

Any member who did not vote for the resolution and any creditor may, within five weeks, apply to the Court for the cancellation of the resolution. The Court on hearing the application may make an order either cancelling the resolution, or confirming it on such terms as it thinks fit. It may also adjourn the proceedings in order to make arrangements for the purchase of shares of dissentient members, or for the protection of dissentient creditors (section 176).

If a company having purchased its shares out of capital is subsequently wound up as being unable to pay its debts, within one year of the purchase, the person from whom the shares were purchased, and the directors who made the statutory declaration, will be liable to contribute to the assets of the company (IA section 76).

A company is not liable in damages if it fails to redeem its redeemable shares or fails to implement an agreement to purchase its own shares. The court will not grant of specific performance in these situations if it can be shown that the company is unable to meet the cost of redemption or purchase out of distributable profits (section 178).

Variation of class rights

It is sometimes necessary to amend or vary the rights of one or more class of shares. If preferential or other special rights are attached to a class of shares, the articles and the memorandum have to be examined to discover if these rights can be varied and by what procedure.

Shareholders may have class rights even though those rights do not attach to any particular class of share. In *Cumbrian Newspapers Group v. Cumberland and Westmoreland Newspapers Ltd.*, in an agreement between the companies, the plaintiff company purchased 10 per cent of the defendant company's shares. The agreement gave pre-emption rights over other shares, rights over unissued shares and the right to appoint a director in the defendant company. It was held that these were class rights which could not be varied without the plaintiff's consent.

The majority of these rights relate to dividend, voting and the distribution of the assets in the winding up of the company.

The procedure to be adopted depends on whether the class rights are defined in the memorandum or in the articles. If the class rights are defined in the memorandum, which provides a procedure for variation, the rights can be varied by following this procedure. If the variation requires the consent of a specified proportion of the class, or the sanction of a general meeting, the minority shareholders can apply to the Court for the cancellation of the variation (section 125).

Section 127 provides that where the articles or memorandum authorise the variation of rights of a class of shares, subject to the consent of a specified proportion of the holders of that class, and such a variation is made, the holders of 15 per cent of the issued shares of the class who did not consent to the variation may, within twenty-one days, apply to the Court to have the variation cancelled. The variation will not become effective unless confirmed by the Court.

If the class rights are defined in the memorandum, but neither the memorandum nor the articles contain a provision for the variation of those rights, they can only be varied by the unanimous consent of all the Company's members (section 125(5)).

If the memorandum prohibits any variation, no variation is possible other than under section 245 which permits compromises to be effected between the company and any class of member.

If class rights are attached to shares other than in the memorandum, for example in the articles or the terms of issue of the shares, and there is a clause permitting their variation (i.e. a variation of rights clause), the class rights can be varied, but only in accordance with the clause. If no provision is made in the articles for variation, class rights may only be varied with the consent in writing of the holders of three-quarters of the issued shares of the class, or with the consent of an extraordinary resolution passed at a separate general meeting of the class. In such a case the rights of the minority shareholders of that class are protected by section 127.

Where the variation of class rights is connected with the giving, varying, revoking or renewing authority to the directors to issue or reduce share capital, then three-quarters of the holders of the class must consent in writing to the variation, or an extraordinary resolution must be passed by a class meeting to sanction the variation (section 125(3)).

Public notice must be given of any special rights attaching to a company's shares and of any variation of these rights. The directors must deliver to the Registrar particulars of any special rights attaching to any class of shares, unless these details are dealt with under some other filing provision – under the company's memorandum or articles, or the resolution within section 380 which deals with the filing of special resolutions (section 128).

An increase in the number of preference and ordinary shares which dilutes the control of existing shareholders is not a variation of class rights.

In *White v. Bristol Aeroplane Co. Ltd*, the issued capital of the company consisted of £600 000 preference and £3 300 000 ordinary stock. The articles of the company provided that class rights could not be altered without the sanction of an extraordinary resolution of the class concerned. The company proposed to issue £600 000 preference shares as bonus shares to the ordinary share-holders which would rank *pari passu* with the existing preference shares. It was held that the issue of new preference shares would affect the enjoyment of the rights of the existing preference stock, not the rights themselves.

In *Re John Smith's Tadcaster Brewery*, a company proposed to increase its capital by creating 280 000 new ordinary £1 shares and issuing them to the ordinary shareholders as fully paid bonus shares from the company's undistributed profits. It was held that the issue of these shares would not affect the rights or privileges of the ordinary shareholder. It would mean that a greater number of people would have similar voting rights.

12
SHARES

A share represents the interest of a shareholder in a company. He does not own any of the company's assets as these belong to the company, a separate legal entity. Nevertheless, he is a proportionate owner of the company and has various rights and liabilities. For example, he has the right to vote, to receive a dividend (if declared), to attend meetings, and he must pay for any amount outstanding on his share.

Each share in a share company must have a nominal value (e.g. £5, £1, 50p) as the memorandum of such a company must state in its capital clause, 'the division thereof into shares of a fixed amount'. It is therefore impossible for a company to issue shares of no par value. Each share must also be distinguished by its number, unless all the issued shares, or all the issued shares of a particular class, are fully paid and rank *pari passu* (section 182).

Application

An application for shares in a company will usually be in writing, although it can be made orally. Such an application, often in response to a prospectus, will be an offer by the applicant. The acceptance of the application will be a letter of allotment from the company. The application form usually reads: 'I agree to accept such shares and any smaller number that may be allotted to me.' Without this clause, a company would be making a counter offer if it allotted any applicant a smaller number of shares than he had applied for, and he could refuse to take any shares.

An application must be accepted within a reasonable time. In *Ramsgate Victoria Hotel Co. v. Montefiore*, Montefiore offered to take shares in the company in June 1864. He did not receive a reply to his letter, but the company allotted him shares in November 1864. By that time the company was in financial difficulties and he refused to take the shares. It was held that the offer had lapsed due to the company's delay in notifying their acceptance.

If the application is subject to a collateral agreement, the acceptance of the application constitutes a binding agreement. If the collateral agreement is not carried out, the applicant's remedy is an action for damages in respect of the collateral agreement. In *Re Elkington's Case Richmond Hill Hotel Co.* Elkington applied for shares and paid 30s (£1.50) per share on allotment. He refused to pay a further call made by the company on the grounds that the company had agreed that, until they had taken and paid for goods to the value of £3 000 from him, no further calls were to be made on the shares. It was held that he must pay the call, and that his remedy lay in action against the company for breach of contract.

Acceptance

The company's acceptance must be communicated to the applicant. Notice of the allotment is generally sent by post and the contract is complete on posting the letter. This is so even if the letter is delayed or lost in the post. In *Household Fire Insurance Co. v. Grant*, Grant applied for 100 shares in a company and was allotted the shares. The letter of allotment was posted by the company, but was not received by Grant. The company went into liquidation and Grant had to pay the balance owing on the shares.

An application for shares may be revoked (i.e. withdrawn) at any time before the letter of allotment is posted. If notice of the revocation of the offer is sent by post the revocation is not effective until the letter is received by the company.

SHARES

──────── Allotment ────────

Directors may not allot shares (i.e. issue shares) unless authorised to do so by the company in general meeting or by the articles. The authority must state the maximum amount of securities that may be allotted, and the date on which the authority expires. The date of expiry must not be more than five years from the date of incorporation when the authority is contained in the company's articles, or five years from the date of passing the resolution giving the authority for altering the articles. The authority may be renewed by the company in general meeting for a further period not exceeding five years (section 80(4)(5)).

Public company

A public company making an allotment is subject to certain restrictions in respect of the allotment of shares.

1. It must not allot shares unless 25 per cent of the nominal value of each share, plus any premium due has been paid (section 101).
2. No allotment may be made unless the capital is fully subscribed for, or the offer states that the shares subscribed for may be allotted in any event, or in the event of the conditions in the offer being satisfied (section 84(1)).
3. If the minimum subscription is not received within 40 days from the issue of the prospectus all money received must be repaid to the applicants within the following eight days. If it is not repaid within the stipulated time, the directors are jointly and severally (collectively and individually) liable to repay it with 5 per cent interest (section 84(2)(3)).
4. The consideration for the allotment may be money, or with the company's consent, money's worth (e.g. goodwill or know how) but a public company may not accept payment by work or service for its shares. Any person who pays for shares by work or services is liable to pay the full value of the shares in money (section 99).
5. A public company may not make an allotment of shares, either fully or partly paid up, other than in cash if part of the payment includes an undertaking that may be performed more than five years after

the date of allotment. If the consideration for an allotment of shares is the transfer to the company of a non-cash asset, it must be transferred to the company within five years of the allotment, and must be valued by a person qualified to be the company's auditor (sections 102, 103). This rule does not apply to an arrangement where the whole or part of the consideration for the allotment is the transfer to the company of shares in another company, or the cancellation of shares in another company; or to an allotment of shares in connection with a proposed merger. An arrangement in this context is any scheme or arrangement, and includes any arrangements under section 425 or IA section 110.

6 The directors must file with the Registrar within one month particulars of any allotment of shares whose rights are not stated in a company's memorandum or articles, or in any resolution or agreement filed with the Registrar, unless the shares are uniform with shares previously allotted (section 128).

7 Whenever a limited company makes an allotment of its shares it must, within one month of the allotment, file with the Registrar a return of allotments, stating the number and nominal amount of the shares and the name of the allottees (i.e. individuals to whom shares have been issued). If the shares have been allotted other than for cash, the consideration for the allotment must also be stated (section 88).

Issue of shares at a discount

A company may not issue shares at a discount (section 100), so that the issue of £1 share for, say, 75 pence is void. Any attempt to achieve an issue at a 'discount' by indirect means is prohibited. In *Moseley v. Koffyfontein Mines*, a company proposed to issue £1 debentures at a 20 per cent discount, namely at 80 pence. The holders were able to have the right to exchange the debentures for fully paid shares at any time before the debentures were repaid. The company was prevented by injunction from proceeding with the issue as there was nothing to prevent a debenture holder from exercising his rights immediately and receiving 100 £1 shares for every £80 that had been paid for the debentures.

Shares issued at a discount will be treated as paid up if payment is made of the nominal value less the discount. The allottee is then liable to pay to the company an amount equal to the amount of the discount, plus interest.

The only exception to the rule is contained in section 97(1) which allows the allottees of shares to deduct or be paid underwriting commission for subscribing for these shares.

Issue of shares at a premium

A company may issue shares at a premium (i.e. at a price in excess of their nominal value) so that the issue of a £1 share for £2 is in order. The Act requires that the premium must be transferred to a share premium account and details of the share premium account must be included in every balance sheet (section 130).

The share premium account may be used to pay up bonus shares to be issued as fully paid to members, to provide a premium on the redemption of shares and to write off the preliminary expenses, commissions and discounts in respect of issues of shares or debentures. Apart from these exceptions the share premiums must be treated as capital.

Relief is given from the provisions of section 130 in certain situations.

1 Premiums on shares issued in exchange for shares in another company (i.e. a merger), where the acquiring company obtains an equity holding of 90 per cent or more, do not have to be credited to the share premium account (section 131).
2 In certain group reconstructions, when the acquiring company issues shares at a premium, only a sum equivalent to the cost of the shares, or equivalent to the amount at which they stood in the company's records, need be transferred to the share premium account (section 132).

Bonus shares

A company makes a bonus or capitalisation issue of its shares when it issues bonus shares to its shareholders. These unissued shares are wholly or partly paid out of the company's reserves and a company may use its undistributed profits, its share premium account, and its capital redemption reserve fund to finance the issue of bonus shares. The articles must allow the capitalisation of profits.

A company does not part with its capital as the shareholders are allotted bonus shares in lieu of cash. Their issue involves an adjustment to a company's balance sheet. For example, a company has an authorised share capital of £100 000 £1 shares. 50 000 shares have already been issued. The company resolves to capitalise £50 000 from its reserves and issue the remaining 50 000 shares as bonus shares on the basis of one new share for each share previously held by the shareholder.

The adjustment is made by reducing the reserves of profit and loss account by £50 000 and adding £50 000 to its issued capital. As both items appear on the liabilities side of the balance sheet, the company's liabilities remain the same.

A shareholder owns the same proportion of the company's share capital as he held before the issue of the bonus shares.

Certificates

A company must have a share certificate ready for issue within two months of allotment or of lodging a valid transfer (not being a transfer which the company is entitled to refuse), unless the terms of issue of the shares provide otherwise. In the case of an allotment of shares the terms of issue normally provide otherwise (section 185), as a company rarely issues share certificates until all the shares are fully paid, which usually takes longer than two months.

If a share certificate is lost or destroyed, the articles usually provide that the company may issue a duplicate on such terms as to indemnify as the directors think fit (Article 7).

Although there is no requirement in the Act that a share certificate must be under seal, the articles usually provide this. Section 186 states that a certificate under the common seal of the company, specifying the shares held by any member, shall be *prima facie* evidence of the title of the member to the shares. It enables him if he so wishes to sell, mortgage or pledge the shares.

'The certificates are the proper (and indeed the only) documentary evidence of title in the possession of a shareholder' (Lord Selbourne).

A share certificate is not therefore conclusive evidence of a member's title to the shares, and the true owner can assert his right to the shares. He can compel the company to restore his name to the register when it has been removed and to pay him any dividends that are outstanding.

Provision is made in the Companies Act 1989 for paperless dealings in securities, i.e. shares and debentures. The Secretary of State may make regulations to enable the title to securities to be evidenced and transferred without certificates. The International Stock Exchange proposes to introduce Taurus, a computerised, paperless trading system, in 1993 (see page 122). Private shareholders will either have an acknowledgement of ownership through an account with their broker or bank, or through an alternative system organised by companies.

A company may be estopped from denying to any person, who has in good faith relied upon the certificate, that the person named on the share certificate is the registered holder (i.e. estoppel as to title).

In *Re Bahia and San Francisco Railway*, a Miss Trittin, who held five shares in the company, left the shares with her broker. The broker sent a forged transfer to the company and the shares were transferred to Stocken and Goldberg, who were issued with share certificates. The company removed Miss Trittin's name from the register. The shares were transferred by Stocken and Goldberg to Burton and Goodburn, who were issued with share certificates by the company. The forgery was subsequently discovered and the company was compelled to restore Miss Trittin's name to the register. As the transfer had been forged no title to the shares passed to Burton and Goodburn, and they claimed damages from the company for the loss of their shares. It was held that they succeeded, for although the shares were not really theirs, the company was estopped from denying the validity of the certificates. The damages awarded were the value of the shares at the time when the company refused to recognise Burton and Goodburn as the shareholders, with interest at 10 per cent from that date.

If the certificate itself is a forgery and has been issued by an officer of the company who does not have the authority to issue certificates, there is no estoppel. In *Ruben v. Great Fingall Consolidated*, Ruben, a firm of moneylenders, lent money to Rowe, the company's secretary, on the security of a share certificate. Rowe signed his own name on the certificate, fraudulently affixed the company's seal, and forged the signature of two of the company's directors. It was held that the certificate was a forgery and the company was not bound.

If the company incurs a loss as a result of acting upon a forged transfer, it may claim an indemnity from the person who sent the forged transfer for registration, that is the transferee and his brokers, who by submitting a transfer impliedly warrants that it is genuine. In *Sheffield Corporation v. Barclay*, two individuals, Timbrell and Honeywill, were joint owners of Sheffield Corporation stock. Timbrell forged Honeywill's signature and transferred the stock to a bank as security for a loan. The bank sent the transfer to the Corporation for registration and was issued with certificates registering the Bank as a stockholder. The Bank later transferred the stock to a third party. On Timbrell's death Honeywill discovered the forgery and the Corporation replaced the stock. The Corporation successfully sued the bank for an indemnity.

A company may, in similar circumstances, be estopped from denying that the amount stated as being paid on the shares has not been paid (i.e. estoppel as to payment).

In *Bloomenthal v. Ford*, Bloomenthal lent £1 000 to a company and was given 10 000 shares as security for the loan. The share certificate described the shares as fully paid, although nothing had been paid on the shares. The company went into liquidation and the liquidator placed Bloomenthal's name on the list of contributories. It was held that the company was estopped from denying that the shares were fully paid and Bloomenthal's name should be removed from the list.

Transfer of shares

A shareholder has an unrestricted right to transfer his shares to any person, subject to any restriction in the articles. The articles may restrict the right to transfer shares; for example Article 24 provides that 'the directors may decline to register the transfer of a share (not being a fully paid share) to a person of whom they shall not approve'. The articles of a large number of private companies contain restrictions on the transfer of shares, while the shares of a public company must normally be free of restrictions on the right of transfer in order to obtain a Stock Exchange quotation.

The directors may be given the power to refuse a transfer of shares without giving reasons for their refusal and, unless there is evidence to the contrary, they will be presumed to have acted in good faith, and in the best interests of the company.

In *Re Smith* and *Fawcett*, there were only two shareholders, who were also the company's directors. Each held 4001 shares. One shareholder died and his son, as executor, applied for the shares to be registered in his name. The other shareholder refused his request (relying on the articles which gave the directors an absolute and uncontrolled discretion to refuse to register a transfer of shares), but offered to register 2001 shares if 2000 shares were sold to him at a certain price. It was held that the director was within his rights to refuse the transfer of the shares.

If the directors give reasons for their refusal, these can be challenged in the Courts, and where they have a discretion to refuse to register the transfer 'to persons of whom they do not approve', their refusal must be on grounds that are personal to the transferee.

In *Re Bede Steam Ship Co.*, the directors of the company refused to register a transfer on the grounds that the shares should not be transferred in small units to individuals with no interest or knowledge of shipping. It was held that this refusal was not on personal grounds and the transfer must be registered.

The board of directors must act positively to refuse a registration of a transfer. In *Re Copal Varnish Co.* there were only two directors, the quorum was two and the chairman had a casting vote. His fellow director deliberately refused to attend meetings to consider transfers of shares, so that a quorum was not present. It was held that the transfers should be registered.

The power of refusal must be exercised within a reasonable time. Section 183 provides that a company must send notice of its refusal to register a transfer to the transferee within two months. It would appear that if the company does not comply with this provision it must register the transfer, as a longer period than two months constitutes unreasonable delay. In *Re Swaledale Cleaners*, share transfer forms were submitted to the company in August 1967. The company's sole director refused to register the transfer although the power of refusal could only be exercised at a board meeting by two directors. In December procedures were commenced to rectify the register. A week later a second director was appointed by the company and at a board meeting the directors refused to register the transfer. It was held that the share transfer was valid as the company had not exercised its powers within a reasonable time.

The articles of a large number of companies contain provisions that a member who wishes to transfer his shares to a person who is not already a member shall first offer them to the other members at a price ascertained in accordance with a formula set out in the articles, or at a fair price estimated by the directors or the company's auditors.

A member may only transfer the shares to a proposed transferee if the other members do not wish to purchase his shares; this is known as a right of pre-emption. If the other members wish to purchase the shares, they must be prepared to purchase all the shares that are being offered for sale. In *Ocean Coal Co. v. Powell Dyffryn Steam Coal Co.* the articles of the Taff Merthyr Steam Co. provided that if a member wished to sell his shares he must first offer the shares to the other members. The company's shares were owned equally by the plaintiff and the defendant. The defendant wished to sell 135 000 shares but the plaintiff sought to purchase 5000 only in order to obtain voting control. It was held that the plaintiff must purchase all the shares offered or reject the offer.

The majority of pre-emption clauses provide for the sale of shares at a fair value. If agreement cannot be reached by the parties as to the value of the shares, provision is usually made for their valuation by the auditor.

Other pre-emption clauses found in the articles of companies include clauses to the effect that:

(a) the transferor may select the shareholder to whom he wishes to sell;
(b) the offer has to be made first to the directors, then to the other members;
(c) on the death of a member, the surviving members and the directors are obliged to purchase the decreased member's shares; *and*
(d) on the bankruptcy of a member, or death of a director, the shares must be offered to the other members.

Pre-emption clauses are usually supplemented by an additional clause which provides that if the existing shareholders do not wish to avail themselves of these pre-emption rights, the directors may decline to register the transfer.

A company proposing to issue equity securities for cash must first offer them to existing shareholders in proportion to their present holding or, if the articles so provide, to shareholders of a particular class (section 89). Equity securities are defined as shares having unrestricted dividend and capital rights which are not subscribers' shares, bonus shares or shares under an employees' share scheme (section 94).

A private company may exclude the pre-emption rights of section 89 by a provision in its memorandum or articles (section 91). A public or private company may vary or exclude section 89 from all its allotments, if its directors have a general authority to issue shares under section 80, by a provision to that effect in its articles or by passing a special resolution (section 95).

Certain rights and obligations are implied in a contract for the sale of shares. The seller undertakes that he will grant the purchaser a valid transfer and will do everything necessary to enable the purchaser to be registered as a member. If the directors decline to register the transfer the purchaser has no remedy, unless he purchased the shares 'with registration guaranteed'. He will be unable to sue the seller for damages for breach of contract, for rescission of the contract, or for recovery of the purchase price from the seller.

Nevertheless, the purchaser has an equitable interest in the shares and the seller holds the shares as a quasi-trustee on the purchaser's behalf until the transfer is registered. Until that time the seller is recognised by the company as the registered owner of the shares and as such will be liable for any instalments or calls outstanding on the shares, and will be entitled to vote and receive dividends in respect of the shares. The purchaser must indemnify the seller for any calls or instalments paid by the seller after the date of the contract of sale, and the seller must vote at company meetings in accordance with the dictates of the purchaser. Shares may be purchased *cum* (with) or *ex* (without) dividend or with a specified sum paid, but if there is no such agreement the purchaser will be entitled to any dividends or benefits declared after the date of the contract.

The form of transfer

A company may only register a transfer of shares if a proper instrument of transfer is delivered to the company; that is, the transfer must be in writing. This is to ensure that stamp duty is paid on transfers. The

Stock Transfer Act 1963 created a simplified method of transferring shares and this applies to the transfer of fully paid securities of companies limited by shares, statutory companies and chartered companies. Securities include stocks, shares, debentures and debenture stock.

A transfer is effected by the seller delivering to the purchaser a signed transfer, accompanied by his share certificate. The purchaser has the transfer stamped and sends the transfer, the share certificate and the registration fee to the company for registration. The company enters the purchaser's name on its register of members, cancels the old share certificate, and within two months issues a new share certificate to the purchaser. If the directors refuse to register the transfer, they must notify the purchaser of their refusal within two months.

The Stock Exchange (Completion of Bargains) Act 1976 has introduced a system called Talisman to simplify the activities connected with the completion of bargains when shares are transferred on a stock exchange. Transfers will be made initially to a stock exchange nominee known as Sepon Ltd, which will subsequently transfer the shares to the ultimate purchaser. The company whose shares are being dealt with will not issue Sepon Ltd with share certificates, but will issue share certificates to the ultimate purchaser.

A new system for the transfer of shares, The Taurus system, is expected to be operational in 1993. This is a new system of electronically recording the transfer of shares on the Stock Exchange. Regulations provide for computer records to be used instead of share certificates where a company's members vote for this by special resolution. The computer records of shareholdings will contain an authorisation code which will be the method by which shares are transferred. Companies must update their record at least once a month.

If a seller is transferring part only of his shareholding he sends a signed transfer and his share certificate to the company for certification. The company certifies (or certificates) the transfer to the effect that a certificate for a particular number of shares has been lodged with the company, and returns the transfer to the seller. The seller hands the transfer to the buyer, who signs and registers the transfer with the company. The company must then issue within two months new certificates – one to the buyer and another to the seller for the balance of his holding. Certification of a transfer is also required when the whole or part of a holding is to be transferred to more than one buyer.

Certification is no longer necessary in stock exchange transactions as the seller's certificate is lodged with Sepon Ltd. At a later date, the company will issue new share certificates to the respective purchasers, and in cases where the seller is not disposing of all his holding, a share certificate for the balance of his holding.

Certification is not a warranty by the company as to the title of the seller, it is a representation by the company that documents have been produced which on the face of them show that the seller has a *prima facie* title to the shares (section 184). The company is liable to any person who acts on the faith of a false certification, if the certification is made either negligently or fraudulently.

Transmission of shares

When a shareholder dies, or in some way becomes incapacitated and no longer has the capacity to contract (e.g. becomes bankrupt or of unsound mind), the power to deal with the shares passes to the person administering the estate (on death), or to the trustee in bankruptcy (on bankruptcy) or to a Receiver under a Protection Order (on becoming of unsound mind). The shares remain initially in the member's name on the company's register. Article 38 provides that notice of general meetings must be given to all persons entitled to a share as a result of the death or bankruptcy of a member.

On the death of a member the shares vest in his personal representative who becomes entitled to deal with them. He may, without being registered as a member, transfer the shares as if he were a member, and does so by signing the transfer in his representative capacity. Alternatively he may choose to be registered as a member.

On the bankruptcy of a member the shares vest in the trustee or receiver in bankruptcy, who like a personal representative becomes entitled either to hold shares in his personal or representative capacity. The trustee can disclaim partly paid shares, if they are onerous (IA section 315). If he does so the company may prove in the shareholder's bankruptcy for any loss it sustains. If the bankrupt's name remains on the register, the bankrupt is entitled to vote and attend meetings, but the company will pay any dividends to his trustee in bankruptcy. Article 31 provides that a person who becomes entitled to a share as a result of the death or bankruptcy of a member has the same rights as the previous owner of the share (i.e. dividends and other benefits), apart from rights relating to meetings. He is not entitled to attend a vote at any meeting until registered as the holder of the shares.

Forged transfers

Such a transfer is a nullity and cannot affect the title of a shareholder whose signature is forged. If a company registers a forged transfer and removes the name of the true owner from the register, it can be compelled to restore his name to the register.

A company incurs no liability in damages by putting the transferee's name on register as a result of a forged transfer, but if it issues a certificate and any person acts on faith of it and suffers damage, the company is liable (*Re Bahia and San Francisco Railway*).

Most companies take precautions to avoid registering forged transfers. When a company receives a transfer for registration, it usually writes to the transferor informing him of the transfer and stating that unless he advises the company by return to the contrary, the transfer will be assumed to be in order and the company will act upon it. If the transferor does not reply, he can still prove the transfer is a forgery.

Companies do not usually accept a transfer for registration unless a share certificate has been surrendered, and will only issue a duplicate certificate after proper enquiry has been made and sufficient indemnity has been provided by the applicant.

Companies may in certain circumstances pay compensation under the Forged Transfer Acts 1891 and 1892. These Acts do not give any right to compensation, they merely give the company power to pay. Most companies insure against liability for forged transfers.

Calls on shares

Most companies provide that if shares are not paid in full on allotment, any sums owing shall be paid by fixed instalments at certain fixed dates. This is financially advantageous to the company and also enables the shares to be converted into stock.

If the shares are not fully paid on allotment and no provision is made for payment by instalment, the company will make a call on these shares when it requires further capital.

A call is a demand by a company, in respect of money unpaid on its shares, where the company does not stipulate a date for payment. The articles generally give the directors power to make calls, and usually provide that no call shall exceed a quarter of the nominal value of the share; that at least a month shall elapse between successive calls; and that each member be given at least fourteen days' notice of the time and place of payment (Article 12). If the articles make no provision for calls, a company may make them by passing an ordinary resolution in a general meeting.

A call must be made for the benefit of the company. If the directors, as in *Alexander v. Automatic Telephone Company*, pay nothing on their own shares but enforce a call on the other shareholders, such a call is improperly made as it deprives the company of capital. The directors must pay a similar amount on their shares.

A company may not make a call upon one particular member without making a similar call on the other members. In *Galloway v. Hallé Concerts Society*, two members of the society, a guarantee company, were in conflict with the society committee. In addition to the guarantee clause in the memorandum, the articles contained a provision that any member should be liable to pay on demand to the company a sum not exceeding £100, termed the contribution. The committee resolved to call up the whole contribution of the dissident members, but made no corresponding call on the other members. Such a call was held invalid.

Calls and instalments are specialty debts; that is, the company can sue to recover the amounts outstanding for up to twelve years after payment is due. If payment is still not forthcoming, the directors may declare the shares forfeit. The articles generally provide that interest may be charged on overdue calls.

The articles usually provide that directors may accept calls in advance, that is accept from a member part or the whole of the amount uncalled and unpaid on his shares. This is regarded as a loan, and usually carries interest at the rate of 5 per cent per annum, which may be paid out of capital if there are insufficient profits. Capital paid up in advance ranks for repayment in a winding up in priority to capital not paid up in advance.

Mortgage of shares

A shareholder wishing to borrow money on the security of his shares may be able to effect a mortgage of his shares. Such a mortgage may be either legal or equitable.

(a) Legal mortgage

A legal mortgage is an out and out transfer of shares to the lender, who is registered as a shareholder in respect of those shares. He is therefore entitled to dividends and other monies in respect of the shares, and is also entitled to exercise the voting powers of those shares. An agreement is made that, on repayment of the loan, the shares will be re-transferred to the borrower.

If the loan is not repaid on the agreed date, the lender may sell the shares, or apply to the court for a foreclosure order. If the document containing the terms of the mortgage is by deed, the lender may also sell the shares if the borrower fails to pay an instalment of mortgage interest for two months after it falls due, or breaks any other covenant of the mortgage.

A legal mortgage is not suitable in all circumstances, for example for shares that are not fully paid up, or for the mortgage of shares by a director who must hold a qualification shareholding. Stamp duty is also payable on the transfer and re-transfer of the shares.

(b) Equitable mortgage

An equitable mortgage may be created by depositing share certificates with the lender. The borrower usually signs a blank transfer form at the same time. There is an agreement that on the repayment of the loan, the share certificate will be handed back to the borrower.

The borrower still remains on the register of members and is entitled to dividends and to exercise his voting powers. The rights of the lender are not recognised by the company, for under section 360 the company cannot take notice of any trust or similar right over its shares. The weakness of an equitable mortgage is that if the borrower fraudulently informs the company that he has lost his certificate he can obtain a new certificate and transfer the same shares to a purchaser.

The only safe course for the lender is to serve a 'Stop Notice' on the company, which provides that the company cannot register a transfer without first notifying the lender. The lender has eight days to obtain an injunction, for after this time the company will be at liberty to transfer the shares.

If the loan is not repaid the lender may, in a case where a blank transfer has been signed, fill in his own name or that of a purchaser and complete the transfer of the shares. If the mortgage consists of share certificates not accompanied by a signed blank transfer, the lender will require a Court order before he can enforce his security.

Forfeiture and surrender

The articles of a company generally contain clauses providing for the forfeiture of shares if a member fails to pay any call or instalment (Articles 18, 19). Such a power must be given by the articles, as forfeiture for any other reason is invalid and amounts to an unlawful reduction of capital.

The power to declare shares forfeit is in the nature of a trust and must be exercised for the company's benefit, not for the benefit of any individual shareholders. In *Re Esparto Trading Co.*, Finch and Goddard were given shares in the company to induce them to become directors and paid nothing on their shares. At a later date both men asked the company to forfeit their shares and this was done. It was held invalid and they were liable to pay in full for their shares.

Its effect is that the shareholder ceases to be a member of the company and is theoretically no longer bound by his obligations as a member, such as to pay any amount outstanding on his shares. The articles, however, usually provide that despite forfeiture he shall be liable for all the money which at the time of forfeiture he owed the company, that is he becomes a debtor of the company (Article 21).

If directors are given the power to accept a surrender of partly paid shares, provision will have to be made in the articles for the surrender of shares. Neither the Act nor Table A make any provision for the surrender of shares.

Surrender is valid only in the circumstances which would justify forfeiture and is used to avoid the formalities of forfeiture. It cannot be used to cancel a member's liability for future calls, as this would amount to an illegal reduction of capital.

Any shares forfeited or surrendered become the company's property, and the articles generally give the directors power to sell such shares. They may be sold for any price they will fetch, but the purchaser will be liable to pay any amounts unpaid on forfeiture or surrender, and will not usually be allowed to vote until the arrears are paid. Shares not disposed of by a public company within 3 years, must be cancelled (section 146).

Lien on shares

A private company possesses a lien on the shares of its members if the articles so provide. The articles frequently provide that a company has a lien on the shares of a member for money that is owed to the company in respect of shares or as a result of any other transaction. Article 18 gives a company a lien on partly paid shares in respect of money due on the shares and in respect of dividends. Article 9 provides that if the debt is not paid a company may sell the shares under a power given in the articles. The company is given an equitable interest in the shares which can be enforced by selling the shares (if this power is given in the articles), by withholding dividends on the shares or by refusing to register any transfer of the shares.

If the company sells the shares, it may retain from the proceeds of the sale the amount owed to the company, but it must return the balance (if any) to the member.

A lien or other charge of a public company on its own shares is void. Two exceptions are permitted:

(i) a charge on any amount outstanding on a partly paid up share.
(ii) a charge taken by a company whose ordinary business includes lending money, on its own shares, whether fully paid or not, in the ordinary course of business (section 150).

13
DIVIDENDS

A shareholder expects a return on his investment in a company. A trading company is expected to earn profits, and these profits are distributed among its shareholders as dividends. A dividend may be defined as that part of the profits of trading that is distributed to members in proportion to their shares and in accordance with their rights as shareholders.

Payment

There are two cardinal principles relating to the payment of dividends (i.e. making a distribution).

1 A dividend may not be paid out of capital.
2 A dividend may only be paid out of the profits available for that purpose.

A company does not require an express power in its memorandum or articles to pay a dividend, although a guarantee company which is allowed to dispense with Ltd in its name may not pay a dividend.

The articles usually determine how, and from which fund, a dividend is to be paid, and provide that 'all dividends shall be apportioned and paid proportionately to the amounts paid or credited as paid on the shares' (Article 104).

A shareholder cannot insist on a company paying a dividend, even though a company has made sufficient profits and is able to make a distribution to its members. This applies to preference shareholders, as well as to ordinary shareholders.

Declaration

The company in general meeting may declare a dividend, but no dividend may exceed the amount recommended by the directors (Article 102).

The declaration of a dividend by a company creates a debt due to its members. If the dividend is stated to be payable at some future date, a shareholder will be unable to enforce payment until the actual date for payment arrives.

Directors are usually given the power to pay such interim dividends (i.e. dividends paid in between two annual general meetings) as appear to the directors to be justified by the company's profits (Article 103). As an interim dividend does not require the approval of a general meeting it is not in the nature of a debt due from the company. If it is not paid, it cannot be sued for.

The articles often give power to the directors, before recommending a dividend, to set aside out of the company's profits such sums as they think appropriate to form a reserve fund, and to carry forward any profits which they think prudent not to divide.

A company may, on the recommendation of its directors, capitalise any part of its reserve accounts or its profit and loss account, and apply that sum in paying up in full unissued shares to be allotted as fully paid bonus shares to its members who would have been entitled to that sum if it had been distributed as a dividend (Article 110).

Unless the articles state otherwise, dividends must be paid in cash, and a shareholder can restrain a company from paying him in any other way. In *Wood v. Odessa Waterworks Co.*, the company proposed to pay a dividend by giving debentures to its shareholders in lieu of cash. It was held that the payment of a dividend meant payment in cash, and the company was prevented from paying a dividend other than in cash.

Profits available

A public or private company (other than an investment company) may only make a distribution to its members out of the profits available for the purpose. These are its accumulated realised profits (not previously utilised by distribution or capitalisation) less its accumulated realised losses (so far as not previously written off in a reduction or reorganisation of capital). Profits and losses include profits and losses made at any time and include both revenue and capital profits and losses. Any profit or loss for an accounting period must not be treated in isolation from other accounting periods, but as a continuation. Therefore, any previous losses must be made good before a distribution can be made (section 263).

A further restriction is imposed on a public company making a distribution. It may only make a distribution if its net assets are at least equal to the aggregate amount of its share capital and undistributable reserves. (Its net assets are the total assets less its liabilities and provisions.)

The undistributable reserves are:

- the capital redemption reserve fund;
- the share premium account;
- the amount by which the accumulated unrealised profits exceeds its current accumulated unrealised losses;
- any of the reserve which a company is prevented from distributing (section 264).

A company may not use its unrealised profits to write off realised losses, or in paying up debentures, or any amounts remaining unpaid on its issued shares. This is to prevent profits not available for distribution being used indirectly to pay dividends. A company may apply its unrealised profits in paying up unissued shares to be issued to its members as fully paid bonus shares.

The right of a company to make a distribution and the amount it may distribute is determined by reference to the relevant items in the 'relevant accounts' (section 270).

Relevant items are any of the following: profits, losses, assets, liabilities, provisions, share capital and reserves (including undistributable reserves). Relevant accounts are normally the last annual accounts which were laid or filed in respect of the last preceding accounting reference period.

If the last annual accounts are taken as the 'relevant accounts':

(a) the accounts must have been properly prepared;
(b) the company's auditors must have made a report in respect of those accounts;
(c) if the report is not unqualified, the auditors must state in writing whether the subject matter of their qualification is material in determining whether a distribution should be made.
(d) a copy of the auditor's statement must have been laid before the company in general meeting or delivered to the Registrar (section 272).

In certain circumstances a distribution may be made on the basis of interim or initial accounts. A company unable to make a distribution if reference were made only to its last annual accounts may make a distribution if more recent (i.e. interim) accounts show that it is able to do so. Initial accounts are drawn up when a company proposes to make a distribution during its first accounting reference period or before any accounts are filed.

Any member who knowingly receives an unlawful distribution is liable to repay it to the company. If the distribution is made other than in cash, the member is liable to pay a sum equal to the value of the distribution.

These restrictions on distributions do not apply to:

(i) An issue of fully or partly paid bonus shares;
(ii) The redemption of shares out of the proceeds of a fresh issue of shares and the payment of any premium payable on their redemption out of the share premium account;
(iii) The reduction of share capital by extinguishing or reducing liability in respect of share capital not paid up, or paying off paid up share capital;
(iv) The distribution of assets to the members on a winding up.

14
GENERAL MEETINGS

The will of the members of a company is normally expressed at the general meeting, when they may vote for or against any resolution that is proposed. If the appropriate majority is obtained for a resolution, the will of the majority of members usually prevails and binds every member.

In this way the majority of members are entitled to exercise the company's powers and control its operations. They are able to appoint directors of their choice and may delegate to the directors the necessary powers to operate the company's business.

The articles of a company invariably give the board of directors the power to convene a general meeting or a class meeting. They will normally do so by passing a resolution at a duly convened board meeting. The articles may provide that a resolution in writing, signed by the directors without a meeting, shall be as effective as a resolution passed at a meeting of the board.

Types of meeting

There are three types of meetings of shareholders: the annual general meeting, an extraordinary general meeting, and a meeting of a class of shareholders.

Annual general meeting

Every company must hold an annual general meeting each (calendar) year in addition to any other meeting which it may hold. Not more than fifteen months may elapse between one general meeting and another. An exception is made for a newly formed company in that it may hold its first annual general meeting at any time within eighteen months of incorporation (section 366).

A private company may by elective resolution dispense with holding annual general meetings. An election has effect for the year in which it is made and for subsequent years, but does not affect any liability already incurred for default in holding an annual general meeting (section 366A).

The election will be cancelled if a member gives notice to the company, no later than three months before the end of the year, requiring the company to hold an annual general meeting in that year (section 366A). The company must then call a meeting in accordance with section 366.

If default is made in holding the meeting the Department of Trade may, on the application of any member, call or direct the calling of the meeting and may give any ancillary or consequential directions as it thinks fit (section 367).

The nature of the business at the annual general meeting depends upon the articles, but the ordinary business at the meeting is generally understood to include the following:

(a) the declaration of a dividend;
(b) the consideration of the accounts and balance sheets;
(c) the consideration of the directors' and auditors' reports;
(d) the appointment of directors and auditors;
(e) fixing the auditors' remuneration.

Any other business is to be regarded as special business. In a notice convening an annual general meeting to transact ordinary business only, it is unnecessary to specify the ordinary business as the members will be aware of the nature of the business from the articles. Members will therefore be entitled to move resolutions without giving notice to other members in respect of ordinary business. In order to prevent a member from proposing a person as a director at an annual general meeting without giving prior warning, the articles often stipulate that any such nomination must be notified to the company not later than a specified number of days before the meeting.

Extraordinary general meeting

Any general meeting other than the annual general meeting is called an extraordinary general meeting. The articles usually give the directors power to call an extraordinary general meeting at any time they think fit (Article 37). This power is used by directors to deal with matters which cannot be held up until the next annual general meeting. In non-urgent matters it is often more convenient to hold a meeting to discuss matters.

The notice convening the meeting is often accompanied by a circular giving the board of directors' views. The board is within its rights in sending out circulars, and it is proper for the company to meet this expenditure as long as the intention is to benefit the general body of members, and is not motivated by self interest (e.g. to stay in office or gain some other advantage). The board is under no obligation to send out the circulars of members who are opposed to its policy.

Members holding not less than 10 per cent of the paid up capital carrying voting rights may at any time compel the directors to call, or requisition, a meeting (section 368). The articles may extend this power by allowing a smaller number of shareholders (e.g. 5 per cent) to requisition the meeting, but they may not restrict this important minority right.

The requisition must state the objects of the meeting and must be deposited at the registered office of the company. If the directors do not convene the meeting within twenty-one days, the requisitionists or a majority of them in voting rights, may themselves convene a meeting. This meeting must be convened in the same manner (or as nearly as possible) as meetings convened by the directors, and must be held within three months of depositing the requisition (section 368).

Any expenses incurred by the requisitionists, due to the failure of the directors to convene a meeting, may be recovered from the company, which must withhold these sums from the fees or other remuneration of the directors who are at fault.

A public company must convene an extraordinary general meeting if there is a serious loss of capital; that is, if the net assets are half or less of the company's called up share capital, the directors must summon a meeting to consider what measures should be taken to deal with the situation (section 142).

Class meetings

If a company has different classes of shares it must hold a meeting of the class in question when required to do so by the Act, or the articles, or the terms of the issue of shares. Any resolution passed at such a meeting will bind the members of that class only, and as the matters under discussion relate only to the members of that class, they alone may attend, vote and speak at class meetings.

Class meetings are usually held to agree to alterations in the rights of that class, or to agree to compromises or arrangements affecting the class. The court may order a class meeting to be convened under section 425.

Notice of general meeting

A meeting cannot be held unless proper notice of it has been given to every person entitled to receive notice.

The persons entitled to notice are *prima facie* the members of the company and the auditor. This may be modified by the articles, which often provide that members with calls in arrear cannot vote and that preference shareholders have no right to notice of meetings or to attend and vote at meetings except in certain circumstances, such as that their dividends are three months in arrear, or a resolution is proposed which affects their rights or is a resolution for winding up the company.

The articles may also provide that notice may be sent by post (Article 111), must be given to a personal representative or to a trustee in bankruptcy if applicable (Article 116) and need not be given to a member who does not have a registered address in the United Kingdom (Article 112).

Failure to give notice to any person entitled to notice will invalidate a meeting. In *Bradman v. Trinity Estates plc*, due to a postal strike some members received late notice of a meeting while others did not receive any notice. It was held that proper notice had not been given and that the meeting should not be held until all the members had been notified.

The articles usually provide that the accidental omission to give notice of a meeting to, or the non-receipt of a notice of a meeting by, any person entitled to receive notice shall not invalidate the proceedings at that meeting (Article 39).

In *Re West Canadian Collieries Ltd* a company's articles contained similar provisions to Article 39. Nine members did not receive notice of a meeting as address plates had inadvertently been left out of a machine used to address the envelopes in which the notices were sent. It was held that the omission was accidental and the proceedings were valid.

The Act provides that no less than twenty-one days' notice must be given for an annual general meeting or for a meeting to pass a special resolution. At least fourteen days' notice is required for any other meeting. The articles can specify longer notice but cannot stipulate shorter notice of meetings (section 269).

A private company may elect to reduce, to not less than 90 per cent, the percentage required for calling a general meeting at short notice (see page 148).

There are instances when meetings may be called by shorter notice. An annual general meeting may be called by shorter notice if all the members entitled to attend and vote agree. In the case of any other meeting, the agreement of a majority holding 95 per cent of the shares having the right to attend and vote, will enable shorter notice to be given (section 269).

The notice must state the date, time and place of the meeting. It must also state clearly the nature of the business to be transacted. If the true nature of the business is not disclosed, such transactions passed at the meeting will be invalid.

In *Baillie v. Oriental Telephone and Electric Co.*, the directors had from 1907 to 1914 received fees from a subsidiary company. At a later date they were advised that payment of the fees should have been approved by the shareholders. They called a meeting to approve their remuneration and to alter the articles to allow directors to receive payment for serving on the boards of subsidiary companies. The notice merely stated that the directors' fees would be a small percentage of the subsidiary's profits, and did not state that the subsidiary had made very large profits, or that the total amount of directors' fees was in the region of £45 000. It was held that the resolution approving the payment of these was invalid, as proper disclosure had not been made to the shareholders.

In *Kaye v. Croydon Tramways Co.*, there was a provisional agreement for the sale of one undertaking to another, with an agreement to pay a substantial sum to the directors for loss of office. The agreement was conditional upon acceptance by the shareholders of the company selling the undertaking. The notice convening the meeting described it simply as an agreement for the sale of the undertaking. It was held that proper disclosure had not been made.

Quorum

In order that a meeting may proceed to business, a quorum of members must be present. The Act provides that two members personally present shall be a quorum, unless the articles state otherwise (section 370). Proxies may only be counted towards the quorum if the articles so provide. If the articles only require a quorum to be present when the meeting proceeds to business, and if the number of members who remain present falls below the stipulated quorum, the meeting may complete its business. If only one person remains present, whether as a member or as a proxy for others, the meeting may not pass valid resolutions as one person alone cannot constitute a meeting.

There are exceptions to this rule in that if the Department of Trade calls an annual general meeting, it may direct that one member present in person or by proxy shall constitute a general meeting (section 367). The Court may make similar directions in cases where it is impractical to call a meeting or conduct a meeting in accordance with the articles or the Act. It may make the order of its own volition, or on the application of any director or shareholder who is entitled to vote (section 371).

In *Re El Sombrero*, the company had three members. Laubscher held 90 per cent of the shares, Salaman and Lewis held 5 per cent each and were the two directors of the company. Laubscher requisitioned an extraordinary general meeting to pass a resolution removing the two directors and appointing others in their place. The two directors did not attend and as there was no quorum present the meeting could not take place. Laubscher successfully applied to the court for an order that the court call a meeting, where these resolutions could be passed, and that one member should constitute a quorum.

Similarly in *Re HR Paul and Son Ltd*, a shareholder holding 90 per cent of the shares called a meeting to alter the articles. The minority refused to attend and there was therefore no quorum. It was held that the quorum provisions in the articles were not a right vested in the minority to enable it to frustrate the wishes of the majority. The court convened the meeting.

In *Re Opera Photographic Ltd* a company's shares were held by two shareholders who were also the company's directors. The majority shareholder who held 51 shares called meetings but as the minority shareholder did not attend, a quorum was not present. It was held that a meeting could be held with a quorum of one, in order to break the deadlock and prevent a minority shareholder from exercising a veto on proceedings.

The articles usually provide that if a quorum is not present within half an hour of the appointed time, a meeting convened on the requisition of members is dissolved, but any other meeting shall be adjourned to the following week at a day, place and time to be determined by the directors. If, at the adjourned meeting, a quorum is not present within half an hour, the members present shall form a quorum (Article 41).

The chairman

The Act provides that if the articles make no provision for the appointment of a chairman to preside at meetings, the members present at the meeting may elect any member as chairman (section 370). The articles generally provide that the chairman of the board of directors shall be the chairman at general meetings (Article 42). If there is no chairman, or he fails to attend or is unwilling to act, then the directors present shall elect one of themselves to be chairman. If there is no director present or willing to act, the members present may elect one of their number to be chairman of the meeting (Articles 42, 43).

The duty of the chairman is to preserve order and to see that the meeting is properly conducted. He must see that the meeting is properly constituted and in particular that a quorum is present. He should restrain irrelevant discussion and intemperate language, and should any persons act in a disorderly manner he should ask them to desist. If they refuse, he may have them ejected, using reasonable force only. Should the meeting become disorderly, the chairman may adjourn the meeting until order is restored.

He must decide points of order and questions of procedure, for example whether a proposed amendment to a resolution should be permitted. An amendment is only allowed if it falls within the scope of the notice convening the meeting.

The chairman must give a reasonable opportunity to the members present to discuss any proposed resolution, and he must allow minority shareholders reasonable time to express their views within the time available. As soon as reasonable time has been given to airing both the views of the minority and majority, he may, with the meeting's consent, close the discussion and put the question to the vote.

In *Wall v. London and Northern Assets Corporation*, Wall and other shareholders wished to continue a discussion at a meeting regarding the proposed amalgamation of two companies. The chairman moved that the question now be put and this resolution was passed, as was a resolution that the amalgamation go ahead. It was held that the resolution was properly passed and that the minority was not entitled to discuss the meeting indefinitely to obstruct the business of the meeting.

In this way he should be able to ascertain the sense of the meeting in regard to any question which is before it. After the questions have been put to the meeting, the votes are counted and the result is declared. The articles usually provide that the chairman's declaration, as to whether or not a resolution has been passed by a specified majority, is conclusive (Article 47). The chairman may have a casting vote where the votes are equal (Article 50), but in the absence of such an article he has no such vote.

He has no general power to dissolve or adjourn a meeting of his own will, unless this power is given to him by the articles. Otherwise his power of adjournment, without the meeting's consent, is limited to adjourning the meeting in case of disorder. Should he prematurely close the meeting and declare it dissolved or adjourned, the meeting may elect another chairman and proceed with the business. Unless the articles otherwise provide, the chairman is not bound to adjourn the meeting even if the members wish him to do so.

Voting at the meeting

The articles usually contain provisions as to voting and may restrict the voting rights of shares (e.g. that preference shares shall carry no voting rights unless their dividend is in arrear). Unless the articles otherwise provide, each shareholder has on a show of hands one vote, irrespective of the number of shares held by him. On a poll, a member has one vote for each share which he holds.

The articles of private companies and guarantee companies may stipulate that certain shares shall have weighted voting rights. In *Bushell v. Faith*, Bushell and his two sisters each held 100 of the company's 300 £1 shares. The articles provided that in the event of a resolution being proposed at a general meeting for the removal of a director, each share held by that director should carry three votes. It was held that such voting rights were valid.

The articles usually provide that in the event of a joint holding of shares, only the first named is entitled to vote. Therefore most joint holders have their names on the register in a different order; for example, Smith and Jones are joint holders of 100 shares, but the shares are registered as fifty shares in the names of Smith and Jones, and fifty in the names of Jones and Smith.

The votes on a resolution are usually taken on a show of hands and the chairman then declares the result. Any member or proxy may demand a poll on any question, except the election of a chairman or adjournment of the meeting, either before or on the declaration of the result.

A poll must be held if it is demanded by not less than five members, or a member or members holding 10 per cent of the voting rights, or 10 per cent of the paid up capital carrying the right to vote (section 373). The articles may provide that a poll can be demanded by less than five members, or by the holders of less than 10 per cent of the capital.

When a poll has been properly demanded, the chairman fixes the time and place for taking it, and the result of any vote on a show of hands is nullified. The chairman is entitled to decide whether a poll shall be taken there and then, unless the articles direct otherwise. This is often the most convenient course of action where the number of votes to be counted is relatively small. He may, however, defer holding a poll until a later date.

On a poll, the votes are recorded by each person signing a paper 'for' or 'against' the resolution and adding the number of votes to which he is entitled. A member holding several shares is entitled on a poll to cast votes for and against the resolution. This provision meets the needs of a nominee (e.g. a bank holding shares on behalf of several persons) to vote in one way in respect of some shares, and in another way, or not at all, in respect of others.

Proxies

A proxy is a document authorising another person to attend meetings and vote on behalf of an absent member. The person who has been so appointed is also known as a proxy.

There are two forms of proxy in use: the ordinary proxy appointing a person to vote as he thinks fit at the meeting; and a special proxy directing the proxy before the meeting to vote for or against a particular resolution. This is known as a 'two-way proxy'. The Stock Exchange makes it a condition for permission to deal, that public companies distribute two-way proxy forms in all cases where special business is to be transacted at a meeting.

Any member who is entitled to attend and vote at a meeting of a company is entitled to appoint another person, whether a member or not, as his proxy (section 372, Article 59). This does not apply to companies not having a share capital, unless the articles state otherwise.

A proxy has the right to attend a meeting of a publc company, but no right to speak at the meeting except to demand or join in demanding a poll. He can only vote on a poll. A member of a public company may appoint more than one proxy, so that a nominee holding shares for various parties can appoint different persons as proxies to represent different interests. The articles of a public company may extend these basic proxy rights.

A proxy at a meeting of a private company has the same right as a member to speak at the meeting, but unless the articles provide otherwise a member of a private company can only appoint one proxy who can only vote on a poll. Presumably this restriction is to prevent a possible abuse of this privilege.

The articles may require the proxy papers to be deposited with the company before a meeting, but they cannot require such deposit more than forty-eight hours before a meeting. The articles cannot deprive a member of his right to appoint a proxy.

Directors, when sending out notices of a meeting, often include proxy forms which enable the members to appoint one or other of the directors as their proxy. It is not unusual for the directors to have in their possession, at the commencement of the meeting, proxies in their favour which will ensure the passing of any resolution supported by the directors.

As long as the directors are satisfied that their policies are in the company's interests they may, at the company's expense, print and distribute such proxy forms. The effect of this may be partially offset by the requirement that in every notice calling a general meeting there must appear with reasonable prominence a statement that any member entitled to attend and vote is entitled to appoint a proxy (section 372).

Should the directors wish to invite members to appoint a person or a number of persons as proxy, such an invitation, if sent out at the company's expense, must be sent to all the members entitled to appoint proxies (section 372), thus preventing the directors from selecting only the members who would grant them proxies of support.

It is also common to make out alternative proxies, for example in favour of one person or in his absence another, so that if the first named is prevented from attending the second named can attend and exercise the rights under the proxy.

A proxy may be revoked by informing the proxy, or if the shareholder after appointing the proxy attends the meeting, he can vote in person – thus impliedly revoking the proxy. A proxy is also automatically revoked by the death or insanity of the person giving it. The articles usually provide that the proxy shall be valid, unless the company has been notified of the member's death or insanity or revocation of the proxy. This is necessary to ensure that resolutions have been validly passed.

If a company is a member of another company, it may appoint any person to represent it at meetings of the company of which it is a member. Such a representative is not a proxy and may exercise the same powers on behalf of the company he represents as if it were an individual shareholder.

— Adjournment of general meetings —

The articles usually empower the chairman, with the consent of the meeting, to adjourn the meeting. He must do so if directed by the meeting (Article 45). A poll may be taken forthwith on the question of adjournment (Article 51). However if a chairman improperly adjourns the meeting, the members who remain may appoint another chairman and continue the business.

A meeting may be adjourned for various reasons. It may be that there is no quorum present, or that the business cannot be completed on that day, or that the adjournment is to take a poll, or the meeting has to be adjourned because of disorder.

An adjourned meeting is regarded for some purposes as a continuation of the original meeting. Fresh notice of an adjourned meeting need only be given if the meeting is adjourned for thirty days or more, but only unfinished business can be transacted at the meeting (Article 45). A resolution passed at an adjourned meeting is to be treated as passed on the date on which it was in fact passed.

Resolutions

There are three types of resolutions which may be passed at a general meeting – special, extraordinary and ordinary. The nature of the business to be transacted determines the type of resolution to be used at a meeting. The Act states that certain matters must be transacted by special or extraordinary resolutions and may not be passed in any other way. All other business may be approved by ordinary resolution unless the memorandum or the articles provide otherwise.

Special resolution

A resolution passed at a general meeting by a majority of three-quarters of the members, voting in person or by proxy, of which twenty-one days' notice has been given specifying the intention to propose the resolution as a special resolution (section 378(2)).

Less than twenty-one days' notice may be given if agreed upon by a majority of those entitled to attend and vote holding 95 per cent of the shares giving those rights (section 378(3)).

A special resolution is required when fundamental changes are proposed by a company, and the twenty-one days' notice required gives members an opportunity to deliberate on the nature and consequences of the proposed changes.

The following are some of the changes requiring a special resolution:

- alteration of the objects clause (section 4);
- alteration of the articles (section 9);
- alteration of the memorandum (section 17);
- modification or withdrawal of pre-emption rights (section 95);
- change of name (section 28);
- creation of reserve capital (section 120);
- reduction of share capital (section 135);
- making directors' liability unlimited (section 307);
- winding up by the Court (IA section 122);
- initiating a members' voluntary winding up (IA section 84);
- sanctioning a sale for a share consideration (IA section 110);
- re-registration of unlimited company as limited (section 51);
- re-registration of a private company as a public company (section 43);
- re-registration of a public company as a private company (section 53);
- financial assistance for the acquisition of shares (section 155);
- off market purchase of a company's own shares (section 164);
- redemption of purchase of a private company's shares out of capital (section 173);
- approval of an *ultra vires* transaction (section 35).

Extraordinary resolution

A resolution passed at a general meeting by a majority of three-quarters of the members voting in person or by proxy, of which notice has been given to propose the resolution as an extraordinary resolution (section 378).

This type of resolution is only required for certain purposes, mainly in connection with the voluntary winding up of a company. The following require the approval of such a resolution:

Initiating a creditors' voluntary winding up (IA section 84);

Granting certain powers to a liquidator in a voluntary winding up (IA section 165);

Variation of class rights (section 125).

Ordinary resolution

This is a resolution requiring a simple majority of those who attend and vote at a meeting. Where the Act or the articles state that the company in general meeting may do some act, this requires an ordinary resolution.

An ordinary resolution is passed initially by a majority on a show of hands. Should a poll be demanded, only a simple majority is required. It is not necessary that the majority of members present should vote in favour of a resolution, merely that a majority of those voting should support the resolution; for example, if 100 members are present and twenty vote in favour, ten against and seventy abstain, the resolution is passed.

There are certain ordinary resolutions which require special notice to be given to a company. These are resolutions for:

(a) removing a director or appointing a person instead of the director who has been removed at that meeting;
(b) appointing or approving the appointment of a director over 70;
(c) appointing as auditor a person other than the retiring auditor;
(d) removing an auditor before the expiration of his term of office;
(e) filling a casual vacancy in the office of auditor;
(f) re-appointing an auditor who was appointed by the directors to fill a casual vacancy.

In these cases twenty-eight days' notice must be given to the company, who must give twenty-one days' notice of such a resolution to its members at the same time and in the same manner as it gives notice of a meeting (section 379).

If it can be shown that all the shareholders with the right to attend and vote at a general meeting agree to a course of action which a general meeting could carry into effect, their assent is as binding as a resolution at a general meeting. In *Re Express Engineering Works*, a company was formed with five members, who were also the directors of the company. They sold property to the company for £15 000 which they had bought for £7 000, to be paid by the issue of debentures. The articles provided that a director could not vote in respect of a contract in which he was interested. It was held that as there was no fraud, the contract could be ratified by the unanimous agreement of the members and the debentures were valid.

In *Cane v. Jones* all the shares in a company were held by members of one family. They agreed that the chairman should no longer have a casting vote, and in the case of an equality of votes an independent chairman would be appointed. Papers were signed to this effect, but no general meeting was held or special resolution passed. A dispute later arose between the members and it was held that the informal agreement was valid and binding.

Written resolution procedure

A written resolution procedure may be used for the general meetings and class meetings of private companies.

Any resolution which may be passed in a general meeting may be passed in this form and applies to ordinary, extraordinary, special and elective resolutions. The written resolution must be signed by or on behalf of all the members who at the date of the resolution would be entitled to attend and vote at a meeting. A copy of every proposed written resolution must be sent to the auditors. If a resolution concerns the auditors as auditors they may, within seven days of receiving a copy, require a company to put the resolution to a meeting. The auditors have a right to attend and address the meeting and the resolution has no effect until it is approved by the meeting.

Such a resolution is only effective if the auditors give notice that the resolution does not affect them as auditors, or that it does not need to be considered by a general meeting; or if the auditors do not respond within seven days. The resolution takes effect from the time of notification by the auditors or the date of the resolution, whichever is the later.

The procedure may be used where a resolution is required as part of an authorisation procedure. Documents containing the same information as would be available at a general meeting must be sent to members before, or at the time the resolution is sent to them for signature. Schedule 15A lists the following situations:

(a) disapplication of pre-emption rights (section 95).
(b) financial assistance for purchasing its own shares or those of its holding company (section 155).
(c) authority for an off-market purchase or a contingent purchase contract of its own shares (sections 164, 165, 167).
(d) approval for redeeming or purchasing its own shares out of capital (section 173).
(e) approval of a director's service contract (section 319).
(f) funding a director's expenditure in performing his duties (section 337).

This procedure may not be used to remove a director from office under section 303 or an auditor under section 391.

Where a written resolution is agreed to, the company may record the resolution and the signatures in a book in the same way as the minutes of the proceedings of a general meeting (sections 381A, 381B, 382).

Elective resolutions (section 379A)

A private company may pass elective resolutions for the following purposes:

(a) to allow directors to allot shares without further authority for an indefinite period or for a fixed period in excess of five years (amending section 80A);
(b) to dispense with laying annual accounts or reports before a general meeting. Shareholders must be sent copies of the documents at least twenty-eight days before the end of the period within which they should otherwise have been laid, and any member or the

auditor may require a general meeting to be called for laying the documents (section 252);
(c) to dispense with holding an annual general meeting (section 366A);
(d) to allow meetings to be held at short notice if agreed by a majority of members holding not less than 90 per cent of the voting shares (section 386);
(e) to dispense with the annual re-election of auditors (section 386).

An elective resolution must either be passed

(i) as a written resolution; or
(ii) with the agreement in person or by proxy of *all* the members entitled to attend and vote at a meeting called on twenty-one days' notice.

A Company may revoke an elective resolution by passing an ordinary resolution to that effect.

Circulation of members' resolutions

Members holding 5 per cent of the total voting rights, or not less than 100 members holding shares on which there has been paid an average sum per member of not less than £100, may on giving six weeks' notice to the company require it to send to all members notice of any resolution they intend to move at the next annual general meeting. (section 376).

They may also require the company, on giving one week's notice, to circulate to members a statement not exceeding 1000 words with respect to any resolution or business to be dealt with at any general meeting. This enables members who are opposed to a course of action or scheme to be submitted to the meeting, to circulate their objections to the other members before the meeting. The requisitionists must deposit a reasonable sum with the company to meet the company's expenses in giving effect to these provisions (section 376).

The directors or any other aggrieved person may apply to the court for an order that the statement should not be circularised as they consider that these rights are being abused to secure needless publicity for defamatory matter (section 377). In practice, members who are opposed to the board's policy will themselves send circulars to their fellow members. They can obtain their names and addresses by inspecting the register of members or obtaining copies of the register from the company. In this way they will not be subject to the directors' possible censorship or limited to 1000 words in their circular.

Registration of resolutions

As a rule any resolution or business transacted at a general meeting is of interest only to the members of the company. As certain resolutions and agreements may affect third party interests copies of the following must be forwarded to the Registrar within fifteen days (section 380). These include:

(a) special and extraordinary resolutions.
(b) resolutions or agreements passed or agreed to by all the members which would otherwise not have been effective unless passed as special or extraordinary resolutions.
(c) resolutions agreed upon by all the members of a class of shareholders.
(d) resolutions requiring a company to be wound up on the effluxion of time. (1.A. section 84).
(e) resolution of the directors to re-register a company as a public or private company (sections 43, 44).
(f) resolution of the directors to comply with a direction to change a company's name (section 32).
(g) resolution of the directors on a company ceasing to be a public company following the acquisition of its own shares (section 147).
(h) resolution giving authority to the directors to make an allotment of securities (section 80).
(i) resolution giving, varying, revoking or renewing authority to a company to purchase its own shares on the Stock Exchange (section 166).
(j) resolution sanctioning the acquisition of a non cash asset from a subscriber to the memorandum (section 104), as required by section 111.

The copies may be printed or in some other form approved by the Registrar.

If a special resolution alters the company's memorandum or articles, the company must send to the Registrar, with the notice of alteration, a printed copy of the altered memorandum or articles (section 18). The

Registrar must then publish in the *Gazette* notice of the receipt by him of those documents (section 711). The latest version of the company's constitution is then available for public perusal at the Registry.

Minutes of meetings

Every company must keep minutes of general meetings and directors' meetings. Any minutes signed by the chairman or by the chairman of the next succeeding meeting are *prima facie* evidence of those proceedings. There is a presumption that, if a meeting has been duly held and convened, the proceedings have been properly conducted and all appointments made at the meeting (e.g. directors, managers, liquidators) are valid (section 382).

The books containing the minutes of general meetings are to be kept at the registered office and are open to inspection by any member, without charge, for at least two hours a day. Any member is entitled, within seven days, to a copy of the minutes at a charge not exceeding 2½p per hundred words (section 383).

15
DIRECTORS

As a company is an artificial legal entity it cannot exercise any of its powers in person, but must of necessity act through the medium of its agents – its directors. Although the Act now stipulates that a public company registered since 1929 must have a minimum of two directors and a private company at least one director (section 282), this has only come about since 1929. Prior to that date there was no statutory obligation on a company to have a director. Article 64 provides that unless otherwise determined by ordinary resolution the number of directors shall not be subject to any maximum but shall not be less than two.

The articles of association of some companies state that a company shall be managed by a 'council' or 'managing committee', whilst the articles of other companies provide that the power of management shall be exercised by a 'governing director', 'life director', or 'permanent director'. Whatever terminology is used such persons will be regarded as directors with certain rights, liabilities and obligations. Section 741 defines a director as 'any person occupying the position of a director by whatever name called'.

A person, who is not a director, is regarded for the purposes of the Act as a shadow director if a company's directors are accustomed to act in accordance with his instructions or directions. He is not a shadow director if the directors act only on advice given by him in a professional capacity (section 741). Certain sections of the Act apply to shadow directors.

Appointment of directors

A statement of a company's first director(s) and secretary must be filed with the application to register a company. The statement must be signed by the director(s) and secretary signifying their consent to the appointment (section 10). The persons named in the statement are deemed to have been appointed as a company's first director(s) and secretary from the date of the company's incorporation (section 13(5)).

The articles often name the first director(s) and secretary but such an appointment is void unless the person is named as director or secretary in the statement (section 10(5)).

The articles usually fix the minimum and maximum number of directors that a company may have. Should the number of directors fall below the minimum set by the company, the remaining directors cannot act unless they are given specific powers in such a situation. Directors are usually given the power to appoint new directors so that the numerical requirements are satisfied. If not, their powers are limited to summoning a general meeting of the company so that new directors can be appointed. Any new directors appointed solely by the board will only hold office until the next annual general meeting when the members may re-elect them if they so wish.

A company can appoint a person a director for life. Such an appointment may be revoked by altering the articles. If such an appointment was made before 18 July 1945, then the director cannot be removed from office.

A director may, if the articles so provide, appoint a person to act for him in his absence. This 'alternate' director will normally be granted the same powers as the director that he represents. The appointment is usually subject to the approval of the majority of the directors. In all probability the alternate director will be a fellow director, and in that case will be able to cast two votes at board meetings. This appointment can be terminated by the original director.

Outside bodies are sometimes given power to appoint directors to the board of an independent company. It is often a condition of a loan made to a company that the lender shall have the power to appoint a certain number of directors to the board to safeguard his interests. A director does not have to be a natural person and so a holding company will nominate the directors of its subsidiary company.

If the articles permit, a director can assign his office, that is transfer his rights and liabilities as a director, to another person. This must be approved by a special resolution of the company (section 308). If a director of a private company has been given the power by the articles to nominate his successor, this is not an assignment and will not require the formality of a special resolution.

Although no qualification by law is required for a director, the articles frequently provide that aliens shall not be appointed to the board of directors. This is often the case with shipping companies where it is sought to preserve British control of the company.

Every company must keep a register of its directors which includes the name, address and business occupation of each director. It must also include details of other directorships currently held by a director, and any other directorship held in the past five years.

Restriction on the appointment of directors

The Company Directors Disqualification Act prohibits certain individuals from acting as directors.

(a) An undischarged bankrupt cannot act as such unless he is authorised by the Court (CDDA section 11).

(b) A person cannot be appointed a director of a public company if at the time of his appointment he has reached the age of 70 (section 293). This provision can be excluded by the articles, and such an appointment may be approved by the majority of members at a general meeting.

(c) A person who is subject to a disqualification order may not act as a director without leave of the Court.

A disqualification order may be made against a person:

(i) who is convicted of an indictable offence in connection with the promotion, formation, management or liquidation of a company or

with the receivership or management of the company's property (CDDA section 2);
(ii) who has been guilty, while an officer of company, of breach of duty or fraud in relation to the company, or of knowingly being a party to fraudulent trading (CDDA section 4);
(iii) who has been persistently in default in filing accounts, returns and other documents with the Registrar (CDDA section 3);
(iv) whose conduct, as a director of a company that has become insolvent, makes him unfit to be concerned with a company's management (CDDA section 6);
(v) where the court has made a declaration that the person concerned is liable to make a contribution to the company's assets as a result of fraudulent or wrongful trading (CDDA section 10);
(vi) where a person's conduct, as revealed by a Department of Trade investigation, makes him unfit to be concerned in a company's management (CDDA section 8).

The maximum period for a disqualification order is 15 years.

Guidelines were recently laid down in *Re Sevenoaks Stationers (Retail) Ltd* as to the periods of disqualification.

(a) Disqualification of 10 years or over should only be used for very serious cases e.g. where a director has previously been disqualified.
(b) Disqualification of 6–10 years for serious cases which do not fall into the top bracket.
(c) Disqualification of 2–5 years where the offences are not serious but disqualification is mandatory.

Qualification shares

An individual may also be prevented from acting as a director unless he holds a certain number of shares in a company. These are known as qualification shares. The reasoning behind this shareholding is that a director should be prepared to have a financial interest in a company whose affairs he is directing but it is not obligatory to have a qualification shareholding. The share qualification is now so small as to be meaningless, or can be a disadvantage in that too high a share qualification can deter suitable persons from becoming directors. Indeed if a director holds a substantial number of shares this could influence his decisions with regard to dividends, or in relation to his tax position.

If a company does specify a share qualification for directors, this must be obtained within two months, or such shorter time as the articles specify. If a director does not obtain the requisite number of shares within the time, he must vacate office and cannot be reappointed director until he has obtained the shares.

The articles frequently state that qualification shares must be held in the director's own name, so that bearer shares or shares held jointly with another person are not suitable (section 291). A director may hold shares as a trustee and this would satisfy a qualification requirement, for although he does not own the equitable interest in the shares his name would appear on the register of members.

Power of management

The management of the company may be exercised by the members in general meeting or it can be delegated by the shareholders to the board of directors. The articles of the majority of the companies delegate this power in words similar to that of Article 70 'The business of the company shall be managed by the directors, who may exercise all such powers of the company'.

The shareholders, having given these powers to the directors, cannot then over-ride the directors' discretion. In *Scott v. Scott*, the shareholders passed a resolution at their general meeting that certain payments in respect of dividends should be made to preference shareholders. The resolution was invalid as it was an attempt by the shareholders to usurp the directors' powers of financial control. Directors have been held to have powers to sell a company's undertaking, to declare an interim dividend, and to sue on behalf of a company without the concurrence of the shareholders.

Board meetings

If the articles vest the power of management collectively in the directors, they must exercise this power only at board meetings. Control of board meetings is in the hands of the chairman of the board. Directors should not take decisions outside meetings unless allowed to do so by the articles. The articles normally provide that the board may delegate its powers to the managing director or a committee of one or more of its directors (Article 72). It is frequently impracticable for all matters to be dealt with at board meetings, and articles such as Article 93 usually provide that if all the directors sign a resolution, it will be as effective as a resolution passed at a board meeting. In practice, a minute is circulated and after each of the directors has signed, it is inserted in the minute book.

The articles usually provide that 'the directors may meet together for the despatch of business, adjourn and otherwise regulate their meetings as they think fit'. Large companies hold board meetings at regular intervals, while small companies tend to hold meetings only where there is a sufficient agenda to justify summoning the board of directors. Unless there are regular meetings at fixed intervals, directors will be entitled to reasonable notice of meetings, but this need not specify the nature of the business to be transacted. If the directors are all present and agree, the formalities of summoning a meeting can be dispensed with and a meeting can be called at any time.

If a director is abroad notice need not be given to him, but if the company inadvertently fails to inform a director of a proposed board meeting, the meeting is irregular. This is a mere technicality as the articles usually declare that a meeting shall be properly constituted, despite an accidental omission to inform a director of a meeting. Even if there were no such article, a later properly constituted board meeting could ratify what had been done irregularly.

The articles generally fix the quorum for a board meeting; this is the number of directors who must be present to enable them to exercise their power as a board. Article 89 states 'The quorum necessary for the transaction of the business of the directors may be fixed by the directors and unless so fixed shall be two'. However, it can be one where a private company has only one director. The quorum must be a disinterested quorum, as the directors present must not have a personal interest in the matters to be voted on, and are therefore by the terms of the articles unable to vote on that particular issue.

Directors exercise their powers at board meetings by passing resolutions approved of by the majority. The articles may provide that in the case of an equality of votes the chairman shall have a second or casting vote (Article 88).

Directors may delegate any of their powers to committees if the articles permit them to do so. A committee may consist of one member; for example, if the board delegates powers to the managing director, he is in effect a committee of one. Regulations are usually embodied in the articles which govern the proceedings of such committees.

Managing director

Larger companies normally appoint a managing director or indeed a number of managing directors to deal with various aspects of the company's business. The powers of such a director are derived solely from the articles. The managing director of a company, to which Table A applies, will initially have to be a director of the company as Article 84 states that 'the directors may from time to time appoint one of their body to the office of managing director'. Such an appointment may be for such a period as his fellow directors think fit, and may even be an appointment for life, although this can be revoked at a general meeting of the company, and he can be removed from office in the same manner as any other director. The articles which delegate this power to a managing director will give the board of directors the right to 'revoke, withdraw, alter or vary such powers'. The members may remove a managing director from his directorship by passing an ordinary resolution (section 303) and this automatically terminates his appointment as managing director.

In *Harold Holdsworth and Co. Ltd v. Caddies*, Caddies acted as the managing director of the major company and its subsidiary. A disagreement arose between him and the board of Harold Holdsworth and Co. Ltd, the parent company, and he was informed that his activities would be solely confined to the subsidiary company. Caddies sued for damages for breach of contract. It was held that the directors had acted within their powers, and Caddies was unable to succeed in his action.

The remuneration of the managing director will be decided upon by his fellow directors, and this may include salary, participation in profits or commission.

A prudent managing director will have a contract of service which clearly states that he is an employee of the company. In *Lee v Lee's Air Farming Ltd*, Lee was the holder of 2999 shares out of the company's total 3000 shares. He was the managing director of the company and drew up a contract between the company and himself for his services as a pilot, where he was described as an employee of the company.

A managing director or any other director may be removed from office, despite having a service contract with the company. Southern Foundries Ltd appointed Shirlaw their managing director in 1933 on a ten year contract. In 1935 the company merged with other companies and in 1937 Shirlaw was removed from the board of directors.

He had to relinquish the post of managing director as the articles stated that only a director could be a managing director. He sued Southern Foundries for breach of contract and recovered damages of £10 000 (*Southern Foundries (1926) Ltd v. Shirlaw*).

A director who is both an employee and managing director will be given all the protection granted to employees under the Employment Protection Consolidation Act 1978 which covers redundancy payments, contracts of employment specification and provisions for unfair dismissal.

Remuneration of directors

The amount of a director's remuneration is usually stated in the director's service contract. The article may make provision for payment of directors' fees, and Article 82 stipulates that the remuneration of the directors shall from time to time be determined by the company in general meeting.

If provision is made in the articles for directors' remuneration, it becomes a debt due from the company to the directors and may be recovered, even though a company has not made any profit; that is, it may be paid out of capital.

It is unlawful for a company to pay a director a fee which is free of income tax (section 311). If a director is paid a sum in excess of that permitted by the company's regulations, he is liable to repay the excess amount to the company. However, a company in general meeting may vote a gratuity which exceeds the director's normal fees.

If a director vacates office during the currency of the year, the articles must be examined to determine the amount, if any, of his remuneration. Article 82 states that the director's 'remuneration shall be deemed to accrue from day to day', and in such a case he will be able to claim. If there is no such article, then the position is not clear. It has been held that to express a director's salary at the 'rate of £1 000 per annum' entitles a director to be paid for the period he has served as a director. If his salary is expressed as £1 000 per annum, or a yearly sum of £1 000, it would appear that a director will only be paid if he completes a full year's service. The Apportionments Act 1870 may apply in this situation, as it states that all annuities and other periodical payments in the nature of income should be apportionable. As annuities include salaries and pensions, it would appear that directors' fees would be covered by this provision.

A company's accounts must give details of directors' remuneration during a current financial year, but it need not disclose each individual director's remuneration. It must give the following details:

(a) the aggregate amount of the directors' emoluments, e.g. fees, expenses, salary, estimated cash value of other benefits.
(b) the aggregate amount of directors pensions or past directors pensions.
(c) the aggregate amount of any compensation to directors or past directors for loss of office.
(d) the chairman's emoluments.
(e) the emoluments of the highest paid director if he is paid more than the chairman.
(f) a scale of directors' emoluments divided into bands of £5 000 and the number of directors in each band.
(g) The number of directors who have waived their rights to emoluments and the aggregate amount of the emoluments. (section 232, schedule 6)

(These disclosure requirements do not apply to a company which is not a holding company, or a subsidiary or where the total directors' remuneration does not exceed £60 000.)

Vacation of office

The articles of the majority of public companies provide that at the first annual general meeting of a company all the directors shall retire from office. They are eligible for re-election, which is usually a mere formality. Article 73 provides for the retirement by rotation of one-third of the directors who have been longest in office each year. They are eligible for re-election. If the number of directors is not exactly three, or a multiple of three, then the number nearest one-third will retire. In compiling this number the managing director is not included, nor are the directors appointed by the board to fill any casual vacancies which have occurred since the last annual general meeting. These directors only hold office until the next annual general meeting at which meeting they must submit themselves for re-election. An example of the working of the formula would be as follows. A company has seven directors (including a managing director). Of the other six directors, two were appointed by the board during the year. These two directors plus one other must stand for re-election. These provisions are rarely found in the articles of private companies.

A retiring director who offers himself for re-election wil be deemed to be re-elected unless it is decided at the meeting not to fill the vacancy, or it is resolved at the meeting that the director be not re-elected.

Section 303 provides that a company may remove a director from office by ordinary resolution, notwithstanding anything in the articles or in the agreement between him and the company. This resolution requires special notice. The director concerned may then require the company to circulate a statement to all the members outlining his defence. If the company fails to do so, or is unable to do so, the director may have the statement read out at the meeting. The company can apply to the Court to be excused from publishing the statement, if it considers that the director is merely making the statement to secure needless publicity for defamatory matter. Additionally, the director is entitled to address the meeting, whether he is a member or not. Section 303 applies to all companies and all directors, with one exception. It does not apply to a director of a private company who was appointed a director for life, on or before 18 July 1945.

Should a director be removed from office in consequence of section

303, the company may appoint another person to take his place. This may be filled by the board as a casual vacancy or there may be an appointment at the same meeting. If an appointment is made at the same meeting, special notice must be given of the intention to fill the vacancy. Such a director holds office only for the unexpired period of office of his predecessor. If the deposed director has a service contract with the company, he may claim compensation and damages for loss of office. The articles may provide that on a resolution to remove a director the shares held by that director shall carry additional voting rights (*Bushell v. Faith* see page 141).

A company's articles may specify other grounds of disqualification, e.g. prohibiting an alien or a minor from holding office as a director, or disqualifying a director who is convicted of a criminal offence.

Article 81 specifies the following additional grounds for disqualification and provides that a director must vacate office if he:

(a) is made bankrupt or makes any arrangement with his creditors generally;
(b) becomes of unsound mind; resigns his office by notice in writing to the company;
(c) is absent, without permission, from board meetings for more than six months. In *Re London and Northern Bank, Mack's Claim* a director who lived in Northern Ireland was unable to travel to London for board meetings over a period of time. It was held that he had not 'absented himself' so as to be disqualified, as his prolonged illness was an involuntary reason for his absence.

Articles frequently provide that a director shall vacate office if he becomes directly or indirectly interested in any contract entered into by the company. On completion of the contract the director may be validly re-appointed.

Compensation for loss of office

Compensation may be paid to a director for loss of his office. Such payment is lawful as long as it is disclosed to the members of the company and approved by the company in general meeting (sections 312–315). In *Re Duomatic Ltd* a payment of £4 000 to a director for loss of office was not disclosed in the company's accounts or to the non-voting preference shareholders. It was held that the directors who had approved the payment were liable to the company for misapplication of funds.

It may arise in three situations:

(i) compensation paid by the company on his retirement, whether voluntary or enforced (section 312).
(ii) compensation paid on retirement following the sale of a company's undertaking. Usually the payment will be made by the purchaser (section 313).
(iii) compensation paid on retirement in connection with an offer for the share capital of the company. If the offer is for one-third or more of the capital, or is conditional on acceptance to a given extent, the approval of the shareholders must be obtained (section 314).

If a director does not disclose payments made to him as compensation, he will hold such payments in trust for the company in situations (i) and (ii). In situation (iii) he will hold the money in trust for the shareholders who have sold their shares as a result of the offer. Money will also be held on trust for shareholders if a director receives a higher price for his shares than is paid to the other shareholders, and this fact is not disclosed.

If there is a scheme of reconstruction providing compensation for displaced directors, any payment made to such a director must be disclosed to members when seeking their approval for the reconstruction. If proper disclosure is not made, the scheme is invalid.

Any bona fide payment of damages for breach of contract, or a payment of a pension for past services is not regarded as compensation and need not be disclosed to, or approved by the shareholders (section 316).

In *Taupo Totara Timber Co. Ltd v. Rowe*, a managing director's five year contract with a company provided that in the event of a takeover of the company he could resign and receive five years salary as compensation. The company was taken over and he resigned. The company refused to pay him compensation unless it was approved by the shareholders at a general meeting. It was held that the approval of the members applied only to voluntary payments and the company was contractually bound to make the payment.

The aggregate amount of any compensation paid to a director for loss of office or retirement from office with a company or its subsidiaries must be disclosed in a company's accounts (Schedule 6).

16
DIRECTORS' DUTIES

Directors must act honestly and in the best interests of the company. If a transaction entered into by the directors is not in the best interests of the company – for example, the power to issue shares being used to retain control (*Piercy v. Mills and Co*) – it is not binding. In *Re Roith (W & M) Ltd*, the memorandum and articles of a company were altered to allow pensions to be paid to dependants of the company's employees. Shortly afterwards a director, in poor health, was appointed general manager for life under a service agreement which provided, *inter alia*, that his widow would be paid a pension for life on his death. It was held that the agreement was not binding, as it was not for the Company's benefit.

A director must account to the company for any profit made by him by virtue of being a director, unless the members give their consent in general meeting. In *Boston Deep Sea Fishing and Ice Co v. Ansell*, a director of the company entered into contracts for constructing fishing smacks, and was paid a commission on the contract by the shipbuilders. He also owned shares in an ice-making company which paid, in addition to dividends, a bonus to shareholders who were owners of fishing smacks and who purchased ice from the ice company for use in their ships. Neither of these transactions was disclosed to the company and

Ansell had to account for the bonus and the commission to the company, even though the company could not have qualified for the bonus.

In *Regal (Hastings) Ltd v. Gulliver*, a company which owned a cinema in Hastings proposed to acquire two other cinemas in order to sell the three cinemas together. It formed a subsidiary company to purchase the cinemas. The subsidiary company was unable to provide all the required capital, so the directors bought some shares in the subsidiary company to enable it to provide the necessary capital. The subsidiary company acquired the two cinemas and the shares of Regal Ltd, and the subsidiary was sold at a profit. It was held that the directors must account to the Regal Company for the profit they had made, as it was only through the knowledge and opportunity they had gained as directors of Regal Ltd that they were able to obtain the shares.

(The directors of Regal Ltd could have obtained ratification of the action by the company in general meeting, but it did not occur to them to do so as they believed their actions were legal and proper.)

A director who, in the course of his employment, obtains a contract for himself, must account to the company for the profit, even though it is debatable whether the company could have obtained the contract.

In *Industrial Development Consultants Ltd v. Cooley*, IDC Ltd, provided construction consultancy services for gas boards. Its managing director was an architect named Cooley. The Eastern Gas Board offered tenders for building four depots, and Cooley was informed that it was unlikely that IDC Ltd would be given the contract. He realised that he had an excellent opportunity of obtaining the contract for himself and represented to IDC Ltd that he was ill. IDC Ltd released him from his contract with them and he then obtained the benefit of the contract for himself. IDC Ltd successfully sued Cooley for the profit he made on the construction of the depots.

A director may retain a personal profit if:

1   the articles permit a director to enter into a contract or to have an interest in a contract; or
2   the company in general meeting passes a resolution to this effect.

If the director concerned controls the voting at the general meeting such a resolution may be regarded as fraud or an oppression of the minority. In *Cook v. Deeks* a company entered into a contract for construction work with the Canadian Pacific Railway. At a later date the company passed a resolution that it had no interest in the contract.

(The directors controlled three quarters of the issued share capital.) The directors obtained the contract in their own names and later formed a new company to execute the contract. It was held that the benefit of the contract belonged to the construction company.

It may be possible for a director to retain a profit made by him if he takes up a proposition in his personal capacity which a company has considered and bona fide rejected.

This was held in *Peso Silver Mines v. Cropper* (a Canadian case) where the Peso company was offered additional claims but rejected the offer. A director of Peso, who took part in the board meeting which considered the offer, later purchased shares in a new company set up to work these claims. It was held that he was acting in his private capacity and was under no obligation to account to Peso for the shares.

The recent case of *Island Export Finance Ltd v. Umunna* shows that the rule in the Regal case is not inflexible. The managing director of IEF negotiated a contract on its behalf with the postal authorities in a West African State. The company did not proceed with the contract and Umunna resigned because of dissatisfaction with company policy. He later obtained for himself a contract with the postal authorities. It was held that he was not in breach of his fiduciary duty and could not be restrained from using expertise and knowledge in exploiting a market which the company was not interested in developing.

Directors as trustees

Directors may be compared to trustees in that they stand in a fiduciary relationship to the company in the performance of their duties. They have possession or control of the company's money and property, and therefore hold these on trust for the company. If these are misapplied, this constitutes a breach of trust.

In *Allen v. Hyatt*, the directors entered into negotiations for the amalgamation of the company with other companies. They informed a number of shareholders that it was necessary to grant the directors an option to purchase their shares at par in order for the amalgamation to take place. The directors then exercised the option and made a substantial profit. It was held that they must account for this profit to the shareholders.

Directors are trustees of the powers entrusted to them; for example, the power to issue shares is granted to directors to enable them to raise capital, when it is required by the company. In *Piercy v. Mills and Co*, the company's two directors made an allotment of shares although the company did not require further capital. The aim of the directors was to maintain control of the company and prevent the appointment of other directors. It was held that the allotment was invalid and void.

In *Lee Panavision Ltd v Lee Lighting Ltd* the directors of a company knowing that a company was proposing to appoint new directors passed a resolution which would in effect remove all managerial powers from the new directors. It was held that the resolution was invalid as directors may not use their powers to retain control of the company where this is not in good faith.

In *Howard Smith Ltd v. Ampol Petroleum Ltd*, the directors of Millers Ltd (a company in which Ampol Petroleum Ltd and another shareholder held 55 per cent of the issued share capital) allotted shares to Howard Smith Ltd in order to destroy the majority holdings of Ampol Ltd and the other shareholders (this was to enable Howard Smith Ltd to make an offer for the shares of the minority shareholders). It was held that the allotment was invalid and void.

The directors of a company are trustees for a company and not for the individual shareholder. In *Percival v. Wright*, the directors of a company purchased shares from Percival at a price based on his valuation. At this time the directors were negotiating for the sale of the company to a third party. If successful, the price realised for each share would have been greater than that paid for Percival's share. The negotiations proved abortive. It was held the directors were not trustees for the individual shareholders and could purchase their shares without disclosing any pending negotiations for the sale of the company.

If it is discovered that the directors have acted from improper motives, they can nevertheless make full disclosure to the shareholders and obtain their approval. (*Bamford v. Bamford*).

The Limitation Act 1980 applies to the acts of directors, as it applies to trustees, and bars any rights against a director for negligence or breach of trust, where the proceedings are commenced more than six years after the alleged wrong or omission.

Directors as agents

As agents of a company directors are limited by the contractual powers of the company, as set out in its objects clause. As long as they contract within the scope of their authority, they incur no personal liability on any contracts made by them. If an agent exceeds his authority when entering into a contract, the agent becomes personally liable for breach of warranty of authority; that is, he is liable as he warrants that he has authority that he does not possess. If the directors make a contract which is beyond the board's power to make, they become personally liable on the contract.

Should a contract be beyond the powers of the directors, but within the power of the company – that is, *ultra vires* the board but *intra vires* the company – the company can in a general meeting ratify the board's actions. This occurred in *Bamford v. Bamford* where the directors of Bamford Ltd, manufacturers of agricultural machinery, allotted unissued shares to a third party to forestall a takeover bid. Although the articles provided that the unissued shares were at the directors' disposal, they exceeded their powers by issuing them for this reason. Nevertheless, it was held that the shareholders, at a meeting one month later, could ratify and validate the directors' actions as they approved of these actions.

If directors hold themselves out as agents to the shareholders in transactions involving the shareholders, they must account for any profit made by them in the course of the transactions (*Allen v. Hyatt*).

Duties owed to employees

Part of a director's fiduciary duty is to have regard to the interests of a company's employees, as well as the interests of the members. This duty is owed to the company and is enforceable by the company in the same way as any other duty owed to it by a director (section 309).

A company may provide for its present and past employees and the employees of its subsidiaries on the cessation or transfer of the whole or any part of its undertaking or that of any subsidiary (section 719). This provision may be exercised even though it is not in the company's best interests. The position of the creditors is safeguarded as payment may only be made out of profits which would otherwise have been available for distribution among members as dividends.

The authority to make such provision must be sanctioned by an ordinary resolution, or a directors' resolution if authorised by the memorandum or articles, or a resolution other than an ordinary resolution if required by the memorandum or articles.

On a winding up of the company the liquidator may make any payment which the company has, before the commencement of the winding up, decided to make under section 719. Payment may be made out of the company assets which are available to members on a winding up, after providing for the costs of winding up and the payment in full of the company's liabilities. It must be sanctioned by an ordinary resolution or a resolution other than an ordinary resolution if required by the memorandum or articles (1A section 187). (A directors' resolution is inoperative as the powers of the directors cease on a winding up.)

Section 719 reverses the decision in *Parke v. Daily News Ltd* where the majority shareholders of a company which had been sold proposed to distribute the whole of the purchase price as *ex gratia* payments to employees who had become redundant. It was held that such payments were not valid as they were not made for the benefit and prosperity of the company and were not incidental to carrying on the company's business.

Directors as employees

A company director who is employed under a contract of employment is entitled to the protection given by the Employment Acts. If a director does not have an employment contract the presumption is that, as an office holder, he is not an employee. (The rights and duties of an office holder are defined by the office he holds and exist independently of the person holding the office.) In certain circumstances, a contract of employment is implied despite the lack of a formal employment contract. In *Folami v. Nigerline (UK) Ltd*, the chief accountant of a Nigerian company was appointed managing director of its English subsidiary company. He was paid a salary but was not given a written contract of employment. It was held nevertheless that he was an employee.

Occasionally clarification of the matter is found in the company's articles of association. In *Parsons v. Albert J Parsons and Sons Ltd*, the sons of the firm's founder were directors of the company. There were no contracts of service, but the articles provided that the directors should be appointed for life. No formal salaries were paid to the directors and they voted themselves a sum described as 'directors emoluments' at the end of every year. One of the sons was removed from office and applied to an industrial tribunal claiming that he had been unfairly dismissed. It was held that he was not an employee as he was regarded and remunerated as a director.

In *Eaton v. Robert Eaton Ltd* the EAT set out some of the factors to consider in deciding the status of a director.

(a) Generally speaking, a director is an office holder and is not in employment.
(b) The use of a descriptive term, e.g. managing director, technical director, may indicate employee status.
(c) Drawing a weekly wage or regular or fixed salary as opposed to director's fees may again indicate employee status.
(d) An agreement to employ a person as managing director minuted at a board meeting or noted by a memorandum in writing is a strong indication of a contract of employment.
(e) Consideration of the director's functions – was he acting in a directorial capacity or under the control of the board of directors?

The degree of skill to be shown by a director

A director must exercise a degree of skill and diligence in the performance of his duties. The degree of skill will vary with the size and complexity of the company. The position of a director of a company carrying on a small retail business is vastly different from that of a director of a multi-national company. The duty owed by a director has been described as the care that an ordinary man might be expected to take in the circumstances.

In *Re City Equitable Fire Insurance*, the directors entrusted the company's investments to its managing director, Bevan, who was also a senior partner in a firm of brokers which handled the company's investments. Some £1 200 000 was lost due to Bevan's fraud and incompetence, including £350 000 left with the brokers. It was held that although the other directors had acted honestly, they had been negligent in not establishing how the company's funds were invested.

In *Re City Equitable Fire Insurance*, Romer J. laid down the following propositions:

1. A director need not exhibit in the performance of his duties a greater degree of skill than may reasonably be expected from a person of his knowledge and experience. (A director of a life insurance company, for instance, does not guarantee that he has the skill of an actuary or physician.)
2. A director is not bound to give continuous attention to the affairs of his company. His duties are of an intermittent nature to be performed at periodical board meetings, and at meetings of any Committee of the board upon which he happens to be placed. He is not however bound to attend all such meetings, though he ought to attend whenever, in the circumstances, he is reasonably able to do so.
3. In respect of all duties that, having regard to the exigencies of business and the articles of association, may properly be left to some other official, a director is, in the absence of grounds for suspicion, justified in trusting that official to perform such duties honestly.

These are general propositions, and outline the minimum standards to be expected from non-executive directors. A far greater degree of skill and commitment will be expected of an executive director and managing director.

A director is not liable for the wrongful acts of his co-directors of which he has no knowledge and in which he has not taken part, but may become liable for the acts and misdeeds of his fellow directors if he habitually abstains from attending board meetings.

A director is not liable for errors of judgement. Brett L.J. stated in *Lagunas Nitrate Co. v. Lagunas Syndicate* that: 'A director must be guilty of such negligence as would make liable in an action. Mere imprudence is not negligence: want of judgement is not. It must be such negligence as would make a man liable in point of law.'

In *Re New Mansholand Exploration Co.*, the directors of a company had power to lend money and promote other companies. They passed a resolution to lend Green a sum of money on his giving security. The company's solicitor handed a cheque for £250 to Green without obtaining any security. Later another cheque for £1 000 was handed to Green without security being obtained, as Green was bringing out a company which the directors believed would benefit their own company. It was held that the directors were not liable for breach of trust or misfeasance as they had exercised their judgment and discretion honestly.

Remedies for breach of duty

The following remedies may be available against a director in breach of his duties.

- The other party to the agreement may apply for rescission of the contract if a director has contravened the rules relating to contracts in which he is interested. This is only possible if the parties can be restored to their former positions and third parties have not acquired rights under the contract.
- Damages may be awarded if the other party has suffered loss as a result of the director's actions.
- An injunction may be granted to restrain a breach which is threatened but which has not yet occurred, for example to prevent the board from taking action which is beyond its power.
- Action may be taken for the restoration of the company's property where the property has remained under the director's control, or it is possible to trace it to a purchaser who was aware of the director's breach of duty.
- A director is liable to account for any profit made by him in his capacity as director, which has not been disclosed to the company.
- A director who is an employee of the company (e.g. a managing director) may be summarily dismissed.
- A director (or any other person) may be criminally liable for fraudulent trading, or wrongful trading (IA sections 213, 214).

It may also be possible to take action against a director by a misfeasance summons. Such a summons may be applied for by the liquidator, any creditor or contributory when the company is in the course of being wound up. The Court may order a director to repay or restore money or property, or compensate a company, where he has misapplied or retained the company's property or money, or has been guilty of any misfeasance or breach of trust (IA section 212).

A director may escape liability if the company in general meeting validly ratifies the breach. In *Pavlides v. Jensen*, it was alleged that the directors had been negligent in selling an asbestos mine owned by the company for £182 000, whereas its true value was in the region of £1 000 000. The company resolved that no proceedings should be taken against them.

Any article of the company seeking to exempt a director from liability for negligence, default, breach of duty or breach of trust in relation to the company is void (section 310). A company may, however, purchase and maintain insurance against such liability for its directors, officers of the company and its auditors (section 110). A company may provide in its articles that it shall indemnify any director against any liability incurred by him in successfully defending any civil or criminal proceedings, or in connection with an application under section 727 in which relief is granted to him by the Court (Article 118).

Relief may also be granted by the Court. Section 727 provides that if in proceedings for negligence, default, breach of duty or breach of trust against a director of a company, it appears that he has acted honestly and reasonably, and having regard to all the circumstances he ought fairly to be excused, the Court may relieve him, wholly or partly, from liability on such terms as it thinks fit.

17
DIRECTORS' BUSINESS INTERESTS

As directors' interests often coincide with those of a company, the Act insists upon disclosure of directors' business interests.

Contracts with the company

As a general rule a director cannot make a contract with a company, as he should not place himself in a situation where his personal interests might conflict with his duty to the company. Such a contract is voidable at the company's option.

In *Aberdeen Railway Co. v. Blaikie Bros*, a railway company entered into a contract with a firm for the supply of certain goods. The company's chairman was at the time of making the contract also the firm's managing partner. It was held that the company was not bound by the contract.

In *Parker v. McKenna*, the directors of the National Bank of Ireland increased the capital of the Bank by issuing 20 000 £50 shares. Any shares not taken up were to be disposed of by the directors at a £30 premium. Stock entered into agreement to purchase 9778 shares for

£30, placing a deposit of £5 on each share, the balance to be paid by instalments. As Stock was unable to take all the shares, the directors took a considerable number of these shares and afterwards disposed of them at a profit. It was held that the directors must account to the Bank for the profits made by them by the sale of the shares.

A director may enter into a contract to take up shares or debentures in a company.

The articles may provide that a director may enter into a contract with the company or have an interest in such a contract (Article 85). Section 317 provides that a director who is in any way, directly or indirectly, interested in a contract or proposed contract with a company must declare the nature of this interest at the first board meeting at which the contract is discussed. The articles usually specify that an interested director may not vote on the contract and that if he does so his vote will not be counted or count in the quorum present (Articles 94, 95). A contract includes any transaction or arrangement, whether it constitutes a contract and a contract with a person connected with a director is deemed to be a contract in which a director is interested. If at that time he had no interest but later becomes interested, he must disclose his interest at the next board meeting after he becomes interested.

A director may give a general notice to the board that he is a member of a company or a firm and is to be regarded as having an interest in any contract made with that company or firm. The notice must either be given at a board meeting or brought up and read at the next board meeting after it is given (section 317).

Section 317 also applies to a shadow director except that a shadow director must declare his interest, not at a board meeting, but by a notice to the directors, which is either:

(a) a specific notice given before the meeting at which, if he had been a director, a declaration would be required to be made; *or*
(b) a general notice which is a sufficient declaration of the interest.

A director who fails to comply with section 317 is liable to a fine and there is also a presumption of a conflict of interest and duty. The contract is voidable at the company's option.

An interest must be declared at a meeting of the whole board and the requirements of section 317 are not fulfilled by disclosure to a sub committee. In *Guinness Plc v. Saunders*, a committee of the board of directors of Guinness Plc agreed to pay Saunders, a director of the company, £5.2m for his services in connection with a take-over bid being made by Guinness. It was held that as the payment had not been approved by the board of directors, Saunders was not entitled to retain the payment.

Connected persons

A person 'connected with a director' includes his spouse (if not a director); his children under eighteen; an associated company in which the director and any person connected with him together are interested in more than one-fifth of the equity share capital or control more than one-fifth of the voting power; and any trustee for, or partner of, the director, or his spouse, children or associated company. A contract entered into in contravention of this section is voidable at the company's option, unless restitution is not possible, or innocent third parties have acquired rights, or the contract is ratified by the company within a reasonable period of time.

A director may give a general notice that he is to be regarded as having an interest in any contract made with a specified company, firm or person.

Substantial property transactions

A general meeting must approve of any contract to transfer to, or acquire from, a director or a person connected with a director, a non-cash asset whose value at the time of the transaction exceeds £50 000 or 10 per cent of the net assets, provided it is not less than £1 000 (section 320).

These restrictions do not apply in the following circumstances:

(a) an arrangement by a holding company and any of its wholly owned subsidiaries, or between two wholly owned subsidiaries of the same holding company;
(b) an arrangement entered into by a company which is being wound up (other than in a members' voluntary winding up);
(c) obtaining an asset from a company in the capacity of a member (e.g. the issue of bonus shares) (section 321).

If the value of the property exceeds the specified limits the transaction must be approved by a resolution of the company in general meeting. If the director is a director of the holding company (or the connected person is connected with that director) the arrangement must also be approved by a general meeting of the holding company.

Any transaction or arrangement entered into in contravention of these provisions is voidable at the company's option unless:

(i) restitution of any money or property is no longer possible or the company has been indemnified for any loss or damage suffered by it; or
(ii) rights have been acquired bona fide and for value by a 3rd party who is unaware of any contravention; or
(iii) the arrangement is confirmed within a reasonable time by the company in general meeting. If the arrangement is with a director of its holding company (or a person connected with him) it must also be approved by a general meeting of the holding company (section 322).

A director and any person connected with him is liable to account to the company for any direct or indirect gain made as a result of the transaction or arrangement and is also liable to indemnify the company for any loss or damage suffered by it. Any other director who authorised the arrangement or any other transaction connected with such an arrangement is also liable unless he can show that he took all steps to secure compliance with the section or was unaware of the circumstances relating to the contravention (section 322).

Loans to directors

The general rule is that a company may not make a loan to a director of the company nor to a director of its holding company. Neither may a company enter into a guarantee or provide any security in connection with a loan made by any person to such a director (section 330).

The Act distinguishes between loans given by relevant companies and other companies. A relevant company is a public company, or a subsidiary or holding company of a public company or forms part of a group which contains a public company. A relevant company may not:

1 make a quasi loan to a director or to a director of its holding company.

2 make a loan or quasi loan to a person connected with a director.
3 enter into a guarantee or provide any security in connection with a loan or quasi loan made by any other person for a director or connected person.
4 enter into a credit transaction for a director or connected person.
5 Enter into a guarantee or provide security in connection with a credit transaction made by another person for a director or connected person.

A quasi loan is a transaction between a company and the director whereby the company pays or promises to pay a third party on terms that the director will reimburse the company, for example the use of credit cards by a director, where the company is the cardholder and promises to pay a third party on the terms that the director will reimburse the company. A credit transaction is a transaction under which a party, i.e. the creditor supplies goods or services or sells, leases or hires land (section 331).

Certain exceptions are allowed and include:

(a) loans or quasi loans or guarantees made to a member of a group of companies (even though a director of one member of the group is associated with another) (section 333).
(b) a quasi loan of up to £5 000 if it is agreed that it is to be repaid within two months (section 332).
(c) the provision of funds for expenses incurred by a director for the purposes of the company or in connection with his duties. In the case of a relevant company there is a ceiling of £20 000 for each director (section 337).
(d) credit transactions made with directors in the normal course of business on commercial terms (section 335).
(e) credit transactions where the 'relevant amount' (i.e. the value of all outstanding transactions made with director and connected persons) does not exceed £5 000 (section 335).
(f) loans made by a money lending company in the ordinary course of business and on normal commercial terms. If the company is not a bank there is a £100 000 limit per director (section 338).
(g) loans made by a money lending company for house purchase and house improvement. This is subject to a limit of £100 000 and is applicable to all companies (section 338).
(h) a loan to a director of the company or its holding company, if the

aggregate of the relevant amounts does not exceed £5 000 (section 334).

Option dealings

It is an offence for a director, including a shadow director, or the spouse or infant children of a director, to deal in options to buy or sell quoted shares or debentures of the company of which he is a director or to deal in securities of associated companies (sections 323, 327).

A director who buys a right to call for, make delivery of, or at his election a right to call for, or make delivery of a specified number of shares, or a specified amount of debentures within a specified time is liable to a fine and/or a term of imprisonment (section 323).

The aim of this prohibition is to prevent a director and his immediate family using inside information to speculate in the securities (i.e. shares or debentures) of companies with which he is closely associated.

A director may acquire an option to buy the securities of a private company, or the unquoted securities of a public company and it is lawful to buy a right to subscribe for shares or debentures directly from the company, or to buy debentures which carry a right to subscribe for or convert into shares.

A director's spouse or infant child, who is accused of contravening these sections, may submit that she (or he) had no reason to believe that the spouse (or parent) was a director of the company in question (section 327).

The Department of Trade may appoint an inspector to investigate cases of suspected option dealing (section 446).

Directors' service contracts

Every company must make available for the inspection of its members the terms of its service contracts with its directors. If the contract is in writing, a copy of the contract must be retained. If it is not in writing, a written memorandum setting out the terms must be available for inspection. Any variations in the terms of the contract must also be shown. The details of a service contract of a director with a subsidiary company must also be available for inspection.

DIRECTORS' BUSINESS INTERESTS

These must be kept at the company's registered office or at the company's principal place of business in England or at the place where the register of members is kept (section 318). These provisions do not apply to a contract which has less than 12 months to run; a contract which may be terminated by the company in the next 12 months without payment of compensation or a contract which requires a director to work wholly or mainly outside the United Kingdom (section 318).

A service contract may contain a provision that a director's employment cannot be terminated by the company by notice, or can be so terminated only in specified circumstances. Such a term can only be incorporated into an agreement if first approved by the company in general meeting. Where an agreement concerns a director of a holding company it must be approved at the general meetings of both the holding company and the subsidiary. Approval is not required in the case of a wholly owned subsidiary (section 319). The aim of this section is to prevent directors from entering into long term service contracts in anticipation of moves to remove them. A breach of contract in these circumstances would entitle them to large sums as compensation.

The resolution may not be passed unless a memorandum setting out the terms of the proposed agreement is available for inspection by the members for 15 days prior to the meeting and at the meeting itself (section 319).

The incorporation of a term into an agreement in contravention of section 319 is void and such agreement is deemed to contain a term that entitles a company to terminate the agreement at any time by giving reasonable notice. However the remainder of the agreement is valid.

A director cannot avoid the provisions of section 319 by entering into a succession of short term contracts of fewer than five years as the unexpired term of one contract must be added to the term of a new contract, e.g. a director who has a four year contract enters into a second four year contract at the end of the second year. The second contract would therefore be of six year duration and subject to the provisions of the section.

Directors' interests in shares and debentures

A director, including a shadow director, is under an obligation to notify a company of his interest in its shares or debentures existing at the time of his appointment. He must notify the company, within five days, in writing of the number and class of shares in which he has an interest, and the amount and class of debentures involved (section 324). This obligation extends to notifying the company of any interest of his spouse or infant children (section 328).

A director is deemed to have an interest in the following situations:

1. if he is the holder of shares;
2. if he enters into a contract for the purchase of shares;
3. if he exercises, or is entitled to exercise, rights conferred by the shares (and he is not the holder of the shares);
4. if a company is interested in the shares and that company or its directors are accustomed to act in accordance with his directions, or he is entitled to exercise or control a third or more of the votes at that company's general meeting. If that company controls a third or more of the voting power at another company's general meeting, he is regarded as having an interest in that other company;
5. if he has an option to take shares or debentures;
6. if any interest in shares is comprised in trust property and he is a beneficiary of that trust. A person is also interested if his spouse, or infant child or step-child is so interested.

He must also inform the company if he ceases to be so interested; or if he makes a contract to sell any shares or debentures; or if he assigns a right to subscribe for the company's shares or debentures; or if a related company grants him a right to subscribe for its shares and debentures (sections 324, 328, 13th Schedule).

Register of directors' interests

A company must keep a register of directors' interests which must be open during business hours for inspection by any member of the company and to other persons on payment of 5p per inspection. The company must supply a copy of the register, or part of it, within 10 days to any person requesting a copy, on payment of 10p per 100 words. Whenever a company grants a director a right to subscribe for its shares or debentures it must inscribe in the register against his name the date on which the right is granted, the period during which it is exercisable, and the consideration for the grant. When a director exercises such a right, the company must inscribe in the register against his name the fact that the right has been exercised, the number of shares or debentures involved, and the name of the person in whose name they were registered (section 325).

The register must be produced at the company's annual general meeting and remain open and accessible during the meeting for persons attending the meeting (section 325, schedule 13).

Insider dealing

The Companies Securities (Insider Dealing) Act 1985 makes it a criminal offence for an individual to deal on a recognised stock exchange in the securities of a company if he has inside information relating to those securities which, if known, would be likely to affect the price of those securities.

An individual who is, or at any time in the previous six months has been, connected with a company shall not deal in that company's securities on a recognised stock exchange if he has information which he holds by virtue of his connection with the company, which he would not be expected to disclose as he is aware that it is unpublished price sensitive information relating to those securities (CSIDA section 1).

Price sensitive information is defined as:

1 information relating either directly or indirectly to specific matters of concern to the company in question;
2 information which is not yet generally known to persons likely to deal in those securities but which if generally known would be likely to affect the price of these securities (CSIDA section 10).

This prohibition also extends to dealings in the securities of another company, if the information relates to any transaction, actual or contemplated, involving that company and the company with which he is connected. This also applies to any transaction involving one of those companies and the securities of the other company (CSIDA section 9).

An individual contemplating, or who has contemplated, making a takeover bid for a company in a particular capacity is prohibited from dealing on a recognised stock exchange in the securities of that company in any other capacity, such as through a nominee (CSIDA section 10).

An individual who is prohibited from dealing by these provisions must not counsel or procure any other person either to deal in those securities or communicate information, if he knows that such information will be used for the purpose of dealing on a stock exchange (CSIDA section 1), or outside Great Britain (CSIDA section 5).

A person who obtains information about a company's affairs, either directly or indirectly, from another individual who is connected with that company, may not deal in that company's securities if he knows or has reason to believe that the information is unpublished and price sensitive.

An individual who is prohibited from dealing in a company's securities on a recognised stock exchange may not deal 'off market' i.e. through an off market dealer making a market in advertised securities (CSIDA section 4).

An individual is connected with a company if he is a director, officer or employee of that company or a related company (CSIDA section 1). A person having a professional or business relationship with the company or related company is connected with the company if this relationship gives him access to unpublished price-sensitive information, which he would not be expected to disclose except in the proper performance of his work (CSIDA section 9).

The prohibition on insider dealings also applies to stock exchange dealings by public servants, obtained in their official capacity.

Certain exceptions are permitted to these prohibitions:

(a) any person dealing in securities other than with a view to making a profit or avoiding a loss, whether for himself or for another person e.g. realising securities to meet a pressing debt.
(b) any person entering into a transaction in good faith while acting as liquidator, receiver or trustee in bankruptcy.
(c) receiving the information in the course of business as a jobber or market maker.

(d) an individual doing anything for the purpose of stabilising the price of securities in conformity with the business rules as laid down under section 48 of the Financial Services Act.

The penalty for insider dealing is a maximum of seven years' imprisonment and/or a fine of unlimited amount. The transactions entered into in breach of the prohibitions on insider dealing are valid, despite the contravention of the Act.

The prohibition on insider dealing does not apply to share transactions in a private company and to other private deals, or to certain dealings in international bonds.

The Secretary of State may appoint an inspector to investigate and report on suspected contraventions of insider dealing legislation. An inspector may compel the production of documents, the attendance of persons and their examination on oath. The evidence provided may be used in evidence in proceedings where prohibited insider dealing is disclosed. The Secretary of State may, at any time, vary the terms of the appointment by limiting or extending the period during which an inspector is to continue his investigation or by confining the investigation to certain matters (FSA sections 177, 178).

18
— MAJORITY RULE —

Every member of a company is by virtue of the articles contractually bound to the company and to his fellow members. As such he undertakes to accept as binding the decisions of the majority as expressed at a general meeting of the company, when a member may attend, put forward his views and (with certain exceptions) vote. If a sufficient majority support a resolution to which he is opposed, he must abide by the majority decision. The majority, who have control of the company, are thus able to formulate policy and appoint the directors of their choice.

Even if a wrong is alleged to have been committed against a company, the members may, by ordinary resolution, validly resolve that no proceedings be taken in respect of the act. The shareholder cannot complain, as he has agreed to the course of action, even if he does not approve of it. A minority shareholder failed in his attempt to prevent a company selling a mine valued at £1 000 000 for £182 000, as no fraud on the minority was alleged (*Pavlides v. Jensen*).

The rule in *Foss v. Harbottle*

The principle of majority rule was established in *Foss v. Harbottle*. In this case the minority shareholders attempted to sue the directors, alleging that the losses incurred by the company were due to the directors' mismanagement. The action was dismissed and the Court formulated various propositions.

1. The proper plaintiff in respect of a wrong alleged to be done to a company is, *prima facie*, the company itself – so preventing a multiplicity of suits.
'The company alone can sue, or be sued; and it matters not whether the dissentients comprise a lone voice or a full 49 per cent minority of the equity voters. (Jenkins L. J. in *Edwards v. Halliwell*.)'
2. The Court will not interfere if the irregularity is capable of being confirmed by the majority, so that it is futile to litigate except with the consent of the majority.
3. An individual shareholder may proceed on a company's behalf if a general meeting does not have the power, or cannot be convened.
4. The rule does not apply to proceedings between shareholders regarding their rights amongst themselves.

Exceptions to the rule

There are exceptions to this rule and the majority cannot:

(a) take advantage of a resolution passed by means of a trick (*Baillie v. Oriental Telephone and Electric Co.*).
(b) commit a fraud on the company.

In *Menier v. Hooper's Telegraph*, the company brought an action against one of its directors, claiming that he had taken the benefit of a contract which belonged to the company. The majority shareholders persuaded the company to drop the action and proposed that the company should be wound up voluntarily. This would have enabled the majority shareholders to obtain the benefit of the contract for themselves. It was held that the company could be prevented from following this course of action.

In *Daniels v. Daniels*, the minority shareholders brought an action against the company and two of its directors alleging that the company had, on the instructions of the directors (a husband and wife who were the majority shareholders), sold land to one of the directors for a figure (£4 250) well below its real value. The land was sold four years later for £120 000 and the court held that the minority could bring an action for fraud. Although the transaction was not fraudulent, the directors' use of their power was a fraud on the minority.

In *Estmanco (Kilner House) Ltd v. Greater London Council*, the GLC entered into a contract to sell a block of flats to individual tenants. A company was formed in which the GLC held all the shares. On the sale of each flat, the GLC transferred one share in the company to each tenant which did not confer any voting rights until all the flats had been disposed of. When the GLC at a later date decided not to continue with the sale of the flats the company's directors brought an action for breach of contract. A general meeting was convened at which a resolution was passed, on GLC votes only, not to continue with those legal proceedings. An individual tenant brought an action on the company's behalf to enforce the contract. It was held that the GLC could not use its voting power to frustrate the purposes for which the company was formed.

(c) take advantage of an act passed by a simple majority vote which requires a special resolution.
(d) exercise their rights merely to discriminate against the majority.

In *Clemens v. Clemens Bros Ltd*, Clemens held 45 per cent of the company's share capital and her aunt held 55 per cent and was one of its five directors. The aunt and her fellow directors wished to alter the articles. She proposed to increase the share capital by issuing 200 shares to herself and 850 shares to be held on trust for the benefit of the company's employees. The appropriate resolutions were passed approving these measures. The effect of this issue of share capital would be to reduce Clemens' percentage holding to less than 25 per cent, and she would be unable to oppose the passing of any special or extraordinary resolution. It was held that the majority's actions were oppressive and discriminatory and the resolutions should be set aside.

(e) use their influence in such a way as to defeat the 'interests of justice'.

A company, Thomas Poole and Gladstone China Ltd, was in severe financial difficulties. Two of its directors conceived a scheme whereby it would sell its assets to Newman Industries Ltd. The two directors were also directors of Newman Industries Ltd. In return, Newman Industries Ltd would take over Thomas Poole and Gladstone China Ltd's debts and pay its shareholders £325 000. This figure was arrived at by a valuation of the assets, based on misleading information supplied by the two directors. Further incorrect information was given by the directors at Newman Industries Ltd's meeting to approve the transaction. The Prudential Assurance Company, a shareholder, successfully brought an action on its own behalf, and on behalf of all the other Newman shareholders, for damages against the two directors for breach of their fiduciary duties to the company (*Prudential Assurance Co Ltd v. Newman Industries Ltd*).

(f) divert profitable contracts away from the company. (*Cook v. Deeks* see page 166).

(g) deprive a member of his individual rights of membership i.e. a member may sue the company to enforce his personal rights against it.

In *Pender v. Lushington* a company's articles provided that a member was entitled to one vote for each 10 shares held, up to a maximum of 100 votes. Pender, a company, transferred shares to nominees to increase its voting power but the chairman refused to accept the votes cast by the nominees. It was held that the plaintiff's votes were property rights which he could enforce by taking proceedings against the company.

If the rule in *Foss v. Harbottle* is not applicable, a minority shareholder may bring:

(i) A derivative action brought by a shareholder in his own name and the names of the other shareholders on the company's behalf to enforce the company's rights or recover its property.

(ii) A representative action, usually combined with a derivative action, on behalf of himself and all the other shareholders to enfore rights common to all shareholders. This may be combined with a personal action if he can show that he has suffered actual loss.

(iii) A personal action in his own name to enforce a personal claim (*Pender v. Lushington*).

A shareholder bringing a representative action may do so at the ultimate expense of the company. In *Wallersteiner v. Moir*, a minority shareholder took a series of actions against the controlling director of a group of companies for the misapplication of £230 000. Although he obtained judgement, he had exhausted his own and other shareholders' finances as the litigation had dragged on for more than ten years. It was held that when the wrongdoers were in control of the company the Court had power to indemnify a shareholder in a representative action, whether he was successful or not.

– Statutory protection of the minority –

Section 459

The minority may always petition the Court to wind up the company on the grounds that it is just and equitable to do so, because of the oppressive conduct of the majority. It is often not in the minority's interest that the company should be wound up, and they may petition the Court for an order under section 459 for relief against the company, on the grounds that the affairs of the company have been conducted in a manner prejudicial to some members.

This section provides that any member may petition the Court on the grounds that 'the affairs of the company are being or have been conducted in a manner which is unfairly prejudicial to the interests of its members generally or any actual or proposed act or omission of the company is or would be so prejudicial'.

If the Court is satisfied that the petition is well founded it may make such order, as it thinks fit, for giving relief with regard to the matters complained of (section 461(1)).

It may also make an order:

(a) regulating the conduct of the company's affairs in the future;
(b) requiring the company to do, or to refrain from doing, any act;
(c) authorising civil proceedings to be brought in the company's name or on behalf of the company by such person and on such terms as the Court may direct;
(d) providing for the purchase of any shares and, if appropriate, any consequent reduction in the company's capital (section 461(2)).

If an order requires the company not to make any alteration to either its memorandum or its articles, the company has no power to make any alteration without leave of the Court.

If the Secretary of State has received an inspector's report, or has exercised his powers to inspect a company's books and papers and it appears to him that a member would have grounds for applying under section 459 instead of presenting a petition for winding up, he may himself petition for an order under this section (section 460).

The following cases illustrate the operation of the section.

In *Re Harmer (H.R.) Ltd*, the eighty-eight year old founder of a company dealing in stamps held the majority of the company's shares. He was, with his wife, able to control general meetings and pass special and extraordinary resolutions. He was the chairman of the board and consistently ignored the other shareholders' wishes and the views of his co-directors and even appointed directors without consulting his fellow directors. His two sons, both directors, petitioned the Court for relief. It was held that he should not interfere in the company's affairs (except in accordance with the board's decisions), and should be given the honorary title of President of the company.

In *Scottish Co-operative Wholesale Society v. Meyer*, both parties had joined forces in forming a subsidiary company to manufacture rayon and cloth. The Scottish co-operative spun the yarn at their mill and Meyer provided the necessary knowledge and expertise to make up the cloth. The co-operative society held 4 000 £1 shares and appointed three directors, while Meyer and his associates held 3 900 £1 shares and appointed two directors. The co-operative society wished to acquire further shares in the subsidiary at par, although the shares were then valued at £6 each. When this was refused, they adopted a policy of deliberately running down the subsidiary by withholding supplies of yarn, so that the subsidiary's shares became almost worthless. The minority petitioned the Court, and an order was made under Section 210 of the 1948 Companies Act (now section 459) ordering the Scottish co-op to buy out the minority shareholders at a price of £3.15s (£3.75 per share).

In *Re A Company (1985)* the directors of a private company, in a letter, advised the shareholders to accept an offer in which the directors had a financial interest, while ignoring a more favourable alternative offer. It was held that the advice given in the letter could be construed as unfairly prejudicial with respect to the future sale of the shares.

In *Re A Company (1987) (ex p) Broadhurst* an individual was the chairman, secretary and majority shareholder of a company which ran a football club. He failed to call annual general meetings, prepare accounts and call extraordinary meetings without giving sufficient notice. Shares were purportedly issued at these meetings. It was held that the failure to comply with the provisions of the Act was unfairly prejudicial and that the issue of the shares was ineffective. The majority shareholder was ordered to sell his shares to the petitioner as he was deemed to be unfit to control the company.

In *Re Sam Weller and Sons Ltd* a private company with an issued share capital of £18 000 in £1 shares had net assets of £500 000, including £296 969 in cash. The profit was £36 330 out of which a dividend of 14p per share was paid, similar to dividends of the previous 37 years. The petitioners became entitled to acquire further shares on the death of members of the family but the company's sole director refused to register the transfer of the shares. It was held that his conduct in refusing to register the shares and his failure to pay larger dividends was capable of amounting to unfairly prejudicial conduct.

In *Re Cumana Ltd* the shares of a company were owned by 2 shareholders, L and B. L (who owned ⅓ of the shares) claimed that B (who owned ⅔ of the shares) had diverted business away from the company to another company owned by him; had not consulted L on major policy decisions; had been paid excessive sums as bonus payments and had attempted to make a rights issue in respect of Cumana Ltd's shares which he knew that L could not finance. It was held that these actions were unfairly prejudicial and B was ordered to purchase L's shares.

It is not necessary for a minority shareholder, seeking relief to come to court with clean hands. In *Re London School of Electronics*, the petitioner owned ¼ of the shares in a company which provided courses in electronics. The other shareholder, company CTC Ltd, removed the petitioner from his directorship after he alleged that CTC Ltd were diverting business from the company to themselves. The petitioner then informed his students that he was teaching for a new college and took some former students with him to this new college. It was held that he was entitled to an order requiring CTC Ltd to purchase his shares. He did not lose his right to relief because of his own conduct.

Other sections protecting minorities

The holders of not less than 10 per cent of the paid up capital carrying a right to vote may at any time compel the directors, by a signed requisition, to call an extraordinary general meeting (section 368).

The holders of not less than 5 per cent of the company's paid up capital, or 100 members who have paid an average of £100 on their shares, may compel a company to give notice of a resolution to be moved at a meeting and circulate statements to members (section 376).

The holders of not less than 15 per cent of any shares affected by a variation of class rights may apply to the Court to have the variation cancelled (section 127).

The holders of not less than 15 per cent of the issued share capital may apply to the Court to cancel a special resolution altering the company's objects (section 5).

The holders of at least 10 per cent of the issued shares of a company, or 200 shareholders whatever their shareholding, may apply to the Secretary of State to appoint inspectors to (i) investigate the company's affairs (section 431), or (ii) investigate the company's ownership (section 442).

Minority shareholders may require a liquidator to acquire their shares on a reconstruction of the company (IA section 11).

In a takeover bid, the dissenting shareholders may compel the company to acquire their shares if the company has not chosen to do so (section 429).

Minority shareholders have the right to demand a poll (section 373).

The holders of not less than 5 per cent of the issued share capital, or 5 per cent of the members (if no share capital) or fifty members can apply to the Court to cancel a resolution for re-registering a public company as a private company (section 54).

The holders of not less than 10 per cent of the issued share capital of a private company may apply to the Court to cancel a special resolution for giving financial assistance for the purchase of shares (section 157).

The holders of not less than 10 per cent of the issued share capital may requisition a company to investigate the ownership of its shares, and may ask the Court to impose restrictions in respect of shares where replies are not received or are unsatisfactory (sections 212, 214).

— Investigations of companies and — their affairs

Occasions may arise which may make it desirable for an investigation to be made into various aspects of a company's affairs. Various Companies Acts have given the Secretary of State for Trade and Industry powers of investigation and inspection.

Investigation into a company's affairs

1. The Secretary of State may appoint inspectors to investigate a company's affairs if requested to do so by 200 members or members holding 10 per cent of the issued shares, or on the application of the company. The application must be supported by evidence showing that the applicants have good reason for requiring the investigation. They may be required to provide security, not exceeding £5 000, for payment of the costs of the investigation (section 431).
2. The Secretary of State may investigate a company's affairs if it appears that a company's affairs are being or have been conducted *(a)* with intent to defraud its creditors or the creditors of any other person; or *(b)* for a fraudulent or unlawful purpose; or *(c)* in a manner unfairly prejudicial to some part of its members (section 432(2)). (This covers any actual or proposed act or omission.)

    The Secretary of State may also investigate if there is evidence of misfeasance, or other misconduct, or if it appears that a company was formed for any fraudulent or unlawful purpose (section 432(2)).
3. The Secretary of State appoints inspectors to investigate and report on suspected cases of insider dealing (FSA section 177).
4. The Secretary of State must appoint inspectors if the Court, by order, declares that the company's affairs ought to be investigated (section 432(1)).

An inspector is given the powers to investigate any related company if he deems it necessary for the purpose of his investigation (section 433).

An inspector may examine on oath past and present officers and agents (including bankers, solicitors and auditors) of the company or related company, and require them to produce all books and documents in their custody. If an officer or agent refuses to co-operate with an inspector he may be punished by the Court as if he had been guilty of contempt of court (sections 434, 436).

An inspector may also require any other person, who may be in possession of any information relating to the company's affairs, to produce any books or documents in his custody relating to the company and may be required to attend before him. Such a person is also required to give an inspector every assistance in connection with the investigation. An inspector also has power to examine a director's bank accounts if he has reason to believe that such accounts have been used in connection with certain offences under the Act (sections 434, 435) e.g. the payment of undisclosed emoluments. He may also obtain information recorded otherwise than in legible form, e.g. computer records.

An inspector may make an interim report to the Secretary of State, and at the conclusion of his investigation he must submit a final report to him. If an inspector was appointed as a result of an order of the Court, the Secretary of State must furnish the Court with a copy of the inspector's report. He may, if he thinks fit, publish the report and make the report available to the company and to other interested parties (section 437).

However, an inspector may be appointed on the terms that any report which he makes is not for publication (section 432).

If as a result of the inspector's report it appears to be in the public interest that a company should be wound up, the Secretary of State may present a petition for winding up on the grounds of 'just and equitable' (section 440).

If the report indicates that civil proceedings ought in the public interest to be brought by the company, the Secretary of State may bring proceedings on the company's behalf and in the company's name (section 438).

If it appears to the Secretary of State that matters have come to light in the course of the investigation which suggest that a criminal offence has been committed and these matters have been referred to a prosecuting authority, he may direct the inspector to (section 437).

If, as a result of the report, it appears to be in the public interest that the company be wound-up the Secretary of State may present a petition under 1A section 122 (g), i.e. under the 'just and equitable' grounds.

If, as a result of the report, it appears that there are grounds for petition by a member under section 459, i.e. that the company's affairs have been conducted in an unfairly prejudicial manner, the Secretary of State may, as well as or instead of petitioning for winding up the company, present a petition under section 459.

Investigation of the ownership of a company

The Secretary of State may also appoint an inspector to investigate and report on the membership of a company to determine the identity of the persons who have been financially interested in a company's success or failure, or who are able to control or materially influence the company's policy (section 442).

An application may also be made to the Secretary of State by shareholders holding 10 per cent of the issued shares of the company, or 200 shareholders for an investigation into the company's ownership (section 442).

If the Secretary of State believes there is good reason to investigate the ownership (though unnecessary to appoint an inspector) he may require any person he has reasonable cause to believe to be, or to have been, interested in a company's shares or debentures to give information of past and present interests (section 444). If it appears that the difficulty in finding out the relevant facts about any shares is due to the unwillingness of the parties concerned to assist the investigation, the Secretary of State may order that:

- any transfer of the shares shall be void;
- no voting rights shall be exercisable;
- no further shares are to be issued in respect of these shares;
- any sums due on those shares shall not be paid, except in a liquidation (section 454).

If the Secretary of State makes such an order, any person aggrieved by it may appeal to the Court for an order that the shares shall not be subject to these restrictions (section 456).

The Secretary of State shall not appoint an inspector if he is satisfied that the application is vexatious. Where an inspector is appointed, he may exclude any matter from the investigation. He may also, before appointing an inspector, require the applicant to provide security (not exceeding £5 000) for the payment of the costs of the investigation (section 442).

The Secretary of State may disclose information relating to share ownership to the following:

(a) the company whose share ownership was under investigation.
(b) any member of the company.
(c) the company's auditors.
(d) any person whose conduct was investigated.
(e) any person whose financial interest appears to be affected by the matters investigated (section 451A).

Investigation of directors' share dealings and interests in shares

The Secretary of State may appoint an inspector to determine whether the provisions of the Act have been contravened (section 446).

Section 323 penalises a director or his/her spouse and infant children (section 327) for dealing in options to buy or sell listed shares or debentures of a company or its related company.

Section 324 imposes a duty on a director of a company to notify the company of his interests and those of his/her spouse and infant children (section 328) in its shares or debentures or those of a related company.

Inspection of a company's book and papers

The Secretary of State may at any time, if it thinks there is good reason to do so, direct a company to produce such books or papers as may be specified, or authorise any officer of his to require their production forthwith (section 447).

Copies of extracts may be taken from the books and papers and any past or present officer of the company may be required to provide an explanation of them.

An application may be made to a Justice of the Peace for a warrant to search premises, when there are reasonable grounds for suspecting that there are books and papers on these premises which have not been produced as requested by the Secretary of State (section 448), or that the documents would be hidden, tampered with or removed from the premises (sections 447, 448).

It is an offence for any officer of the company to be a party to the destruction, mutilation or falsification of any document relating to the company or to fraudulently part with, alter or make an omission from any document (section 450). It is also an offence for any person to knowingly or recklessly give a false explanation or statement in response to the directions of the Secretary of State.

19
BORROWING POWERS

Every trading company has an implied power to borrow for purposes that are incidental to its business. Nevertheless most trading companies include in their objects clause an express power to borrow, and the clause may limit the amount which may be borrowed.

A company's articles usually give the directors authority to borrow on a company's behalf. A commercial company which states that its object is to carry on business as a general commercial company has the power to do all such things as are incidental or conducive to its carrying on any trade or business (Article 70). The directors may be given a specific authority e.g. an article which provides that the directors may exercise all the company's powers to borrow money but limits the amount to the nominal amount of the shares.

The articles may impose a limit on the directors' borrowing powers; for example, the directors may be given authority to borrow up to a certain sum, with any borrowing in excess of this amount requiring the approval of a resolution. If the directors borrow in excess of this amount, without obtaining the company's approval, such borrowing is *ultra vires*. The company may ratify such an act by passing an appropriate resolution or altering its articles and so validating the transaction.

In these circumstances the lender may be able to rely on the rule in *Royal British Bank v. Turquand.*

The rule in Royal British Bank v. Turquand

This rule provides that if a transaction is within a company's powers and within the ostensible authority of the directors, a person contracting with the company is entitled to assume that all the necessary internal procedures have been complied with. In *Royal British Bank v. Turquand*, the directors of a company were empowered to issue bonds if authorised by a general resolution of the company. The company borrowed £2 000 from the Royal British Bank and, when sued on the bond, claimed that no resolution had been passed. It was held that the Bank had a right to assume that a resolution had been passed and the bond was binding on the company.

A person contracting with the company may be able to rely on the rule if it later transpires that a director did not have the authority or was not properly appointed as a director, if it can be shown that the director was acting within the scope of the authority conferred upon him by the company. The authority may be actual or apparent.

(a) Actual authority, which may be express or implied. Lord Denning MR in *Hely-Hutchinson v. Brayhead Ltd* observed that authority:

'... is express when it is given by express words, such as when a board of directors passes a resolution which authorises two of their number to sign cheques. It is implied when it is inferred from the conduct of the parties and the circumstances of the case, such as when the board of directors appoint one of their number to be managing director. They therefore impliedly authorise him to do all such things as fall within the scope of that office.' In *Hely-Hutchinson v. Brayhead Ltd* the chairman of B Ltd acted as the company's managing director although he had not been appointed as such. The company's articles allowed the appointment of a managing director. The chairman purported to issue various guarantees and undertakings in respect of takeover on the company's behalf. It was held that B Ltd were liable on these for although the chairman had no actual authority, the company had implied that he had the authority which had never been granted to him.

(b) Apparent authority. A company may be bound by the actions of a director who enters into a contract on the company's behalf without the board's authority as a whole or with the board's acquiescence i.e. the director is *held out* as the company's authorised agent.

In *Freeman and Lockyer v. Buckhurst Park Properties*, an individual named Kapoor acted as managing director, even though he was not appointed as such. He appointed architects to act on the company's behalf and they successfully sued the company for their fees. It was held that as Kapoor had acted with the board's acquiescence – he had been held out as having authority – the company was liable.

The rule has certain limitations and does not apply in the following circumstances:

1. if the transaction is known to be irregular. In *Howard v. Patent Ivory Manufacturing Co.*, the articles provided that the directors could borrow up to £1 000 without the shareholders' approval, but any borrowing in excess of this amount required a resolution. The directors lent the company £3 500 without a resolution being passed, and debentures were issued to them for that amount. The company was later wound up, and the debentures were held valid for £1 000 only as the directors were aware that a resolution had not been passed sanctioning the borrowing.
2. if the transaction is so unusual that the person should be put on enquiry as to its regularity. In *Underwood (AL) Ltd v. Bank of Liverpool and Martins Ltd*, the sole director of a company paid cheques drawn in favour of the company into his own bank account in order to pay his debts. A debenture holder brought an action against the bank for conversion of the cheques. It was held that the bank could not rely on the rule, as the payment of a company's cheques into a private account was unusual and should have put the bank on enquiry.
3. if the person relies on a document which turns out to be a forgery (*Ruben v. Great Fingall Consolidated*).
4. when the person who seeks to rely on the rule purported to act as a director in the transaction. In *Morris v. Kanssen*, the first directors of a company C & D quarrelled. C then forged an entry in the board minutes appointing L as a director. C & L then purported to appoint M as a director. M was aware that a dispute had arisen

prior to his 'appointment' as a director but made no enquiries. At a later board meeting C & L purported to 'allot' shares to M. It was held that M could not rely on the rule to validate the allotment as M purported to act as a director in the transaction.

A lender who is unable to sue the company, or rely on the rule in *Royal British Bank v. Turquand* may have recourse to other remedies. *(a)* If the money borrowed has not been spent, or it can be identified (e.g. specific investments have been purchased with the money) the lender may apply to the Court for a tracing order to recover the money or the investments. *(b)* If the money has been used to pay legitimate debts, the lender may be subrogated to the rights of the creditors paid off; that is, he stands in the shoes of the creditors that have been paid off and may sue the company to the extent of their debts. *(c)* If the money cannot be identified, but it can be shown that the assets of the company have increased, the lender may claim repayment out of such an increase. *(d)* The lender may also bring an action against the directors for a breach of an implied warranty of authority.

The securities offered

A company may offer one or several of the following as security for a loan:

(a) a legal mortgage of specific parts of its property.
(b) an equitable mortgage created by depositing title deeds with a lender.
(c) a mortgage of chattels.
(d) a bill of exchange or a promissory note.
(e) a bond.
(f) a charge on uncalled capital if allowed by the memorandum or the articles.
(g) debentures and debenture stock.

A company usually borrows by means of debentures.

20
DEBENTURES

There is no precise legal definition of a debenture as the Act merely states that debenture 'includes debenture stock, bonds and other securities of a company whether constituting a charge on the assets of a company or not' (section 735). In *Levy v. Abercorris Slate and Slab Co.*, it was defined as 'a document which creates or acknowledges a debt'.

It is a document which sets out the terms of a loan and is normally issued under a company's seal. It provides for the repayment of the loan at some future specified date and for the payment of interest to the debenture holder at a specified rate at fixed intervals.

A document which is not in this format may nevertheless be a debenture. In *Lemon v. Austin Friars Investment Trust Ltd*, a company issued 'income stock certificates' as an acknowledgement of a debt. The certificates did not create a charge, no date was fixed for repayment, and they were not issued under the company's seal. They provided that three-quarters of the company's profits were to be applied in redeeming the certificates, and that a register of certificate holders was to be kept by the company. It was held that the certificates were debentures.

It is an attractive form of security to the lender as he is given certain rights in the event of a company not meeting its obligations under the terms of the debenture, and it also offers a degree of flexibility to the company.

A debenture holder is not a member of the company, and as a creditor is entitled to interest on his debentures whether a company earns profits or not. A company may issue 'income debentures', which provide that payment of interest or the repayment of capital is dependent on the company earning sufficient profits.

Issue of debentures

A debenture may be issued at a premium or at a discount and the prohibition imposed on the issue of shares at a discount does not apply to debentures as they do not form part of the company's capital. A debenture may be issued which allows the holder, within a certain period of time, to convert the debenture into shares. Such a debenture may not be issued offering an immediate option to convert, as this would be in effect issuing shares at a discount (*Moseley v. Koffyfontein Mines*).

Debentures issued to the public are normally issued in a series and are said to rank *pari passu* (i.e. equally), otherwise they would take priority as to security and payment in the order of their serial numbers or date of issue. A single debenture may be issued privately and is usually of a high nominal value, providing security for a bank loan or overdraft.

The usual form of debenture creates a floating charge over the company's undertaking, with or without a fixed charge on its freehold property. A debenture not secured by a charge is termed a naked or unsecured debenture, and offers no more than an unsecured promise by the company to repay a loan.

Most debentures issued to the public stipulate that they are redeemable on or before a certain date (e.g. 1990–4). This means that a company will redeem the debentures within those years. The redemption may be financed out of a sinking fund, a sum set aside annually to provide for redemption out of a new issue of debentures. A partial redemption may be accomplished by 'drawings', when a company draws lots and redeems an agreed number of debentures. The drawings may be at the company's option, or it may be stated in the terms of issue of the debentures that drawings will take place at fixed intervals.

A company may purchase its debentures in the market. It is clearly to the company's advantage if the debentures stand at a discount in the market as it may extinguish part of its liability in this way. It may redeem debentures at their issue price or at a higher price. They may be re-issued unless:

(a) the company has passed a resolution that they may not be re-issued; *or*
(b) the articles specify that they may not be re-issued; *or*
(c) the terms of the debenture stipulate that they may not be re-issued (section 194).

Types of debentures

A *debenture* may be classified as *irredeemable* in that no date is fixed for its redemption. It may only be redeemed if the company is wound up, or there is a breach of a condition of its issue (e.g. default in the payment of interest).

A *perpetual debenture* is similar, in that no time is fixed for redemption, but the company does have the right to redeem the debenture at its option.

A *debenture* may be *registered*, in that the lender is entered in the register of debenture holders. This register must be kept at the registered office of the company, or at any other office of the company where it is made up, and must be open for the inspection of debenture holders and other persons for not less than two hours each day (sections 190, 191).

A *bearer debenture* may be issued by a company. It is similar to a registered debenture, except that it is stated to be payable to bearer. It is a negotiable instrument which may be transferred by mere delivery. Coupons are attached to bearer debentures and these are submitted to the company when interest is payable.

Companies also issue *debenture stock*. This may be transferred in fractional amounts, although the terms of issue or the articles may specify that stock may only be transferred in minimum amounts. The lender is issued with a stock certificate.

Fixed and floating charges

A debenture may be secured by a fixed charge or a floating charge or a combination of both.

Fixed charge

A fixed charge or mortgage is expressed to cover specific assets of the company, such as land or interests in land or ships. Although the company normally remains in possession of such property, it may not dispose of the property, free from the charge, without the prior consent of the holders of the charge. A debenture holder secured by a fixed charge ranks as a secured creditor in a winding up of a company.

Floating charge

A floating charge is a charge on a company's undertaking which allows a company to offer as security assets that are constantly changing (e.g. stock, cash, book debts).

In *Re Yorkshire Woolcombers Association*, Romer L. J. stated that a floating charge has three characteristics:

- It is a charge on a class of assets present and future;
- It changes from time to time in the ordinary course of business;
- A company can carry on its business in the ordinary way until steps are taken to enforce the charge.

A floating charge 'crystallises' (i.e. becomes a fixed charge) when the company ceases to carry on business, or is wound up, or on the occurrence of some event specified in the terms of issue of the debenture; for example, if a company defaults in the payment of interest or fails to redeem the debentures, the debenture holders may take steps to enforce their rights, e.g. by appointing a receiver.

Disadvantages of floating charges

1 A floating charge has certain disadvantages and is deferred to the following:

(a) to a fixed charge. As a fixed charge is a legal mortgage of a specific asset it will have priority over a floating charge which is equitable. This is so even if the fixed charge is created after the floating charge, with one exception. If the individual taking the fixed charge is aware of a clause in the floating charge prohibiting the creation of any fixed or floating charge ranking before it, the holder of the fixed charge will not rank before the floating charge.

DEBENTURES

(b) to a landlord who distrains for rent. If the rent is in arrear the landlord can seize goods on the tenant's premises and sell them.
(c) to the interests of a judgment creditor. That is, a person who obtains judgment in the Court against the company, with the goods being seized and sold by the sheriff.
(d) to the following preferential debts:
   (i) value added tax up to six months before the relevant date.
   (ii) employees' arrears of wages or salary for four months prior to the relevant date up to £800.
   (iii) PAYE deductions for 12 months before the relevant date.
   (iv) Social security and occupational pension scheme contributions (IA section 386, schedule 6).
(e) to owners of goods supplied to the company under a hire purchase agreement.
(f) to a seller of goods who has inserted a retention of title clause, i.e. a Romalpa clause in a contract of sale.

2 A floating charge created within twelve months of the commencement of the winding up or the making of an administration order is invalid if the company was unable to pay its debts when it created the charge, or becomes unable to do so as a result of the transaction. The charge is however valid to the extent that the holder of the charge gives value to the company i.e. in cash, goods or services supplied or the discharge or reduction of a debt (1A section 245).

3 A floating charge created within 2 years of the commencement of the winding up of the company or the making of an administration order is invalid if created in favour of a person who is 'connected' with the company (1A section 245).

4 Any charge created by a company within six months of the commencement of winding up or the presentation of an administration petition is void if it is a preference of any creditor i.e. preferring one creditor at the expense of another. In the case of a connected person the time is 2 years from the commencement of winding up etc (1A sections 239, 240. See page 26.)

5 Any charge created within two years of the commencement of winding up or the presentation of an administration petition is void if it is a transaction at an undervalue i.e. a transaction entered into

by the company without consideration or for a consideration which is significantly less than that provided by the company (1A section 238. See page 258.)
6   Any charge created by a company within three years of the commencement of winding up or presentation of an administration petition is void if it forms part of an extortionate credit transaction i.e. if the terms of an agreement require grossly exorbitant payments to be made for the provision of credit or it otherwise grossly contravenes the ordinary principles of fair dealing (1A section 244. See page 259).
7   A charge must be registered with the Registrar within twenty-one days of its creation (section 395). Failure to register renders the charge void as security on the company's property against an administrator or liquidator of a company, or any person who for value acquires any interest in, or right over, the property subject to the charge, e.g. a purchaser or a mortgagee. The charge will not be void as against the company's creditors generally (section 398).

Registration of charges

Charges created by a company must be registered in two registers, at the Companies Registry and in the company's register of charges.

(a) The Companies Registry

Particulars of charges created by a company must be registered with the Registrar within twenty-one days of creation (section 395). This section relates to, among others:

- floating charges;
- charges on land;
- charges on book debts;
- charges on uncalled capital;
- charges on goodwill, patents, trade marks, service marks, registered designs, copyright or design rights and any licence in respect of any such right; *and*
- charges to secure any issue of debentures.

The statutory particulars of the charge must be submitted to the

Registrar within twenty-one days and may be effected by the company or any person interested in the charge. Particulars of the charge need only be submitted and a receipted copy of the particulars will be issued to the person who submitted the charge (normally the company's solicitor), the company and the chargee. A certificate of registration of the charge, will only be issued by the Registrar if specifically requested. It is only conclusive evidence that the particulars described in the certificate were delivered to the Registrar not later than the date specified in the certificate.

If a company purchases property, subject to an existing charge, the charge must also be registered within twenty-one days.

Where particulars of a charge are filed late the charge will nevertheless be effective as at the date of its creation providing:

(i) the company was solvent at the date of filing;
(ii) the charge is not invalid as a preference, 1A section 239 (see page 261) or under provisions relating to avoidance of certain floating charges, 1A section 245 (see page 207); *and*
(iii) a purchaser for value without notice of the charge has not obtained an interest in the charged property between the expiry of the twenty-one day period and the date of filing.

If a third party has obtained such an interest, the priority gained over the charge will remain.

Where the charge is invalidated by sections 239 or 245 of the Insolvency Act 1986 or where the charge is postponed to a person who takes a prior interest in the charged property the money becomes repayable, with interest, on demand on the happening of a 'relevant event' i.e. the liquidation or administration of the company or the acquisition of an interest in the property which will defeat the charge.

The chargee will therefore rank as an unsecured creditor in the liquidation or administration of the company.

If incorrect particulars of a charge are registered, correct particulars may later be filed with the Registrar, subject to the same reservations as apply to filing late particulars (see above). The charge will retain its priority against the liquidator, administrator, creditor and any purchaser from the company, from the date of filing the correct particulars subject to:

(i) the rights of a purchaser obtaining an interest in the property after the twenty-one day registration period but before the date of filing; *and*
(ii) the charge not being invalidated in that time under section 239 or section 245 of the Insolvency Act.

On payment of the debt or release of the property charged a memorandum of satisfaction is filed. This must be signed by both the company and the chargee. A memorandum of satisfaction may still be filed if either party fails to sign it and if any person interested in the charge has obtained a court order that it should be filed. This provision should ensure that a charge is removed from the register once it is discharged.

(b) The company's register of charges

Every limited company must keep at its own registered office a register of charges containing particulars of any property of the company that is subject to a charge; the amount of any charge; and the names of the chargees. If there is a trust deed the names of the trustees are entered as chargees.

Failure to register a charge does not affect the validity of the charge, but renders the defaulting officers and the company liable to a fine.

The trust deed

Debentures and debenture stock are often secured by a trust deed, which conveys the company's property to trustees in favour of debenture holders.

Whether a trust deed is appropriate depends on the circumstances of the loan. If the loan is short term (e.g. issued to a bank to secure an overdraft or to the directors of the company) it is generally dispensed with. When debentures are offered for sale to the public in a large scale borrowing, a trust deed is invariably drawn up appointing trustees (e.g. a trust corporation to safeguard the interests of the debenture holders).

A trust deed usually contains provisions dealing with:

1 the amount and terms of issue of the debentures;
2 the date and method of redemption and details of any sinking fund set up by the company to provide for redemption;

3 the nature of the charge, which is usually a fixed charge on the land and buildings and a floating charge on the undertaking and assets of the company;
4 the powers of the trustees to act if the company defaults in the payment of interest or other major breach of conditions (e.g. to enter into possession and sell, to appoint a receiver or manager);
5 covenants for insurance and repair of property by the company;
6 the remuneration of trustees;
7 the exemption of the trustees from liability;
8 meetings of debenture holders. Sometimes a clause is included providing for the modification of rights, if approved by a majority, at a meeting of debenture holders. All debenture holders are then bound.

The appointment of trustees is advantageous to the company and to its debenture holders. A company is able to deal directly with the trustees instead of a number of individual debenture holders. The title deeds and company investments are in the safe custody of the trustees. The trustees may authorise the company to deal with the property charged, thus enabling the company to carry on the business. The trustees may also allow a company to create mortgage of specific assets.

The interests of debenture holders are better served by the employment of a professional trust corporation which acts for the benefit of all the debenture holders. The trustees can ensure that a legal mortgage is created over the company's property so that any charges created at a later date cannot gain priority. This is also accomplished by having custody of the title deeds. The trustees can ensure that the company observes the various covenants contained in the trust deed, for example to repair and insure property. If a company defaults, the trustees may take immediate steps to protect the interests of the debenture holders, as a trust deed usually gives the trustees various powers to sell the property, to appoint a receiver or manager, and to carry on the company's business.

Any provision in a trust deed which exempts a trustee from liability for breach of trust, if he fails to show the required degree of care and diligence, is void. However, the deed may provide that he should be excused in respect of specific acts or omissions, or on ceasing to act, or on his death, if three-quarters in value of the debenture holders so resolve at a meeting called for the purpose (section 192).

Remedies of debenture holder

(a) *If a debenture is not secured by a charge* and the company defaults in the payment of interest or in the repayment of capital, the debenture holder has three remedies only available to him. He is in a similar position to any other trade creditor of the company.

  (i)   He may sue for the principal and interest that are owed by the company and obtain judgment from the Court. If the company does not pay the judgment debt he may levy execution against the company's property.
  (ii) He may apply to the Court for an administration order on the grounds that the company, is or is likely to become, unable to pay its debts (IA sections 8, 9).
  (iii) Alternatively he may petition for the winding up of the company by the Court under IA section 124 on the grounds that the company is unable to pay its debts (IA section 122 (1)(f)), so that he may prove for his debt in the winding up.

If the company is already being wound up, he can prove in the winding up for the amount that is owed to him.

(b) *If a debenture is secured by a charge*, the holder of the debenture is in a far stronger position than an unsecured debenture holder. He has the above remedies and usually the deed creating the charge (i.e. the debenture or the trust deed) contains remedies for enforcing the security without having to seek the Court's aid, e.g. the power of sale and appointment of a receiver.

The remedies available to the secured debenture holder are:

(i)   *A debenture holder's action.* Any debenture holder may bring an action against the company when the company defaults in the payment of interest or repayment of capital. He sues on behalf of himself and the other debenture holders. The Court usually appoints a receiver (and manager) and either orders a sale of the property or gives permission to apply for a sale of the property.
(ii) *Valuation of security.* If a company is insolvent and is being wound up, a debenture holder may value his security and prove for the balance of the debt, or he may surrender his security and prove for the whole debt.
(iii) *Foreclosure.* He may apply to the Court for a foreclosure order.

This is rarely applied for, as all the debenture holders must be parties to the action. Its effect would be to vest the title in the property in the debenture holders, free from the company's equity of redemption (i.e. the company's right to repay the loan and recover its property free from the charge).

(iv) *Sale.* The power to sell the property is usually found in a trust deed and may be exercised without the Court's consent. The power of sale may also be sought in a debenture holder's action where the trust deed or debenture does not give this power. If a debenture is a single debenture, with a charge over the company's assets, it will usually contain an express power of sale, but even in the absence of an express power the holder may be given an implied power of sale under section 103 of the Law of Property Act 1925.

(v) *Receiver.* The usual remedy is to appoint a receiver. The debenture or trust deed usually provides for the appointment of a receiver. If no such provision exists, application may be made to the Court in a debenture holder's action for such an appointment.

The receiver

A company may not be appointed receiver (IA section 30), nor may an undischarged bankrupt (IA section 31), except by the Court. A receiver may be disqualified by the court from acting as such under the Company Directors Disqualification Act. Most receivers are administrative receivers who are given additional powers under the Insolvency Act. An administrative receiver is a receiver who takes possession of the whole, or substantially the whole, of the company's property.

A receiver appointed by the debenture holders is an agent of the debenture holders and they are liable on his contracts, unless the terms of issue provide otherwise. The debenture or trust instrument usually provides that he is to be the agent of the company. He is entitled to the same indemnity and subject to the same personal liability as a receiver appointed by the Court. He is paid by the debenture holders, but if the company is wound up the Court may review the payments made to the receiver and reduce the amount, if considered excessive. He may apply to the Court for directions in connection with the performance of his duties.

An administrative receiver is deemed to be the company's agent unless and until the company goes into liquidation. He is also personally liable on any contracts entered into by him but is entitled to an indemnity in respect of that liability out of the company's assets (IA section 44).

An application may be made to the Court for the appointment of a receiver when:

- the principal or interest is in arrear;
- the company is being wound up;
- the security is in jeopardy, that is when there is a risk of the security being seized and used to pay claims which do not rank in priority to the claims of the debenture holders.

In *Re London Pressed Hinge Co. Ltd* the debenture holders had a floating charge on the company's undertaking and sought the appointment of a receiver and manager of the company. Default had not been made in the payment of interest or principal, but a creditor had obtained judgement against the company and was in a position to issue execution. The appointment of a receiver would mean that the debenture holders, to whom nothing was due, would be paid in priority to the creditor who was owed money. It was held that a receiver should be appointed.

A receiver appointed by the Court is an officer of the Court and any interference with him is a contempt of Court. No proceedings may be commenced against him or in respect of the property, without the Court's consent. Since the Court cannot be liable, he is personally liable on any contracts entered into by him, although he is entitled to an indemnity out of the company's assets in priority to the debenture holders.

When a company is being wound up by the Court, the Official Receiver may be appointed receiver (IA section 32).

A manager may be appointed if the debentures give a charge over the 'business' or undertaking of the company. Usually the person appointed as receiver will also act as manager.

He is appointed to sell the business as a going concern and so his term of office will be for a comparatively short period of time.

On the appointment of receiver (and manager):

(a) the floating charges crystallise and so become fixed.
(b) the powers of the directors are suspended.
(c) if the receiver is appointed by the Court, the company's employees are automatically dismissed. If appointed by the debenture holders there is no dismissal, unless the business is sold.

(d) other contracts bind the company but not the receiver. He must not refuse to carry out current contracts if such a refusal would injure the company's goodwill.
(e) every invoice, order and business letter issued by the company must contain a statement that a receiver has been appointed (IA section 39).
(f) within 7 days of his appointment he must give notice of the fact to the Registrar, who must enter the fact in the register of charges. (section 409)
(g) on ceasing to act he must notify the fact to the Registrar who must enter the fact in the register of charges (section 409).

Within two months of receiving a statement of affairs the receiver must submit the statement, with his comments, to the Registrar and the Court. He must also send a summary of both to the Registrar. He must send the company a copy of his comments, or a notice that he makes no comments. A copy of the summary must also be sent to the debenture holders and to the trustees.

Within one month of each anniversary of his appointment or of ceasing to act, the receiver or manager must submit an abstract of receipts and payments to the Registrar, the debenture holders, and the trustees (IA section 38).

Where (vi) is not applicable, the receiver or manager if appointed by debenture holders must file with the Registrar a similar abstract at intervals of six months and within one month of ceasing to act (IA section 38).

Distribution of assets

If a receiver realises the company's assets, and they are insufficient to meet all the company's debts, he must apply them in the following order:

1. the costs of realising the property.
2. the costs of the receiver, including his remuneration.
3. the costs and remuneration of the trustees for the debenture holders, if provided for by the trust deed.
4. the costs of the plaintiff in a debenture holder's action.
5. the claims of the preferential creditors, if the debentures are

secured by a floating charge and the company is not being wound up.

Any sums due to debenture holders in respect of principal and interest.

21
ACCOUNTS

Every company must keep proper accounting records which are sufficient to show and explain the company's transactions. They must disclose at any time, with reasonable accuracy, the financial position of the company at that time, and thus enable the directors to ensure that any balance sheet or profit and loss account complies with the Act. The accounts must be prepared in accordance with generally accepted accounting principles.

A company's directors must prepare a balance sheet, profit and loss account, group accounts (if applicable), auditors' report and directors' report in respect of each accounting reference period. Certain other information must also be given to supplement the balance sheet and profit and loss account. A company's annual accounts must be approved by the board of directors and signed on the balance sheet, on the board's behalf, by a director.

If annual accounts are approved which do not comply with the requirements of the Act, every director who is a party to their approval and who knows they do not comply, or is reckless as to whether they comply, is guilty of an offence and liable to a fine (section 233).

The accounts must be laid before the general meeting and copies of the documents must be delivered to the Registrar within a specified time.

An unlimited company need not file its accounts, or the directors' report, or the auditors' report. A company which does not trade for profit must prepare an income and expenditure account in place of a profit and loss account. (section 227).

A copy of the company's annual accounts, with a copy of the directors' report for that financial year and the auditors' report on the accounts, must be sent to every member, debenture holder and person entitled to receive notice of a general meeting, at least twenty-one days before the date of the meeting (section 238). A public company whose shares are listed need not comply with these provisions and may send its members a summary financial statement, derived from its annual accounts and directors' report. The company must however supply a copy of the full accounts and related documents to any member who wishes to receive them (section 251).

Various exemptions are granted to small and medium-sized companies. A small company need only file an abbreviated version of its balance sheet, and is not required to file a profit and loss account or directors' report. A medium-sized company must file a full balance sheet and directors' report, but only a modified profit and loss account. These companies will have to prepare full accounts for their shareholders.

In particular the accounting records must contain:

1 entries from day to day of all money received and expended by the company and the matters in respect of which the receipt and expenditure take place;
2 a record of all the company's assets and liabilities.

In the case of a company dealing in goods:

(a) statements of stock held by the company at the end of each financial year;
(b) statements of stocktaking;
(c) statements of all goods purchased and sold (except by way of ordinary retail trade) and the buyers and sellers of these goods (section 221).

These records must be kept at the company's registered office or at such other place as the company's directors think fit, and must be open to inspection at all times to the company's officers (section 222).

They must be preserved for six years by a public company and for three years by a private company. If a company fails to comply with these requirements any officer of a company in default is guilty of an offence, unless he shows that he acted honestly and that in the circumstances in which the business was carried on the default was excusable.

Revision of Accounts

Directors may prepare revised accounts or a revised directors' report if it appears to them that any annual accounts or directors' report do not comply with the requirements of the Act. The Secretary of State may challenge any apparent non compliance in published accounts. If the directors do not provide a satisfactory explanation or revised accounts, he may apply for a court order requiring the latter. The directors who had approved the original accounts may then be personally liable for the costs of the court application and for the preparation of revised accounts.

—— Accounting reference periods ——

A company's directors must prepare annual accounts based on the company's accounting reference period, which must coincide with the company's financial year.

A company may give notice to the Registrar within nine months of its incorporation specifying a date on which its accounting reference period is to end, otherwise its accounting reference period will run from 1st April of each year to 31st March of the following year (section 224). A company may alter its current and future accounting reference periods by giving notice to the Registrar and specifying a new accounting reference date (section 225).

The balance sheet

The directors of every company must prepare a balance sheet as at the date to which any profit and loss account is made up. It must give a true and fair view of the state of a company's affairs as at the end of its financial year (section 227). Companies (other than banking, insurance and shipping companies) must adopt format 1 or 2 in the presentation of their balance sheets. (Most United Kingdom companies will probably adopt format 1, as this closely resembles current United Kingdom practice.)

The formats are as follows:

Format 1

A	Called up share capital not paid	
B	Fixed assets	
	I Intangible assets	
	1	Development costs
	2	Concessions, patents, licences, trade marks and similar rights and assets
	3	Goodwill
	4	Payments on account
	II Tangible assets	
	1	Land and buildings
	2	Plant and machinery
	3	Fixtures, fittings, tools and equipment
	4	Payments on account and assets in course of construction
	III Investments	
	1	Shares in group undertakings
	2	Loans to group undertakings
	3	Participating interests
	4	Loans to undertakings in which the company has a participating interest
	5	Other investments other than loans
	6	Other loans
	7	Own shares
C	Current assets	
	I Stocks	
	1	Raw materials and consumables
	2	Work in progress
	3	Finished goods and goods for resale

ACCOUNTS

       4 Payments on account
- II *Debtors*
  1. Trade debtors
  2. Amounts owed by group undertakings
  3. Amounts owed by undertakings in which the company has a participating interest
  4. Other debtors
  5. Called up share capital not paid
  6. Prepayments and accrued income

  1. Shares in group undertakings
  2. Own shares
  3. Other investments

Prepayments and accrued income

E *Creditors: amounts falling due within one year*
  1. Debenture loans
  2. Bank loans and overdrafts
  3. Payments received on account
  4. Trade creditors
  5. Bills of exchange payable
  6. Amounts owed to group undertakings
  7. Amounts owed to undertakings in which the company has a participating interest
  8. Other creditors including taxation and social security
  9. Accruals and deferred income

F *Net current assets (liabilities)*

G *Total assets less current liabilities*

H *Creditors: amounts falling due after more than one year*
  1. Debenture loans
  2. Bank loans and overdrafts
  3. Payments received on account
  4. Trade creditors
  5. Bills of exchange payable
  6. Amounts owed to group undertakings
  7. Amounts owed to undertakings in which the company has a participating interest
  8. Other creditors including taxation and social security
  9. Accruals and deferred income

I *Provisions for liabilities and charges*
  1. Pensions and similar obligations
  2. Taxation, including deferred taxation
  3. Other provisions

- **J** *Accruals and deferred income*
- **K** *Capital and reserves*
  - *I Called up share capital*
  - *II Share premium account*
  - *III Revaluation reserve*
  - *IV Other reserves*
    1. Capital redemption reserve
    2. Reserve for own shares
    3. Reserves provided for by the articles of association
    4. Other reserves
  - *V Profit and loss account*

Format 2

ASSETS

- **A** *Called up share capital not paid*
- **B** *Fixed assets*
  - *I Intangible assets*
    1. Development costs
    2. Concessions, patents, licences, trade marks and similar rights and assets
    3. Goodwill
    4. Payments on account
  - *II Tangible assets*
    1. Land and buildings
    2. Plant and machinery
    3. Fixtures, fittings, tools and equipment
    4. Payments on account and assets in course of construction
  - *III Investments*
    1. Shares in group undertakings
    2. Loans to group undertakings
    3. Participating interests
    4. Loans to related undertakings in which the company has a participating interest
    5. Other investments other than loans
    6. Other loans
    7. Own shares
- **C** *Current assets*
  - *I Stocks*
    1. Raw materials and consumables
    2. Work in progress
    3. Finished goods and goods for resale

ACCOUNTS

    4 Payments on account
- *II Debtors*
  1. Trade debtors
  2. Amounts owed by group undertakings
  3. Amounts owed by undertakings in which the company has a participating interest
  4. Other debtors
  5. Called up share capital not paid
  6. Prepayments and accrued income
- *III Investments*
  1. Shares in group undertakings
  2. Own shares
  3. Other investments
- *IV Cash at bank and in hand*

D *Prepayments and accrued income*

LIABILITIES

A *Capital and reserves*
- *I Called up share capital*
- *II Share premium account*
- *III Revaluation reserve*
- *IV Other reserves*
  1. Capital redemption reserve
  2. Reserve for own shares
  3. Reserves provided for by the articles of association
  4. Other reserves
- *V Profit and loss account*

B *Provisions for liabilities and charges*
  1. Pensions and similar obligations
  2. Taxation including deferred taxation
  3. Other provisions

C *Creditors*
  1. Debenture loans
  2. Bank loans and overdrafts
  3. Payments received on account
  4. Trade creditors
  5. Bills of exchange payable
  6. Amounts owed to group undertakings
  7. Amounts owed to undertakings in which the company has a participating interest
  8. Other creditors including taxation and social security
  9. Accruals and deferred income

D *Accruals and deferred income*

The following information is required to supplement the information given in the balance sheet, or is otherwise relevant to assessing the company's affairs in the light of the information so given.

1. The authorised share capital, and the issued share capital (if the company has allotted shares of more than one class).
2. Details of any allotment of shares, or the issue of any debentures during the financial year.
3. Where part of the allotted share capital consists of redeemable shares – the dates of redemption, whether the redemption is optional, and details of any premium due on redemption.
4. Particulars of any shares for which anyone has an option to subscribe.
5. The amount of any fixed cumulative dividends and the period for which they are in arrears.
6. Particulars of valuations of fixed assets and total amounts acquired and disposed of during the financial year.
7. Particulars of any charges on the company's assets on behalf of others.
8. The general nature of contingent liabilities.
9. Future capital expenditure under contract or authorised by the directors.
10. Details of investments.
11. The nature of the reserves and provisions during the year, and the amounts (if any) transferred.
12. The amount set aside for taxation.
13. Details of any creditor's future indebtedness.
14. Details of guarantees and any other financial commitment, entered into by the company on its own behalf or on behalf of its holding company or subsidiary, (which is not included in the balance sheet) which is relevant to assessing the company's state of affairs.

The following documents must be annexed to the balance sheet:

(a) the profit and loss account.
(b) any group accounts.

ACCOUNTS

Profit and loss account

The directors of a company must prepare a profit and loss account in each accounting reference period of a company. The period in respect of which the account is prepared must be a financial year of the company, and must show the amount of the company's profit or loss on ordinary activities before taxation (section 227).

Every profit and loss account of a company shall give a true and fair view of the profit or loss of the company for the financial year, and must show the items listed in one of the four profit and loss formats set out in the Act.

Format 1

1. Turnover
2. Cost of sales
3. Gross profit or loss
4. Distribution costs
5. Administrative expenses
6. Other operating income
7. Income from shares in group undertakings
8. Income from participating interests
9. Income from other fixed asset investments
10. Other interest receivable and similar income
11. Amounts written off investments
12. Interest payable and similar charges
13. Tax on profit or loss on ordinary ativities
14. Profit or loss on ordinary activities after taxation
15. Extraordinary income
16. Extraordinary charges
17. Extraordinary profit or loss
18. Tax on extraordinary profit or loss
19. Other taxes not shown under the above items
20. Profit or loss for the financial year

Format 2

1. Turnover
2. Change in stocks of finished goods and in work progress

3. Own work capitalised
4. Other operating income
5. (a) Raw materials and consumables
   (b) Other external charges
6. Staff costs:
   (a) wages and salaries
   (b) social security costs
   (c) other pension costs
7. (a) Depreciation and other amounts written off tangible and intangible fixed assets
   (b) Exceptional amounts written off current assets
8. Other operating charges
9. Income from shares in group undertakings
10. Income from participating interests
11. Income from other fixed asset investments
12. Other interest receivable and similar income
13. Amounts written off investments
14. Interest payable and similar charges
15. Tax on profit or loss on ordinary activities
16. Profit or loss on ordinary activities after taxation
17. Extraordinary income
18. Extraordinary charges
19. Extraordinary profit or loss
20. Tax on extraordinary profit or loss
21. Other taxes not shown under the above items
22. Profit or loss for the financial year

Format 3

A *Charges*
1. Cost of sales
2. Distribution costs
3. Administrative expenses
4. Amounts written off investments
5. Interest payable and similar charges
6. Tax on profit or loss on ordinary activities
7. Profit or loss on ordinary activities after taxation
8. Extraordinary charges
9. Tax on extraordinary profit or loss

ACCOUNTS

    10   Other taxes not shown under the above items
    11   Profit or loss for the financial year

B *Income*
1. Turnover
2. Other operating income
3. Income from share in group undertakings
4. Income from participating interests
5. Income from other fixed asset investments
6. Other interest receivable and similar income
7. Profit or loss on ordinary activities after taxation
8. Extraordinary income
9. Profit or loss for the financial year

Format 4

A *Charges*
1. Reduction in stocks of finished goods and in work in progress
2. *(a)* Raw materials and consumables
   (b) Other external charges
3. Staff costs:
   (a) wages and salaries
   (b) social security costs
   (c) other pension costs
4. *(a)* Depreciation and other amounts written off tangible and intangible fixed assets
   (b) Exceptional amounts written off current assets
5. Other operating charges
6. Amounts written off investments
7. Interest payable and similar charges
8. Tax on profit or loss on ordinary activities
9. Profit or loss on ordinary activities after taxation
10. Extraordinary charges
11. Tax on extraordinary profit or loss
12. Other taxes not shown under the above items
13. Profit or loss for the financial year

B *Income*
1. Turnover
2. Increase in stocks of finished goods and in work in progress
3. Own work capitalised

— 227 —

4 Other operating income
5 Income from shares in group undertakings
6 Income from participating interests
7 Income from other fixed asset investments
8 Other interest receivable and similar income
9 Profit or loss on ordinary activities after taxation
10 Extraordinary income
11 Profit or loss for the financial year

Formats 1 and 2 are closest to current United Kingdom practice and it is envisaged that most companies will adopt either of these formats, with most large companies adopting format 1, and most small companies choosing format 2.

In addition, every profit and loss account must show separately as additional items:

(a) any amount to be carried or proposed to be carried to the reserves, or withdrawn or proposed to be withdrawn from reserves.

(b) the aggregate amount of any dividends paid and proposed.

The following information is required either to supplement the information given in the profit and loss account, or to provide particulars of income or expenditure or of the circumstances of the items shown in the profit and loss account.

- The amount of the interest on loans made to the company, including long term loans, bank loans and overdrafts.
- The amount provided for the redemption of the share capital or loans.
- The amount of income from listed investments.
- The amount of rent received from land (if material).
- The amount paid for hire of plant and machinery.
- The amount of the auditor's remuneration.
- The basis on which the charge for corporation tax is computed and the amount of the charge.
- If the company has carried on two or more classes of business which in the directors' opinion differs substantially from each other, a statement of:

(i) the proportions in which the turnover for that year is divided amongst these classes:

(ii) the extent to which the carrying on of the business of that class contributed to or restricted the profit or loss of the company for that year, before taxation.
- Particulars of turnover where the company has supplied different markets during the course of the year.
- The average number of persons employed by the company in each week in the year and the aggregate remuneration paid to them in the year.
- Details of any extraordinary income or charges arising in the financial year.
- The effect of any transactions that are exceptional by virtue of size or incidence, although within the company's ordinary activities.

Group accounts

The contents of the balance sheet and profit and loss account will vary according to whether the company is an ordinary company with normal shareholders or whether it is a parent or a subsidiary undertaking.

The following terms are used for group accounting purposes – parent undertaking, parent company and subsidiary undertaking. A parent company is a parent undertaking which is a company. These definitions differ from the traditional definitions of holding and subsidiary companies in that they focus on effective control rather than on equity participation.

A parent/subsidiary undertaking relationship exists if the parent undertaking:

1 has the majority of the voting rights in the undertaking; or
2 is a member of the other undertaking and has the right to appoint or remove directors having a majority of the voting rights at board meetings; or
3 has the right to exercise a dominant influence over the undertaking under the constitution of the other undertaking or under a control contract; or
4 is a member of the undertaking and controls alone, under an agreement with the other shareholders or members, the majority of the voting rights of the undertaking; or

5   has a participating interest in the undertaking and actually exercises a dominant influence over the subsidiary undertaking;
6   *or* both it and the subsidiary undertakings are managed on a unified basis.

An interest is 'participating' if the parent hold 20 per cent or more of the subsidiary's shares.

A 'dominant influence' is the right of an undertaking to give directions with respect to the operating and financial policies of another undertaking which its directors are obliged to comply with whether or not they are for the benefit of that other undertaking.

An undertaking is a 'member' of another if 'any of its subsidiary undertakings is a member of that undertaking, or if any shares in that other undertaking are held by a person acting on behalf of the undertaking, or any of its subsidiary undertakings (section 258).

Where a company has a subsidiary undertaking it must prepare, at the end of its financial year, group accounts dealing with the state of affairs and profit or loss of the company and its subsidiary undertakings. The group accounts must give a true and fair view of the state of affairs and profit and loss of the group undertakings (section 227).

Group accounts must be prepared as consolidated accounts, comprising a consolidated balance sheet and a consolidated profit and loss account of the company and its subsidiary undertakings (section 227).

The financial year of each subsidiary should normally coincide with that of the holding company, but where it does not the consolidated accounts must now be based on interim management accounts, or on statutory accounts if the subsidiary's year end was in the previous three months.

The parent company of a small or medium-sized group need not prepare group accounts as long as any two of the criteria defining a medium sized company are satisfied (see page 42). This exemption will not apply if any member of the group is a public, banking, insurance or financial service company.

Group accounts are not necessary if:

(i)   The holding company is a wholly owned subsidiary of a parent undertaking established within the EC;
(ii) that parent undertaking holds more than 50 per cent of the shares

in the holding company, provided that notice has not been received from minority shareholders requesting group accounts (section 228).

A subsidiary undertaking *may* be excluded from inclusion in consolidated accounts if:

(i) its inclusion is not material for the purpose of giving a true and fair view;
(ii) severe long-term restrictions hinder control by the parent company;
(iii) the necessary information cannot be obtained without disproportionate expense or undue delay;
(iv) the interest of the parent company is held exclusively with a view to re-sale and the subsidiary has not previously been included in consolidated group accounts (section 229).

A subsidiary undertaking *must* be excluded from consolidation if its activities are so different from the other companies in the group that its inclusion would be incompatible with the obligation to give a true and fair view, e.g. an industrial company with insurance or banking subsidiaries.

Additional information to be given in the accounts (Schedules 5, 6)

- A statement of the aggregate amount of the following:
  (a) directors' emoluments, including the estimated value of non cash benefits
  (b) payment made to a director for accepting office.
- The chairman's emoluments.
- The emoluments of the highest paid director, if greater than those of the chairman's.
- The number of directors who waived the right to receive emoluments.
- A scale dividing directors' emoluments into bands of £5 000 showing the number of directors whose emoluments fell within each band.

(The disclosure of items 2–5 is only required if item 1 exceeds £60 000.)

- Directors' or past directors' pensions.
- Compensation paid to directors or past directors for loss of office.
- Sums paid to third parties for making available the services of a director.
- *(a)* Any loan, quasi loan or credit transaction or arrangement, made by a public company with its directors, or directors of its holding company or persons connected with directors. Disclosure is not required if the aggregate amount does not exceed £5 000.

(A credit transaction involves the supply or lease of goods, services or land on deferred terms.)

  (b) Any agreement to enter into such a transaction or arrangement.

  (c) Any other transaction or arrangement with the company and its subsidiary in which a director of the company or its holding company has a material interest, e.g. property transactions, consultancy agreements. Disclosure is not required if the aggregate amount does not exceed £1 000 or in a company whose assets are £100 000-£500 000 and the aggregate amount does not exceed 1 per cent of the company's net assets.

- Any loans, quasi loans, or credit transactions or arrangements made by a company with its officers (other than its directors) which are in excess of £5 000.
- Where the company has subsidiary undertakings, the names of the subsidiaries, the country of incorporation, particulars of the shares of the subsidiary undertakings held by the company, the aggregate amount of the capital and reserves of the subsidiary undertakings and the amount of their profit or loss
- Where the company is a subsidiary, the name and country of incorporation of its holding company.
- Where a company holds 20 per cent of the allotted share capital of another company, it must state the aggregate amount of the capital and reserves of that company and must provide the amount of the profit or loss of that company.
- Where the company holds 10 per cent of the allotted share capital of another company which is not a subsidiary undertaking, particulars of these shares and the identity and place of incorporation of such a company.

Auditors' report

The auditors of a company must make a report to the members on the accounts examined by them, and on every balance sheet, every profit and loss account and all group accounts of which a copy is laid before the company in general meeting during their tenure of office.

The auditor's report shall be read before the company in general meeting and must be open to inspection by any member. The report must state whether, in the auditors' opinion, the balance sheet and profit and loss account and (if applicable) the group accounts have been properly prepared in accordance with the provisions of the Act. They must also consider whether the information given in the directors' report relating to the financial year is consistent with the accounts. If they do not consider it so, they must state that fact (section 236).

The report must also state whether in their opinion a true and fair view is given:

1. in the case of the balance sheet, of the state of the company's affairs as at the end of its financial year;
2. in the case of the profit and loss account, of the company's profit or loss for its financial year;
3. in the case of group accounts submitted by a holding company, of the state of affairs and profit or loss of the company and its subsidiary undertakings (section 236).

It is the auditors' duty in preparing the report to carry out such investigations as will enable them to form an opinion as to whether:

(a) Proper accounting records have been kept by the company and proper returns adequate for their audit have been received from branches not visited by them; and
(b) The company's individual accounts are in agreement with the accounting records and returns (section 237).

If the auditors are of the opinion that *(a)* and *(b)* have not been complied with they must state that fact in their report.

If the auditors fail to obtain all the information and explanations which, to the best of their knowledge and belief, are necessary for their audit, they must also state that fact in their report.

If the directors do not disclose any loan, quasi loan, credit transaction or arrangement made between themselves with the company as required by the Act, the auditors must include in their report (as far as they are able to do so) a statement giving these particulars.

Directors' report (schedule 7)

Every company must attach to the balance sheet a report by its directors which must give:

1. a fair review of the development of the company's business and those of its subsidiary undertakings during the financial year, and of their position at the end of it (section 235);
2. the amount (if any) which they recommend should be paid as a dividend and the amount (if any) which they propose to carry to the reserves;
3. the names of the persons who at any time during the financial year were directors of the company;
4. the principal activities of the company and its subsidiary undertakings in the course of the financial year, and any significant change in the activities;
5. particulars of any important events affecting the company or any of its subsidiary undertakings which have occurred since the end of that financial year;
6. an indication of likely future developments in the business of the company and of its subsidiary undertakings;
7. an indication of the activities (if any) of the company and its subsidiary undertakings in the field of research and development;
8. any significant change in the fixed assets of the company or its subsidiary undertakings;
9. the extent of a directors' shareholding or acquisition of debentures in the company at the end of the financial year, according to the register of director shareholding;
10. the right of a director or member of his immediate family to subscribe for shares or debentures in the company;
11. information regarding health, safety and welfare provisions in respect of the company's employees;
12. if a company has 250 or more employees, a statement as to the

company's policy for employment, training, career development and the promotion of disabled persons;
13 particulars of contributions exceeding £200 given for political or charitable purposes;
14 particulars of the acquisitions by a company (or its nominee) of its own shares;
15 the purchase or maintenance of insurance of officers or auditors against liabilities in relation to the company.

Every member of the company, every debenture holder and any other person who is entitled to receive notices of general meetings of a company, must be sent a copy of the directors' report (section 240).

A company which has not entered into any significant accounting transaction from its formation or from the end of the previous financial year (i.e. a dormant company) is not required to appoint an auditor. This course of action must be approved by special resolution. The accounts, however, must contain a director's declaration that the company was dormant throughout the financial year. This concession is only applicable if the company is eligible to be treated as a small company and is not a public, banking or insurance company.

The directors of a small company are not required to file a copy of the directors' report with the annual accounts. If a company does not take reasonable steps to comply with the requirements relating to the directors' report, every person who was a director during the relevant period is guilty of an offence unless he can prove that he took all reasonable steps to secure compliance with these requirements (section 235).

Approval of Accounts

The accounts must be approved by the board of directors and the balance sheet must be signed on their behalf by a director. The directors' report must be approved by the board of directors and signed on their behalf by a company secretary or director.

22
AUDITOR AND COMPANY SECRETARY

The auditor

Appointment

The articles usually provide for the appointment of an auditor and the auditing of a company's accounts. The first auditor of a newly created company may be appointed by the directors. Unless removed midterm he will hold office until the conclusion of the first general meeting of the company, before which annual accounts are laid. If the directors fail to appoint the first auditor, the general meeting may do so (section 384).

Every company (except a dormant company) must, at every general meeting of the company at which accounts are laid, appoint an auditor to hold office from the end of that meeting until the end of the next general meeting at which accounts are laid. A retiring auditor may be re-appointed (section 384), but only if a resolution is passed for his re-appointment.

If the meeting fails to appoint an auditor, the Department of Trade may appoint an auditor on the company's behalf.

Special notice must be given of a resolution to appoint anyone other than a retiring auditor. The company must then notify the retiring auditor of the proposal. He may make representations to the company in writing and request that the company notify these representations to each member. The company must then send notice of the resolution to the members, accompanied by the auditor's representations. If the company does not send a copy of the representations to the members, the auditor may request that they be read out at the meeting (section 388).

A private company which has elected to dispense with laying accounts must appoint an auditor within twenty-eight days of sending accounts for the previous financial year to its members. The auditor will hold office from the end of that period or the conclusion of the general meeting until the end of the time for appointing auditors for the next financial year. The first auditors of such a company may be initially appointed by the directors (section 385A).

A private company may elect, by elective resolution, to dispense with the obligation to appoint auditors annually. The auditors are deemed to be re-appointed for each succeeding financial year unless, as a dormant company, the company is not required to appoint an auditor, or a member has served notice proposing the ending of the appointment (section 386).

Qualifications

The Companies Act 1989 establishes Recognised Supervisory Bodies (RSB) for the authorisation and supervision of auditors and Recognised Qualifying Bodies (RQB) for their examination and training. An RSB will maintain and enforce rules regarding eligibility to seek appointment as an auditor and the conduct of audit work. All auditors must be members of an RSB or be subject to its control and authorisation, and must hold an appropriate qualification. This is defined as one of the following:

1 membership of a recognised body of accountants, *or*
2 authorisation by the Department of Trade as having similar qualifications obtained outside the United Kingdom, or as having adequate knowledge and experience, *or*
3 authorisation by the Department to act as auditor as he retains

authorisation previously granted by the Department (section 389); *or*
4   the holder of a recognised United Kingdom professional qualification, *or*
5   the holder of an approved overseas qualification, *or*
6   a person who began his training before 1 January 1990 and who will obtain his qualification before 1 January 1996. The body awarding the qualification must be recognised by the Secretary of State.

An auditor may be a partnership or a company. In the case of a partnership, the appointment is that of the partnership and not of the partners, unless a contrary intention appears.

The following may not act as an auditor of a company:

(a)   an officer or employee of the company, for example any director, manager or secretary;
(b)   any partner, or person in the employment of an officer or employee of the company;
(c)   the officer or employee, or the partner, or the employee of the officer or employee of any associated undertaking (section 389).

Duties of an auditor

Lord Denning, in *Fomento (Sterling Area) v. Selsdon Fountain Pen Co.*, observed that: 'An auditor is not to be confused to the mechanics of checking vouchers and making arithmetical computations. He is not to be written off as a professional "adder-upper and subtractor". His vital task is to take care to see that errors are not made, be they errors of computation, or errors of commission or downright untruths. To perform this task properly, he must come to it with an enquiring mind – not suspicious of dishonesty, I agree – but suspecting that someone may have made a mistake somewhere and that a check must be made to ensure that there has been none.'

He has a right of access at all times to the company's books, accounts and vouchers and is entitled to require from the officers of the company such information and explanation as he thinks necessary for the performance of his duties.

1   His principal duty is to make a report to the members on the accounts examined by him and on every balance sheet, profit and

loss account and all group accounts laid before the company during his tenure of office. The report must state whether in his opinion the balance sheet, profit and loss, and (if applicable) group accounts have been properly prepared in accordance with the provisions of the Act (section 235, 236).

The auditor must also state whether proper returns have been kept by the company; whether the accounts are in agreement with the accounting records and returns; whether he has obtained all the information and explanations necessary for the purposes of the audit (section 237).

The report must be annexed to the balance sheet and must be read before the company in the general meeting. It must also be open to inspection by any member. The auditor fulfils his duty to members by sending his report to the company secretary. He is not responsible if the report is not placed before the members.

An auditor is also required to append a report to a statutory declaration made by the directors of a company which proposes to purchase its own shares out of capital, or to give financial assistance for the acquisition of its shares. The auditors must endorse the directors' opinion as to the company's ability to meet its financial obligations after adopting either of these courses, and must state that having inquired into the company's affairs they are not aware of any matter which would render the directors' opinion unreasonable in the circumstances.

2 It is also his duty to ascertain the company's true financial position as shown by the company's books. He is not responsible for matters that are concealed from him, but if there are suspicious circumstances he must fully investigate them.

In *Re Thomas Gerrard and Son Ltd*, the managing director had falsified the accounts in various ways. The auditors noticed that invoices had been altered, but failed to investigate the matter further and gave a favourable view of the company's profits. It was held they were liable for the dividends and tax that had been paid by the company as a result of their negligence.

In *Re London and General Bank*, the greater part of the capital of the bank was advanced to companies and a few select customers upon securities which were insufficient and difficult to realise. The auditors pointed this out to the directors in a confidential report, but their report to the shareholders merely stated that the value of the assets was dependent on realisation. As a result of this, dividends were declared which were in effect paid out of capital. It was held that the auditors had failed in their duty to ascertain the true financial position of the company, by not reporting to the shareholders, and were liable to make good the dividend declared.

The auditor must not confine himself to checking the mere arithmetical calculations, but must ensure that the books show the correct financial position. He is not responsible for tracking ingenious and skilful schemes of fraud when there is nothing to arouse his suspicion.

3 He must satisfy himself that the company's securities exist and are in safe custody. This should be done by personal inspection, but if the securities are in the possession of a trustworthy individual who normally holds securities in the ordinary course of business, a certificate given by such a person that they are in his custody is sufficient. In *Re Kingston Cotton Mill Co.*, an auditor accepted the certificate of the company's manager as to the value of the company's stock in trade. As a result dividends were paid out of capital. It was held that the auditor was not liable, as he was entitled to rely on the manager's certificate.

It is not part of an auditor's duties to take stock, but if he forms the opinion that the stock is overvalued he should report this to the shareholders. It is generally accepted that an auditor should carry out a check on some sample items in the audit.

4 He must familiarise himself with a company's articles, with the Act and with other relevant statutes. If an audited balance sheet does not show a company's true financial position, the onus is on the auditor to show that this is not as a result of a breach of duty on his part.

5 An auditor may have to value a company's shares, as the articles of a private company often contain pre-emption clauses (e.g. a member selling his shares must first offer them to the existing members at a price to be determined by the auditor). An auditor need not give the reasons for his valuation, and the burden of proving that it is unfair or improper lies on the person objecting to it. It can only be challenged by showing that the auditor made a

fundamental mistake; or materially misdirected himself in the course of his valuation, for example by making a serious computational error; or that he was negligent in his valuation. Where a company is in a poor financial condition he may rightly value the shares on the basis of the break up value of the company. If the shares concerned constitute a controlling block he need not value the shares on the basis of the control of the company, if there is no reason to assume that the shares will be purchased as one block.

In *Arenson v. Casson, Beckman, Rutley and Co.*, it was held that an auditor owes a duty of care to a shareholder when valuing shares. Arenson, the controlling shareholder and chairman of a private company, took his nephew into the business and gave him a parcel of shares in the company. The nephew agreed that in the event of terminating his employment with the company he would sell his shares to his uncle at their 'fair value' that is the value of the shares as determined by the auditors 'acting as experts and not as arbitrators'. His employment ceased in 1970 and he transferred the shares to his uncle for £4 916 – the auditors' valuation. A few months later the company 'went public', and the shares were seen to be worth six times that amount. It was held that the auditors had been negligent in their valuation.

6   An auditor does not owe a duty of care to individual shareholders when preparing the audit. In *Caparo Industries plc v. Dickman*, Caparo claimed damages against the auditor of a company taken over by Caparo for loss allegedly suffered as a result of relying on inaccurate and misleading accounts. It was held that the purpose of an audit is to fulfil the statutory requirements of the Companies Act with a view to circulating the accounts to the shareholders and laying the accounts before the general meeting. A duty of care is owed to the shareholders as a body, not to individual shareholders or to members of the public who rely on the accounts in deciding whether to purchase a company's shares.

An auditor does not owe a duty of care to a lending bank. In *Al Saudi Banque v. Clarke Pixley* a bank sued an insolvent company's auditors alleging that the auditors were negligent in their examination of the company's accounts and in compiling the audit report. The bank stated that it relied on the report in deciding whether to maintain and finance the company. It was held that the auditor was not under a statutory duty to report to the bank and did not provide the accounts with the knowledge or intention that they were to be supplied to the bank.

An auditor does not owe a duty of care to a bidder in a takeover bid because accounts prepared for a company are for the use of that company alone. In *James McNaughton Ltd v. Hicks Anderson and Co* JM Ltd entered into negotiations with a rival company with a view to a takeover. The rival company's accountants prepared draft accounts for use in negotiations and a takeover was completed. Discrepancies were later found in the draft accounts and the accountants were sued for negligence by JM Ltd. It was held that the accounts were prepared for the rival company and a duty of care was not owed to JM Ltd as it could not have foreseen that JM Ltd would treat them as final accounts.

If a company's financial advisers make representations to a bidder in a takeover bid, they owe the bidder a duty of care not to be negligent in making representations which might mislead him. In *Morgan Crucible v. Hill Samuel Bank Ltd* a company made a takeover bid relying on accounts and an unaudited statement prepared by the other company's auditors. A month later the auditors, in a circular, forecast a substantial increase in profits. The accountants in a letter stated that it had been properly prepared and the company's bank stated that it had been made with due care and inquiry. In reliance on these statements the company increased its bid and the takeover was successful, but claimed later that the profit forecast had been negligently prepared. It was held that the company's financial advisers and its directors had made express representations which gave rise to a duty of care.

7   An auditor must consider whether a written resolution of a private company affects him in his capacity as an auditor or whether such a resolution should be considered by a general meeting (section 381B) (see page 147).

Liability of an auditor

If an auditor fails to discharge his duties he is liable to a company for any loss resulting from his negligence or default. Any provision in the company's articles or in any contract with a company exempting him from liability, is void. A company may, however, purchase and maintain insurance against the liability of its auditor (section 310).

An auditor who is liable may be wholly or partly relieved from liability by the court if it appears that he acted honestly and reasonably and ought to be excused (section 727).

Removal and resignation

Although an auditor is appointed to hold office until the next general meeting at which accounts are to be presented, a company may at a general meeting pass an ordinary resolution removing an auditor before the expiration of his term of office, notwithstanding the terms of his contract with the company. Notice of the fact that a resolution for removal of the auditor has been passed must be given to the Registrar within 14 days (section 386).

Special notice is required for a resolution at a general meeting:

(a) to appoint as auditor a person other than a retiring auditor; or
(b) to fill a casual vacancy in the office of auditor; or
(c) to reappoint as auditor a retiring auditor appointed by the directors to fill a casual vacanacy; or
(d) to remove an auditor before the expiration of his term of office. (section 388).

An auditor who is removed in this manner may be entitled to compensation for loss of his position as auditor, or for the loss of any other office with the company he held as a result of being its auditor, and which he also loses on his removal. The Act specifically reserves this right. Whether such compensation is payable, and its assessment, will depend on the terms of the auditor's contact with the company and his ability, if any, to mitigate the loss.

An auditor may resign his appointment by depositing a written notice to that effect at the company's registered office. His resignation will take effect on the date of the notice or on such later date as the notice specifies. Where an auditor ceases, for any reason, to hold office, he must deposit a statement that there are no circumstances connected with his resignation which he considers should be brought to the attention of the company's members or creditors; or if there are any such circumstances, a statement of them (section 390).

The company must then send a copy of the statement to every

person entitled to receive a copy of the company's accounts; it may apply to the court if it considers that the auditor is seeking needless publicity or defamatory matter. If the court agrees, the statement need not be sent.

Where an auditor's notice of resignation contains a statement that there are circumstances which should be brought to the attention of the members or creditors, he may deposit a requisition with the company calling on the directors to convene an extraordinary general meeting to consider these matters. The directors must comply with his request (section 391).

He is also entitled to receive notice to attend any general meeting at which it is proposed to fill the vacancy caused by his resignation, or at which his term of office would have otherwise expired. He may there speak on any part of the business of the meeting which concerns him as the company's former auditor (section 391).

If a company's auditor was ineligible to act as an auditor during any part of a company's audit, the Secretary of State may direct the company to appoint another auditor to re-audit the accounts or review the first audit and report whether a second audit is required.

Remuneration

An auditor's remuneration is determined by the person or body who appointed him, i.e. the directors, the general meeting or the Secretary of State. The amount of the remuneration must be stated in a note to the accounts and applies to benefits in kind (with the estimated money value), as well as to payments in cash.

The secretary

Appointment

Every company must have a secretary, but a sole director cannot be secretary. The secretary may be another company, but a company may not be the secretary if its sole director is also the sole director of the company (section 283).

Qualifications

It is the duty of the directors of a public company to take all reasonable steps to ensure that the company's secretary is a person who appears to them to have the requisite knowledge and experience to discharge the functions of secretary of the company. The qualifications laid down are that he should be a person who:

(a) on 22nd December 1980 held the office of secretary or assistant or deputy secretary of the company; *or*
(b) for at least three of the five years immediately preceding his appointment as secretary held the office of secretary of a company other than a private company; *or*
(c) is a member of one of the following bodies: The Institute of Chartered Accountants in England and Wales; The Institute of Chartered Accountants of Scotland; The Association of Certified Accountants; The Institute of Chartered Accountants in Ireland; The Institute of Chartered Secretaries and Administrators; The Chartered Institute of Managements Accountants; The Chartered Institute of Public Finance and Accountancy; *or*
(d) is a barrister, advocate or solicitor called or admitted in any part of the United Kingdom; *or*
(e) is a person who, by virtue of his holding or having held any other position or his being a member of any other body, appears to the directors to be capable of discharging those functions (section 286).

Duties

A secretary's duties vary with the size of the company and his terms of employment with a company. He is an officer of the company and as such is liable to penalties if he fails to comply with certain requirements of the Act.

Until recently it was thought that a secretary had a very 'humble role' to play in a company's activities *Whitechurch (George) v. Cavanagh.* However, in *Panorama Developments (Guildford) Ltd v. Fidelis Furnishing Fabrics Ltd,* it was held that 'times have changed'. Lord Denning stated that: 'A company secretary is a much more important person than he was in 1887.' (In *Barnett, Hoares and Co. v. South London Tramway C.*, it was stated that 'He (the secretary) is a mere servant . . . no one can assume he has any authority'.) He is an officer of the company with extensive duties and responsibilities. This appears not only in the modern Companies Acts, but also by the role which he plays in the day-to-day business of companies. He is no longer a mere clerk. He regularly makes representations on behalf of the company and enters into contracts on its behalf which come within the day-to-day running of the company's business. So much so that he may be regarded as held out as having authority to do such things on behalf of the company. He is certainly entitled to sign contracts connected with the administrative side of a company's affairs, such as employing staff, and ordering cars, and so forth. All such matters now come within the ostensible authority of a company's secretary.'

In this particular case, Bayne, the company secretary of Fidelis Furnishing Fabrics Ltd, ordered cars from Panorama Developments, ostensibly for business purposes. He told the car hire firm that the cars were required to carry important customers of the firm. Bayne wrote on the company's paper ordering the cars and signed himself 'Company Secretary'. He gave references for the company which showed that the company was of good standing. The car firm sent hiring agreements naming Bayne as the hirer. Bayne used the cars himself. It was held that the Fidelis Furnishing Fabrics were liable for the hire of the cars as Bayne had ostensible authority to enter into contracts for the hire of cars.

Certain statutory duties are imposed upon a secretary, for example his signature is required on the annual return, and he must also certify a copy of the accounts sent with the annual return. His other duties include the maintenance of the company's registers, dealing with share transfers and the issue of share certificates, registration of charges, preparation of returns, preparation of notices and agendas for meetings and subsequent action after meetings.

23
COMPULSORY LIQUIDATION

A company's existence is terminated by:

(a) the company being struck off the register as a defunct company;
(b) the early dissolution of the company;
(c) the company being wound up as a result of (i) the court making a winding up order; or (ii) the members passing a resolution for winding up.

Striking off the register

If the Registrar has reason to believe that a company is not carrying on business or is not in operation he may send a letter of inquiry to the company. If no reply is received within one month, he may send a registered letter to the company stating that unless an answer is received to the second letter within one month, a notice will be published in the *Gazette* with a view to having the company struck off the register. If he receives no answer within one month after sending the second letter, or if he is informed by the company that it is no longer carrying on a business, he may publish in the *Gazette* a notice that, unless cause is shown to the contrary, the company will be struck off the register and dissolved within three months (section 652).

Similar notices may be sent by the Registrar if the company is in liquidation and he has reasonable cause to believe that the liquidator is no longer acting; or if he has reason to believe that the company's affairs have been fully wound up, but the liquidator has failed to submit the returns required by the Act.

This is a simple and relatively inexpensive method of dissolving a company. It does, however, deprive creditors and members of the safeguards provided for by the normal procedures of winding up, and the Act makes certain provisions for this type of dissolution. The liability of every director, officer of the company and member shall continue as if the company had not been dissolved, and the Court can wind up a company despite the fact that the company has been struck off the register (section 653). Any property of the company, including land, which remains after its dissolution becomes vested in the Crown (or the Duchy of Cornwall or the Duchy of Lancaster) as *bona vacantia* (section 654).

The Court may, at any time within 2 years of a company's dissolution, declare a dissolution void on the application of the liquidator or other interested person. The Court may make an order on such terms as it thinks fit and proceedings may be taken as if the company had not been dissolved. This time limit is extended where the purpose of the application for restoration is to bring an action against the company for damages for personal or fatal injuries or an action for damages under the Fatal Accidents Act. The Court may in these circumstances restore a company to the register at any time. (section 651).

The Court may also within twenty years of the dissolution, order a company to be restored to the register on the application of a company or any member or creditor. Any property which had vested in the Crown (or Duchies of Cornwall or Lancaster) may be sold by the Crown, even though orders reviving the company have been made, provided the Crown pays the company an amount equal to the amount received by it for the sale of the property. This provision deals with the situation where a company was carrying on business when it was struck off, and also allows a company to be revived to take advantage of any monies or assets that subsequently come to light (section 653). In *Re Vickers and Bott Ltd*, a company was restored to the register to enable it to take advantage of £700 that became payable to the company as a result of a dividend being declared in the bankruptcy of a debtor.

Early dissolution of the company

If the Official Receiver is the liquidator and it appears to him that the company's assets are insufficient to cover the expenses of winding up and the company's affairs do not require further investigation he may apply to the Registrar for early dissolution of the company.

The Official Receiver must however give twenty-eight days notice of his intention to apply for an early dissolution to the creditors and contributories (IA section 202). Any creditor or contributory may within three months, apply to the Secretary of State for directions on the basis that:

1. the company's assets are sufficient to cover the expenses;
2. the company's affairs require further investigation;
3. the company's early dissolution would be inappropriate (IA section 203).

If there is no such application the company is automatically dissolved three months after the Registrar receives the application (IA section 202).

Winding up by the Court

An order for the compulsory winding up of a company is obtained by presenting a petition to the appropriate Court. The petition must contain the company's name, the date of its incorporation, the amount of its nominal and paid up capital, the company's objects, and the grounds on which the petition is made. It concludes with the prayer 'that the company may be wound up by the court under the provisions of the Insolvency Act 1986 or that such other order may be made as the court thinks fit.'

The petition is normally initiated in the County Court if the company's paid up share capital does not exceed £120 000, otherwise the petition will be heard in the Companies Court.

A copy of the petition must be served on the company, and at least seven days before the petition is heard it must be advertised in the *Gazette* and in one local or London newspaper.

The petitioners

The petition may be presented by the company itself. Such a petition is rare as it is quicker, more convenient and less expensive to pass a special resolution to wind up voluntarily. If the company passes an ordinary resolution that it should be wound up by the Court, the directors may present a petition for a winding up order.

A creditor may petition for a compulsory winding up whatever the amount of his debt, whether his debt is secured or unsecured, and whether payable immediately or at some future date or time. An order will not be made if the debt is less than £750 (IA section 123), unless the petitioner is able to join with other creditors and their total debts exceed £750. Should the company appear to have a substantial defence, no order will be made. It is advisable for a creditor to obtain judgement on a debt before presenting such a petition. If a creditor satisfies these conditions the Court may nevertheless pay regard to the wishes of the other creditors, and if the majority, in value, of creditors object, with good reason, to a winding up order, the Court has a discretion to refuse the order. If the debt is disputed on some substantial grounds, the creditor cannot generally obtain a winding up order.

Any contributory may petition for winding up if the number of members has fallen below the statutory minimum, or if the shares were originally allotted to him, or have been held by him for at least six out of the last eighteen months, or have devolved on him through the death of a former holder (IA section 123).

A contributory in this context not only includes 'every person who is liable to contribute to the assets of the company in the event of its being wound up', that is the holders of partly paid up shares and those who were the holders of such shares in the last twelve months, but also the holders of fully paid shares and persons who ceased to be members more than a year before the commencement of the winding up (IA section 79).

The Court will only make an order on the petition of a contributory if he has an interest which can only be protected by winding up the company. A holder of partly paid up shares, a member of an unlimited company, a member of a guarantee company – all of these would have an interest in preventing a company from incurring further debts towards which they would have to contribute. If a company is insolvent, or is a guarantee company, the contributory is entitled as of right to a winding up order, but in other cases the Court has a discretion whether to make an order.

The Official Receiver may also petition for a winding up order where the company is already being wound up voluntarily, or under the supervision of the Court. An order will only be made if the Court is satisfied that the existing winding up cannot be continued with due regard to the interests of the creditors or contributories. In *Re Ryder Installations*, the liquidator had on five occasions failed to submit reports to the Registrar. His accounts, when audited, were unsatisfactory. It was held that the Official Receiver's petition should be granted.

The Department of Trade may present a petition for winding up if, as a result of information or documents obtained from an inspection of the company's books or papers or from an inspector's report, it appears to be in the public interest that the company should be wound up (1A section 124).

An administrative receiver or administrator may present a petition for a winding up order (IA section 42). A petition presented by an administrator must be combined with the discharge of the administration order as a resolution for a winding up order cannot be made while an administration order is in force. A supervisor of a voluntary arrangement may also petition for a winding up order.

The Attorney General may also petition in the case of a company which has been formed for a charitable purpose.

The grounds for winding up

A company may be wound up by the Court if one or several of the following grounds exist (IA section 122).

1 The company has passed a special resolution that it should be wound up by the Court.
2 The company has not been issued with a section 117 certificate. (This only applies to a public company).
3 The company does not commence business within a year of its incorporation, or suspends its business for a year.

If there are prospects of commencing business in the future and the majority of members do not wish the company to be wound up the Court will not grant the order. In *Re Middlesbrough Assembly Rooms Co.*, the company suspended building operations for three years during a trade recession. It intended to resume operations as soon as trading prospects improved. The petition was opposed by 80 per cent of the shareholders and it was held that it should be dismissed.

4   The number of members is reduced below two.
5   The company is unable to pay its debts. This is the most common ground for a petition. As it would be extremely difficult for a petitioner who had no access to a company's books to prove that a company is unable to pay its debts, a presumption of inability arises in the following circumstances:
   (a)   a creditor, to whom the company owes £750 or more, has served on the company a demand for payment, and the company has for three weeks thereafter neglected to pay the sum or compound for it to the reasonable satisfaction of the creditor.
   (b)   an execution or judgment remains unsatisfied.
   (c)   if it is proved to the Court's satisfaction that the company is unable to pay its debts, taking into account its contingent and prospective liabilities as well as the debts which are immediately payable.
   (d)   if it is proved to the court's satisfaction that the value of the company's assets is less than the amount of its liabilities, taking into account its contingent and prospective liabilities (IA section 123).
6   If the Court is of the opinion that it is just and equitable that the company should be wound up.

If a petition is presented on this ground, the Court may grant relief to the petitioner by some other means (e.g. section 459 provides an alternative remedy for an oppressed minority on the grounds of unfair prejudice).

There are numerous instances of companies being wound up under this provision.

In *Re German Date Coffee Co*, it was held that the company should be wound up as the sub-stratum of the company had gone. The company was formed to work a German patent to extract coffee from dates.

It never obtained this patent, but purchased a Swedish patent, and successfully manufactured coffee in this way. It was held that the company should be wound up as it was formed basically to work a German patent in Germany.

In *Re T. E. Brinsmead and Sons*, it was held that as the company's objects were illegal it should be wound up. The company was formed to trade on the goodwill of a similarly named company. It had no capital of its own and was hopelessly embarrassed by numerous actions brought by its shareholders on the grounds of fraud.

In *Re Yenidje Tobacco Co Ltd*, it was held that as there was deadlock in the company's affairs, the only course open to the Court was to wind up the company. The company's two director shareholders held equal voting power and were not on speaking terms due to a disagreement. Despite the fact that substantial profits were being made by the company, it was wound up.

In *Loch v. John Blackwood Ltd*, a company was wound up because of mismanagement in its conduct towards its minority shareholders. The company was formed to carry on John Blackwood's business and to divide the profits amongst the members of his family. The managing director was the majority shareholder. He omitted to hold meetings and failed to submit accounts or recommend a dividend. His purpose was to keep the shareholders in ignorance of the company's affairs so as to acquire their shares at an undervaluation.

The petition and its effect

The petition sets out the grounds on which an order is sought and must be verified by an affidavit of the petitioner. The petition, (unless presented by the company itself) must be served on the company at its registered office. If there is no registered office it must be served at its principal or last known place of business. A copy of the petition must also be sent to the liquidator, receiver or administrator if the company is being wound up, is in receivership, is subject to an administration order or a voluntary arrangement is in force.

The Court may dismiss the petition, or adjourn the hearing, or make an interim order (e.g. adjourn the hearing, appoint a provisional liquidator), or make any other order that may be just.

A provisional liquidator is usually appointed before the hearing in cases where there is likely to be a lengthy period of time between the presentation of the petition and the hearing, in order to preserve the company's assets. The Official Receiver or a qualified insolvency practitioner may be appointed provisional liquidator (IA section 135).

The provisional liquidator takes into his custody or under his control all the company's property (IA section 144). In *Re Union Accident Insurance Co Ltd*, it was held that a provisional liquidator was entitled to terminate loss-making contracts, for by doing so he was preserving the company's assets for the benefit of its creditors and shareholders. He can apply to the Court for the appointment of a special manager to manage the company's business (IA section 177).

Consequences of the winding up order

(a) The Official Receiver becomes the liquidator of the company, unless the Court appoints the person who was the administrator of the company under an administration order or the supervisor under an approved voluntary arrangement (1A sections 136, 140).

(b) No action can be commenced, or proceeded with, against the company without the Court's leave (1A section 130).

(c) Any disposition of the company's property, any transfer of shares or alteration in the status of the company to members is void, unless the court orders otherwise (1A section 127).

(d) Any execution against the company's property is void (1A section 128).

(e) The directors' powers cease.

(f) The company's employees are dismissed.

(g) A copy of the winding up order must be sent to the Registrar who enters it in his records relating to the company. (1A section 130) and publishes notice of its receipt by him in the *Gazette* (section 711).

(h) The winding up is deemed to commence from the date of granting the petition, although if a voluntary liquidation is already in progress, the winding up is deemed to commence from the date of the resolution for voluntary winding up (1A section 129).

The statement of affairs

Within 21 days of making a winding up order or appointing a provisional liquidator the Official Receiver may require a statement of the company's financial affairs. This gives particulars of the comany's assets, debts and liabilities, its creditors, the securities held by them and the dates when such securities were given, and any further information which the Official Receiver may require. This statement must be verified by affidavit by one or more of the directors and the company's secretary.

Official Receiver's investigation

The Official Receiver must investigate the reasons for the company's failure and the promotion, formation, business dealings and affairs of the company. He may make such report to the court as he thinks fit (IA section 132).

He may apply to the Court for the public examination of any person who

(a) is or has been an officer of the company; or
(b) has acted as liquidator, administrator, or receiver or manager of the company; or
(c) has taken part in the promotion, formation or management of the company.

He *must* apply for an examination if requested to do so by one half in value of the creditors or three quarters in value of the contributories (IA section 133).

Meetings of creditors and contributories

The Official Receiver may summon separate meetings of creditors and contributories to choose a person to be liquidator in his place. He must decide within 12 weeks whether or not to do so. If he decides not to convene meetings he must inform the creditors and contributories of his decision. He must convene the meetings if requested to do so by one quarter in value of the creditors (IA section 136).

The liquidator

The Official Receiver, by virtue of his office, becomes the liquidator and continues in office until the appointment of another person (IA section 135), who must be a qualified insolvency practitioner.

(a) He may summon separate meetings of creditors and contributaries to choose another person to be liquidator in his place (section 136).
(b) He may apply to the Secretary of State or appoint another person in his place (IA section 137).
(c) He may be replaced if one quarter of the creditors summon a meeting to appoint another person in his place (IA section 139).
(d) If a winding up order follows immediately on the discharge of an administration order, the Court may appoint the administrator as liquidator (IA section 140).
(e) If a winding up order is made at a time where there is a supervisor of a voluntary arrangement approved by the Court, the Court may appoint the supervisor as liquidator (IA section 140).

Liquidation Committee

Where a winding up order has been made by the court and separate meetings of creditors and contributories have been summoned for the purpose of choosing a liquidator, these meetings may establish a liquidation committee. Alternatively, a liquidator, who is not the Official Receiver may at any time, if he thinks fit, summon general meetings of the creditors and contributories to decide whether such a committee should be established. He must summon a meeting if requested to do so by 10 per cent in value of the creditors.

The liquidation committee is not able or required to carry out its functions at the time when the Official Receiver is the liquidator (IA section 141).

The liquidator's powers and duties

A liquidator's duties are to collect and realise the company's assets, to settle a list of contributories and creditors, to pay the company's debts and liabilities, and to divide the surplus (if any) among the members of the company in accordance with their rights.

In order to achieve this, he may sell and transfer the company's property and borrow money on its security. He may also execute any documents in the name of the company; appoint an agent to undertake business which he is unable to do himself; prove in the bankruptcy of a contributory; take out letters of administration to the estate of a deceased contributory, raise money on the security of the assets; and do anything necessary for winding up the company's affairs and distributing its assets.

With the sanction of the Court or liquidation committee, he can also bring and defend actions on the company's behalf, carry on the company's business, make a call, rectify the register of members, pay any class of creditors in full and compromise with creditors, contributories and debtors. He may summon general meetings of creditors and contributaries to ascertain their wishes. He must do so if requested by 10 per cent in value of the creditors or contributories, or at such times as the creditors or contributories by resolution may direct. Where a liquidator, who is not the Official Receiver disposes of any of the company's property to a connected person or employs a solicitor to assist him in carrying out his functions, he must give notice of the fact to a liquidation committee, if such a committee is in existence (IA sections 165, 167, 169).

Without sanction he may sell any of the company's property by public auction or private contract and execute deeds, receipts and other documents. He may draw, accept and indorse bills of exchange in the company's name and raise money on the security of the company's assets. He may prove in the bankruptcy or insolvency of any contributory and appoint an agent to do any business which he is unable to do himself. He may do all such other things as are necessary to wind up the company's affairs and distribute its assets (1A schedule 4).

He therefore takes custody or control of all the property to which the company is or appears to be entitled. This does not vest in the liquidator and he may apply to the court for a vesting order. He can then bring or defend proceedings in relation to that property or take necessary action for winding up the company and recovering its property (IA section 145).

The liquidator will require payment by the contributories of the amount, if any, uncalled on their shares. A contributory is any person liable to contribute to the assets of the company in the event of its being wound up.

In a company limited by shares, a member holding partly paid up shares is liable for the amount which remains unpaid on his share and is placed on the 'A' list of contributories. A past member, who was a member within a year of the commencement of winding up, is placed on the 'B' list. Such a member is only liable where the existing holder of the shares fails to pay the amount due. The 'B' list is only prepared if it appears that the present members are unable to meet the calls made on them. The liability of a past member only extends to the debts incurred by the company while he was still a member.

A member of a company limited by guarantee is liable to the extent of his guarantee. If the company has a share capital he is also liable for the amount which remains unpaid on his shares. The liability of past members is similar to that of past members of companies limited by shares. A member of an unlimited company is liable to contribute to the company's assets in proportion to his interest in the company.

The liquidator informs each contributory of the amount of his liability and appoints a day for hearing any objections. A contributory has a further right of appeal to the Court. Before the liquidator makes a formal call, he must obtain the consent of the committee of inspection, or if there is no committee, the Court.

A liquidator may set aside transactions, recover property and receive compensation in respect of certain transactions that are forbidden by the Act.

1 Transactions at an undervalue

A transaction is deemed to be at an undervalue when a company makes a gift to a person or enters into a tranaction with a person for either no consideration or for a consideration which is less than that provided by the company (IA section 238).

Such a transaction may be challenged by the liquidator, if made within 2 years of the commencement of winding up or the presentation of a winding up order, on the grounds that it was entered into at a time when the company was unable to pay its debts or is unable to do so as a consequence of the transaction (IA section 240).

If the transaction is entered into with a connected person there is a presumption, which may be rebutted, that the company is insolvent. An order will not be made if the court is satisfied that

(a) the company entered into the transaction in good faith and for the purpose of carrying out its business and

(b) that at the time it did so there were reasonable grounds for believing that the transaction would benefit the company (IA section 238).

2 Extortionate credit transaction

A liquidator may apply to the court for an order with regard to a transaction providing credit to the company, if

(a) the terms were extortionate; or

(b) it otherwise contravened the principles of fair trading, and it was entered into within 3 years of winding up or making an administration order. It is presumed, unless the contrary is proved, that a credit transaction is extortionate if an application is made to the court in respect of the transaction.

The court may:

(i) set aside the whole or any obligation created by the transaction,
(ii) vary the terms of the transaction or the terms on which any security is held,
(iii) require a party to the transaction to repay any sums paid by the company in respect of the transaction,
(iv) require any person to surrender to the liquidator any property held as security,
(v) direct accounts to be taken (IA section 244).

3 Certain floating charges

A floating charge created by the company within twelve months, of winding up or making an administration order is invalid as a security for a debt, if at the time of its creation the company was unable to pay its debts or became unable to pay its debts as a result of the transaction under which the charge was created. (The time is extended to two years if it was made in favour of a connected person).

There are exceptions to the rule, in that the following will be binding on the liquidator if made at the same time as, or after, the creation of the charge and in consideration of the charge: money paid, goods or service supplied, the discharge or reduction of any debt of the company and the payment of contractual interest (in relation to the above) (IA section 245).

4 Fraudulent trading

If in the course of a winding up it appears that a company's business has been carried on with intent to defraud creditors, or for any other fraudulent purpose, the Court may declare that any individuals who were *knowingly* responsible for carrying on business in this way are liable to make such contributions to the company's assets as the Court thinks proper (IA section 213).

In *Re Leitch*, a company continued trading and incurred further debts when the directors knew that there was no reasonable prospect of the creditors ever being paid. It was held that the company's business was being carried on with intent to defraud creditors. In *Re Peake and Hall*, a father and son were the sole directors of a company. The father was not in good health and his wife dealt with the company's affairs and managed its business. The company became insolvent in 1977 but continued trading until 1980. It was held that the son was not liable, for although he was a director, he had not concerned himself with the company's financial affairs.

The Court may make a disqualification order against a person:

(a) if it appears that he has been guilty of fraudulent trading, whether or not he is convicted; *or*
(b) it makes a declaration under IA section 213 that he is liable to contribute to the company's assets (CDDA sections 4, 10).

5 Wrongful trading

If in the course of a winding up it appears to a liquidator that a director is guilty of wrongful trading he may apply to the court for a declaration that the director make a contribution to the company's assets.

To establish wrongful trading a liquidator must show that:

(a) the company has gone into insolvent liquidation; at some time before the commencement of the winding up the director knew, or ought to have concluded, that there was no reasonable prospect of the company avoiding insolvent liquidation;
(b) on realising that there was no prospect of the company avoiding insolvent liquidation, the director took insufficient steps to minimise the potential loss to the company's creditors (IA section 214).

The standard to be applied is that of a reasonable diligent person having both the general knowledge, skill and experience expected of a person carrying out that director's duties and the general knowledge, skill and experience possessed by the particular director (IA section 214).

In *Re Produce Marketing Consortium*, a liquidator brought an action against two directors of a company claiming £107 946 contribution from them as a result of their wrongful trading. It was held that the directors had a minimum obligation to keep proper accounting records within the time limits set down by the Companies Acts. As this had not been done, they were liable to make a contribution to the company's assets on the basis of the amount by which those assets had been depleted by their conduct which amounted to wrongful trading. They were ordered to make a contribution of £75 000.

6 Preference

Where a company has given a preference to any person, within six months of the commencement of winding up or the presentation of a petition for an administration order, the liquidator may apply to the court for an order to restore the position to what it would have been had not the company given that preference.

A company gives a preference if:

(a) the person preferred is a creditor, and
(b) the company's act has the effect of placing that person in a better position in the event of the company going into insolvent liquidation (IA section 239).

(The time is extended to two years in the case of a preference of a connected person).

In order to establish a preference, the company must either have been unable to pay its debts at the time of giving the preference, or as a result of giving the preference (IA section 240).

7 Disclaimer of onerous property

A liquidator may, on giving notice, disclaim onerous property i.e., property of the company which is more of a liability than an asset. This includes:

(a) property which is either unsaleable or not readily saleable; property which may give rise to a liability to pay money or perform any onerous act;
(b) unprofitable contracts.

A liquidator may disclaim, even though he may have taken possession of the property, endeavoured to sell it or in some other way exercised rights of ownership in relation to it.

A liquidator may not give notice of disclaimer if a person who is interested in the property applies to him in writing requiring him to decide within twenty-eight days whether or not to disclaim and the liquidator has not given notice of disclaimer within that time (IA section 178).

8 Misfeasance

An application may be made to the Court by the Official Receiver, a liquidator, a creditor or contributary, if in the course of the winding up it appears that a promotor, director, liquidator or officer of the company has misapplied or retained property of the company or has been guilty of misfeasance, that is a breach of duty involving the misapplication of a company's assets. Examples of misfeasance are where directors sold their own property to the company or used a company's property to make a profit for themselves, and where an auditor sanctioned the payment of dividends out of capital.

Directors who sell a business as a going concern are not guilty of misfeasance if they fail to gain a higher price by breaking up a company which is in financial difficulty. In *Re Welfab Engineers Ltd* the directors of a company sold the business as a going concern for £110 000 with the purchaser taking on the workforce. The liquidator contended that the company's freehold premises could have been sold for £125 000. It was held that the directors were not guilty of misfeasance for although they were not entitled to sell the business on terms which worsened the position of the creditors, they were entitled to allow the survival of the business.

The creditors

A creditor must submit proof of his debts in writing to the liquidator giving details of the debt, the amount claimed and whether the debt is secured. The creditor's remedy is solely against the company and the debts for which he can prove are specified in the Insolvency Act. If the company in solvent, then all claims are provable. If the company is insolvent all debts and liabilities owing at the dates of the commencement of the liquidation are provable.

A creditor must submit proof of his debts, in writing, to the liquidator giving details of the debt, the amount claimed and whether the debt is secured. The creditor's remedy is solely against the company and the debts for which he can prove are specified in the Act.

If the company is solvent then all claims are provable, including sums payable on a contingency, sums payable in the future and claims in respect of unliquidated damages for which a just estimate can be made.

If the company is insolvent all debts and liabilities owing at the date of the commencement of the liquidation are payable (as above), except for debts incurred with the knowledge of the winding up and claims in respect of unliquidated damages, other than for breach of trust or contract. The liquidator may set off against any debt owed by the company, a debt due to the company from the creditor. Only the balance is proved or paid.

The creditor who is the most favoured is the secured creditor. As he holds some security for the debts owed to him by the company, such as a mortgage, charge or lien, he has four courses open to him. He can rely on his security and not prove in the winding up. If the security covers part only of the debt, he can realise the security and prove for the balance. Alternatively, he can surrender the security to the liquidator and prove for the whole debt, or he can value the security and prove for the balance, in which case the liquidator may redeem at the assessed value.

The payment of debts

If the company is solvent, the liquidator can settle the company's debts in any order he wishes, but if the company is insolvent he must follow a strict order for the payment of debts.

The assets are applied first in paying the cost, charges and expenses properly incurred in the winding up. This includes the remuneration of the liquidator.

The next group of debts to be paid are the preferential debts. They all rank equally and must be paid in full, unless there are insufficient assets when they abate in equal proportions. The main classes of preferential debts are listed in section 386 and Schedule 6 of the Insolvency Act. They are:

- income tax (PAYE deductions) for twelve months before the relevant date;
- value added tax for six months before the relevant date;
- wages or salaries of an employee during the four months preceding the relevant date, up to £800, and all accrued holiday remuneration;
- contributions payable in respect of national insurance during the twelve months before the relevant date and certain other claims under Social Security legislation.

The relevant date in a compulsory winding up is usually the date of the winding up order.

If a person such as a bank, has advanced money to a company to enable the wages, salaries or holiday remuneration of the employees to be paid, that person is regarded as a preferential creditor to the same extent as an employee would have been.

Preferential debts have priority over a floating charge created by the company.

After the preferential debts have been paid, the claims of the ordinary creditors are met. These debts also rank equally among themselves, and if there are insufficient assets to meet their claims in full, they will abate equally. The payment to a member of any unclaimed dividend will be deferred until the ordinary creditors have been paid.

COMPULSORY LIQUIDATION

Should there be a surplus, the liquidator must repay any calls on shares which have been paid in advance, followed by the repayment of capital to the shareholders. Any further surplus will be distributed amongst the shareholders according to the rights set out in the articles.

— Termination of office of liquidator —

A liquidator who wishes to resign his office must summon meetings of the creditors to obtain their consent. The notice summoning the meeting must be accompanied by an account of his administration. He may only resign on the grounds of ill-health, or if he intends ceasing to practise as an insolvency practitioner, or if there is a conflict of interest, or change of personal circumstances which makes it impractical for him to continue as liquidator.

A liquidator may otherwise only be removed by order of the Court or by a general meeting of creditors summoned especially for that purpose. He must, however, vacate office if he ceases to be a qualified insolvency practitioner.

A liquidator, other than the Official Receiver, will be released on completion of the winding up on filing a notice that the creditors' final meeting has been held. If the creditors, at that meeting oppose his release it will take effect at such time as the Secretary of State determines (IA section 174).

If the Official Receiver is the liquidator he is released from office on giving notice to:

(a) the Secretary of State that the winding up is complete; or
(b) the Court if he is replaced by another liquidator.

A liquidator may be removed from office by the Court if good cause is shown. Should a receiving order in bankruptcy be made against a liquidator, then he will be removed from office. When the liquidator has completed winding up the company's affairs, he may, after giving notice to every creditor who has proved, and to every contributory, apply to the Department of Trade for a report on his accounts to be prepared. The Department of Trade will consider the report and any objections made by any creditor or contributory, and will either grant or withhold the liquidator's release.

A release relieves the liquidator from liability for any breach of duty committed in the course of the winding up. A release can be revoked if it is shown that it was obtained by fraud or by the concealment of some material fact.

Neither resignation nor removal releases a liquidator from liability, and he must follow a similar procedure in applying to the Department of Trade for his release.

⎯⎯ Dissolution of the company ⎯⎯

When a liquidator (who is not the Official Receiver) notifies the Registrar that the final meeting of creditors has been held *or* the Official Receiver notifies the Registrar that the winding up is complete, the Registrar registers the notice. The company is automatically dissolved three months from the date of the registration of the notice (IA section 205).

24
VOLUNTARY LIQUIDATION

Procedure

A company may resolve to wind up voluntarily. This is the usual method of winding up a company and there are fewer formalities to be complied with than in a compulsory winding up.

A voluntary winding up is initiated by passing one of the three types of resolutions (IA section 84).

An *ordinary resolution* is required if the articles specify that the company shall be wound up after a certain period of time, or on the occurrence of a certain event. Such articles are rarely found in practice, and a company is not automatically dissolved on the occurrence of either of these events. The Court is not bound to make a winding up order in these circumstances.

The company may pass a *special resolution* to wind up voluntarily. No reason need be given for the passing of such a resolution as it is sufficient that a 75 per cent majority at a meeting of the company has resolved upon a winding up. Should the voluntary liquidation be the first step towards an amalgamation or reconstruction of the company, a special resolution is required. Such a resolution can only be challenged on the grounds that it is unfairly prejudicial to the minority, or that it is not in the interests of the members as a whole.

If the company decides that it cannot continue in business by reason of its liabilities, it will pass an *extraordinary resolution* to wind up voluntarily. Usually such a resolution signifies that the company is insolvent. This is not necessarily so, as a company may decide that the payment of its debts will leave it with insufficient working capital to continue in business.

The resolution must be advertised in the *Gazette* within fourteen days of its being passed (IA section 85). A voluntary winding up dates from the passing of the winding up resolution (IA section 86).

There are two kinds of voluntary winding up:

1 members' voluntary winding up;
2 creditors' voluntary winding up.

A members' voluntary winding up

A members' voluntary winding up takes place where the company is solvent. The liquidation will be under the control of the members themselves and they will appoint the liquidator. As the creditors will be paid in full they have no role to play in the winding up.

The first step is for the directors to make and file a declaration of solvency to the effect that they have made a full inquiry into the affairs of the company, and having done so have formed the opinion that the company will be able to pay its debts in full, within a period not exceeding twelve months from the commencement of winding up. This declaration must be made within the five weeks immediately preceding the passing of the winding up resolution, and must include a statement of the company's assets and liabilities. The declaration must be filed with the Registrar within fifteen days of passing the resolution (IA section 89).

At the subsequent extraordinary general meeting, two resolutions are passed: a resolution to wind up; and a resolution to appoint a liquidator. The winding up resolution and the notice of the liquidator's appointment must be advertised in the *Gazette*, and filed with the Registrar (IA section 91).

If in the course of the winding up the liquidator forms the opinion that the company will be unable to pay its debts in full, within the specified time, he must summon a meeting of the creditors. Creditors must be given at least seven days' notice of the meeting which must be advertised in two local newspapers and published in the *Gazette*. The liquidator must lay before the meeting a statement of affairs which contains: Particulars of the company's assets, debts and liabilities. The names and addresses of creditors and any securities held by them (1A section 95).

Summoning the meeting does not convert the winding up into a creditors' voluntary winding up, it merely ensures that the creditors are given information relating to the company's financial position so that they may, if they so wish, petition for a compulsory winding up order. Otherwise the voluntary winding up continues, with the liquidator summoning annual and final meetings of creditors, as in a creditors' voluntary winding up (IA sections 95, 96).

If the winding up continues for more than a year the liquidator must summon a general meeting of the company at the end of the first and each successive year, and lay before it an account of his acts and dealings and the progress of the winding up during the preceding year (IA section 93).

As soon as the company's affairs are fully wound up the liquidator calls a final meeting of the company, which must be advertised in the *Gazette*, and submits his final account. A copy of this account, and a return of the meeting, must be filed with the Registrar within one week before the meeting.

The company is automatically dissolved three months after the registration of the return (IA section 201).

Creditors' voluntary winding up

If the directors are unable to file a declaration of solvency, the winding up proceeds as a creditors' voluntary winding up (IA section 90). In addition to summoning an extraordinary general meeting of the company to pass a resolution for winding up (a minimum of seven days' notice to be given) the company must also summon a meeting of its creditors. The notice of the creditors' meeting must be sent to each creditor at the same time as notices convening a general meeting (IA section 98).

The creditors' meeting must be held either on the same day as the extraordinary general meeting, or on the following day, and will be presided over by one of the directors (1A section 98). The directors must lay before the meeting a full statement of the company's affairs, together with a list of creditors and the estimated amounts of their claims (IA section 99).

At the company's meeting a resolution may be passed to nominate a liquidator. The creditors likewise have the right at their meeting to nominate a liquidator. Should different persons be nominated, the nomination of the creditors will prevail, subject to any order made by the Court. The creditors may also appoint a liquidation committee of up to five persons to act with the liquidator (IA section 101).

The company may then nominate up to five persons to act as members of the committee, but the creditors may disallow the company's nominations, subject to appeal to the Court (IA section 101).

If the winding up continues for more than one year, the liquidator must not only summon a general meeting of the company, but also a meeting of the creditors at the end of the first and each successive year, and lay before the meetings an account of his acts and dealings and the progress of the winding up during the preceding year (IA section 105).

As soon as the company's affairs are fully wound up, the liquidator calls final meetings of the company and creditors and submits his final accounts to both meetings. The meetings are advertised in the *Gazette*. The liquidator sends to the Registrar a copy of the accounts and a return of the meetings within one week after the date of the later meeting (IA section 201).

The company is automatically dissolved at the end of three months from the registration of the return (IA section 201).

The effect of a voluntary winding up

When the company resolves to wind up voluntarily it ceases to carry on its business except in so far as it is necessary for its beneficial winding up (IA section 87). It still retains its corporate personality until it is dissolved. Shares can only be transferred with the sanction of the liquidator and any alteration in the status of the members is void (IA section 88). The employees of the company are dismissed only if the company is insolvent. The powers of the directors cease on the appointment of the liquidator, unless their continuance in office is sanctioned (IA section 91).

The liquidator's duty is to pay the company's debts and adjust the rights of the contributories among themselves.

He applies the company's property, first in paying preferential debts, and then in discharging the company's liabilities *pari passu*. Any surplus will be distributed amongst the members according to their rights.

In order to achieve this he may, without sanction, make calls, settle a list of contributories, summon general meetings and exercise most of the powers of a liquidator in a compulsory winding up.

With the sanction of an extraordinary resolution in a members' voluntary winding up, or the sanction of the Court, liquidation committee or the creditors (if there is no liquidation committee), the liquidator may make any compromise or arrangement with creditors, pay any class of creditors in full, and compromise any calls, debts or liabilities. For example, a compromise could be sanctioned if a contributory was unable to pay the full amount of a call or a debt (IA section 165, Schedule 4).

25
VOLUNTARY ARRANGEMENTS

The Insolvency Act 1985 introduced two new procedures which provide an alternative to company liquidation in circumstances where a company is, or is likely to become, insolvent. These provisions are now to be found in the Insolvency Act 1986.

The two alternatives are:

1. company voluntary arrangements;
2. administration order.

Voluntary arrangements

The Insolvency Act (sections 1–7) provides a relatively simple procedure under which a company, which is insolvent or almost insolvent, enters into a legally binding arrangement with its creditors for:

(a) a composition in satisfaction of its debts, i.e. an agreement to take a proportion of what is due to them; *or*
(b) a scheme of arrangement of its affairs, i.e. a comprise or arrangement.

VOLUNTARY ARRANGEMENTS

The voluntary arrangement must be supervised by a qualified insolvency practitioner who is known as the *nominee* (IA section 1). The initial proposal for a voluntary arrangement may be made by the company's directors, or by an administrator if an administration order is in force, or by a liquidator if the company is being wound up (IA section 1).

If the nominee is not the company's administrator or liquidator he must submit a report to the court, within twenty-eight days of being given notice of the proposals. He must also be given a statement of the company's affairs which contains particulars of its assets, liabilities, creditors and debts (IA section 2).

The report must state:

1 whether, in his opinion, meetings of the company and its creditors should be summoned to consider the proposal; *and*
2 if, in his opinion, such meetings should be summoned and the time, date and place of the meetings (IA section 2).

Where the nominee is the company's liquidator or administrator he may summon meetings of the company and its creditors to consider the proposal and decide whether to approve the proposed voluntary arrangement.

A voluntary arrangement may be approved with or without modifications. Any modification which so alters a proposal so that it is no longer a proposal (within the definition of the Insolvency Act) will not be permitted. The following proposals will not be approved:

(a) those affecting the rights of any secured creditor to enforce his security, without his concurrence; *or*
(b) those affecting the rights of any preferential creditor to be paid otherwise than in priority to non preferential debts, without his concurrence; *or*
(c) those affecting the rights of preferential creditors to be paid *pari passu* with each other, without their concurrence.

After the conclusion of either meeting, the chairman must report the result of the meeting to the Court and to such persons as may be prescribed (IA section 4).

Where both meetings approve the proposed voluntary arrangement either with or without modification, the composition or scheme takes effect as if made by the company at the creditors' meeting and binds every person who had notice of, and was entitled to vote at that meeting, whether he did so or not, as if he were a party to the voluntary arrangement (IA section 5).

If the company is being wound up or an administration order is in force the court may stay all proceedings in the winding up or discharge the administration order. It may also give such directions as it thinks fit to enable the voluntary arrangement to be implemented (IA section 5).

The decision to approve the voluntary arrangement may be challenged by:

- a person entitled to vote at the meeting; *or*
- a liquidator (if the company is being wound up); *or*
- an administrator (if an administration order is in force)

within 28 days on the grounds that it is unfairly prejudicial to the interests of a creditor, member or contributory, or there has been some material irregularity in the conduct of the meeting. The court has wide powers and may revoke or suspend the approval given or it may summon further meetings to consider revised proposals (IA section 6).

Where a voluntary arrangement is approved the person carrying out the functions of the nominee will be known as the supervisor who may be the previous nominee or a substitute for the nominee. He may apply to the Court for directions for the company to be wound up, or for an administration order to be made in relation to it (1A section 7).

A creditor who is dissatisfied with any act, decision or omission of a supervisor may apply to the Court which has overriding powers in relation to the supervisor's acts and may make directions as to his future conduct (IA section 7).

Administration orders

The aim of an administration order is to ensure the rehabilitation and survival of a company as a going concern, or failing that to ensure a more advantageous realisation of a company's assets that would ensue from a winding up.

An administration order is an order directing that, during the period for which the order is in force, the company's affairs, business and property shall be managed by an administrator appointed by the Court (IA section 8).

A court may make an administration order if it is satisfied that a company is, or is likely to become, unable to pay its debts and considers that making an order will achieve one or more of the following purposes:

1. the survival of the company and the whole or any part of its undertaking as a going concern;
2. the approval of a voluntary arrangement under the Insolvency Act;
3. sanctioning a compromise or arrangement between a company, its members and creditors; *and*
4. a more advantageous realisation of the company's assets than would be affected on a winding up (IA section 8).

An application may be made to the Court by petition, by the company, its directors, creditors or any combination of these.

Notice of the presentation of the petition must be given to any person who has appointed, or is entitled to appoint an administrative receiver. The Court must dismiss a petition if it is satisfied that an administrative receiver has been appointed, unless the person who appointed the receiver has consented to the order being made, or the appointment of the receiver could be challenged on the grounds of transactions at an undervalue, preferences or the avoidance of a floating charge (IA section 9).

During the time between the presentation of the petition and making the order (or dismissing the petition):

(a) no resolution may be passed or order made for winding up the company;
(b) no steps may be taken to enforce any security over the company's property (other than by appointing an administrative receiver) or repossess goods under the company's possession without the court's leave; *and*
(c) no other proceedings may be commenced or continued and no distress levied against the company or its property without the court's leave (IA section 10).

The Court may dismiss the petition, adjourn the hearing conditionally or unconditionally, or make an interim order, or any other order that it thinks fit.

A holder of a floating charge who has not yet appointed a receiver may nevertheless prevent an administration order from being made by appointing a receiver before the Court arrives at a decision on the petition.

Effect of the Order

On making an order:

1. any petition for winding up the company must be dismissed;
2. any administrative receiver of the company must vacate office;
3. any receiver of part of the company's property must vacate office if required to do so by the administrator.

During the time the order is in force:

(a) no resolution may be passed, or order made, for winding up the company;
(b) no administrative receiver may be appointed;
(c) no steps may be taken to enforce any security over the company's property or repossess goods under a hire-purchase agreement, without the administrator's consent or leave of the court;
(d) no proceedings, execution, or other legal process may be commenced or continued, or distress levied, against the company or its property without the consent of the administrator or leave of the court;
(e) every invoice, order for goods of business letter issued on the company's behalf or the administrator must state the name of the administrator and the fact that the company is subject to an administration order (IA sections 11, 12).

Powers of an administrator

He may do all such things as are necessary to manage the company's affairs, business and property.

The following powers are listed in Schedule 1 of the Insolvency Act. He may:

(a) take possession of the company's property;
(b) raise or borrow money and grant security over the company's property;

VOLUNTARY ARRANGEMENTS

- *(c)* sell or dispose of the company's property;
- *(d)* carry on the company's business;
- *(e)* bring or defend any action or other legal proceedings in the company's name and on its behalf;
- *(f)* refer questions relating to the company to arbitration;
- *(g)* appoint a solicitor or accountant or other professionally qualified person to assist him in the performance of his functions. He may also appoint an agent to conduct any business which he is unable to do himself or which is more conveniently done by an agent;
- *(h)* effect insurances in respect of the company's business and property.
- *(j)* establish subsidiaries and transfer to subsidiaries the whole or any part of the company's property;
- *(k)* grant or accept a surrender of a lease or tenancy of the company's property and take a lease or tenancy of any property required or convenient for the company's business;
- *(l)* execute any deed receipt or document in the company's name and on its behalf;
- *(m)* draw, accept, make and endorse any bill of exchange or promissory note in the company's name and on its behalf;
- *(n)* use the company's seal;
- *(o)* name any payment necessary to the performance of his functions;
- *(p)* do all such things (including carrying out works) as are necessary to realise the company's property;
- *(q)* make any arrangement or compromise on the company's behalf;
- *(r)* call up any of the company's uncalled capital;
- *(s)* rank and claim in the bankruptcy, insolvency or liquidation or any person indebted to the company;
- *(t)* present or defend a petition for the winding up of the company;
- *(u)* change the situation of the company's registered office;
- *(v)* employ and dismiss employees;
- *(w)* do all other things incidental to the exercise of all the powers listed above;
- *(x)* remove and appoint directors (IA section 14);
- *(y)* call a meeting of creditors or members (IA section 14);
- *(z)* apply to the court for directions relating to any particular matter connected with his administration (IA section 14);
- (i) without the court's permission, to deal with and dispose of prop-

erty of the company which is subject to a floating charge as it if were not subject to a charge (IA section 14).

(ii) to dispose of, with the court's permission, any property subject to a charge, or goods subject to a hire-purchase agreement, as if the property were not subject to the charge and the owner's rights under the hire-purchase agreement were vested in the company. The court must be satisfied that the disposal would be likely to promote the purposes set out in the administration order (IA section 15).

Duties of an administrator

1. On his appointment he must take into his custody all the property to which the company is entitled (1A section 17).
2. He must manage the affairs, business and property of the company (1A section 17).
3. He must publish a notice of the administration order and send it to the company, the creditors (within twenty-eight days) and the Registrar (within fourteen days) (1A section 21).
4. He must require a statement of the company's affairs to be submitted to him. This must be submitted by the company within twenty-one days of the administrator's appointment. It must show particulars of the company's assets, debts and liabilities, the creditors and any securities held by them. This must be submitted by present or past officers of the company, any person who took part in the company's formation in the previous twelve months, present or past employees (within the previous twelve months), any officer or employee of a company, who in the previous twelve months was an officer of the company (1A section 22).
5. Within three months of making the administration order the administrator must send to the members, the creditors and the Registrar a statement of his proposals for the company (1A section 23).
6. He must then summon a meeting of creditors, on giving fourteen days notice, to consider the proposals. The creditors at the meeting may approve the proposals or approve the proposals with modifications, but only with the administrator's consent (1A section 24).
7. The administrator must then send a report of the meeting to the Court and to the Registrar. If the meeting refuses to approve the

administrator's proposals the Court may discharge the administration order or adjourn the hearing, and make any other order that it think fit (1A section 24).

A creditors' meeting which has approved an administrator's proposals may, if it wishes, establish a committee of creditors. It may, on giving not less than seven days notice, require the administrator to attend before it at any reasonable time and provide it with such information relating to the carrying out of its functions as it may reasonably require (IA section 26).

A creditor or a member of the company may petition the court for an order on the grounds that;

(a) the company's affairs, business and property are managed or have been managed by the administration in a manner which is unfairly prejudicial to the interests of the creditors or members; or

(b) an actual or proposed act of the administrator is, or would be, prejudicial.

On receipt of the petition the court may make an order as it thinks fit for giving relief, or adjourn the hearing conditionally or unconditionally, or make an interim order. In particular the order may:

- regulate the future management by the administrator of the company's affairs, business and property;
- require the administrator to do, or refrain from doing, an act or summoning a meeting of creditors or members to consider certain matters;
- discharge the administration order.

A court order must not prejudice or prevent any composition or scheme approved by the committee of creditors, or any compromise or arrangement from being implemented. An application for an order must be initiated within twenty-eight days of the meeting at which the approval of the creditors was given (IA section 27).

Discharge or variation of the order

An administrator may at any time apply to the court for an administration order to be discharged or varied in order to specify an additional purpose:

(a) if it appears that the purposes specified in the order have been achieved; or
(b) are incapable of being achieved; or
(c) if he is required to do so by a meeting of the creditors.

On hearing the application the Court may order the administration order to be discharged, adjourn the hearing conditionally or unconditionally, make an interim order, or make any order it thinks fit. If the order is discharged or varied, the administrator must within fourteen days, send a copy of the order to the Registrar.

Vacation of office

1 An administrator may be removed from office by order of the Court.
2 He may in certain prescribed circumstances resign his office by giving notice of his resignation to the Court.
3 He must vacate his office: if the administration order is discharged; *or* if he is no longer qualified to act as an insolvency practitioner.

On ceasing to hold office his remuneration and expenses are deemed to be a preferential charge over the company's property which was in his custody at the time he ceased to hold office, as are any sums payable in respect of debts or liabilities in respect of contracts entered into or contracts of employment adopted by him, while he was administrator (IA section 19).

A person who has ceased to be administrator has his release from the following time:

(a) a person who has died, from the time notice is given to the Court;
(b) in other cases, from such time as the Court may determine (IA section 20).

26
THE RECONSTRUCTION AND AMALGAMATION OF COMPANIES

These are commercial terms, which are widely used, but are not given any legal definition in the Act. The term 'reconstruction' is used to describe a scheme which involves the re-organisation of a company's capital structure. It is also used to describe a scheme in which a company transfers its whole undertaking and property to a newly formed company, in exchange for shares in that company.

An amalgamation occurs when the undertakings of two or more companies are brought under single control.

A reconstruction or an amalgamation, as the case may be, may be achieved in one of four ways: by sale under the memorandum, by reconstruction under IA section 110 by scheme of arrangement or by takeover.

Sale under the memorandum

A company may sell the whole of its undertaking and property to a new company in return for shares in that company. Although a company has no implied power to dispose of its undertaking in this way, most companies reserve such a power in their objects clause. A company may decide upon this course of action when it does not require further capital from its shareholders. It can be used if no arrangement or composition is to be made with the company's shareholders, creditors, or debenture holders.

The old company sells its undertaking to the new company in exchange for shares in the new company. The old company is then wound up. The shares in the new company are distributed amongst the members of the old company, in accordance with their rights. If a member dissents he obtains the same protection as a member is given under IA section 110.

In this way it is possible to extend the objects, reduce capital, obtain new capital and perform other operations which might otherwise be difficult to accomplish.

Reconstruction under IA section 110

IA section 110 gives a company the power to effect a reconstruction by means of a voluntary liquidation. If a company is not already in liquidation, it will circulate details of the scheme to its members, convene a general meeting, pass the necessary resolutions to wind up, and appoint a liquidator.

If the company is in liquidation, the procedure laid down by the section can be carried out at any time. Should the liquidation be a creditors' voluntary winding up, the liquidator must also obtain the Court's sanction, or that of the committee of inspection to a reconstruction.

The liquidator will invariably seek the Court's approval in a members' voluntary winding up, for without its approval the special resolution for the sale of the company's assets will be void, if a winding up order or supervision order is made within a year of passing the resolution.

This form of reconstruction is often used when a company requires further capital from its existing shareholders. The liquidator transfers the whole of the old company's undertaking to a new company for shares in the new company, credited as partly paid. The shares of the new company are distributed to the members of the old company *pro rata* to their holdings. The amount unpaid on the new shares is then called up to provide the additional capital. As the shareholders have the right to refuse or dissent, it is usual to arrange the underwriting of the new capital.

It has also been used for altering a company's objects. A company may wish to extend its activities, but finds that the alteration of its objects clause would not be permitted under section 4. It may form a new company with the desired objects, and by proceeding under IA section 110, transfer its undertaking to the new company.

IA section 110 is also an effective method of varying shareholders' rights, where these are set out in the memorandum and are stated to be unalterable.

An amalgamation can be conveniently achieved under IA section 110. An existing company can sell the whole of its undertaking to another company. The shareholders of the first company become shareholders of the second company. The business and property of both companies become amalgamated into one company.

An amalgamation of two or more companies may be effected by transferring their undertakings to a new company formed for the purpose. The new company issues shares credited as fully paid to the shareholders of the old companies, in exchange for their shares. The old companies are dissolved and the new company usually assumes the name of one of the old companies to complete the amalgamation.

Rights of dissenting shareholders

A member who is opposed to the scheme may express his dissent by serving written notice on the liquidator at the company's registered office within seven days, requiring him either to refrain from proceeding with the scheme or to purchase his shares. As the liquidator is bound to carry out the resolution, he must purchase the shares. The purchase money must be paid before the company is dissolved. This provision only applies to a shareholder who did not vote in favour of the scheme (IA section 111).

If the parties agree on the purchase price the shares will be purchased at that price. Should they be unable to agree, the matter will be referred to arbitration. In determining the purchase price, regard must be had to the value of the shares before the reconstruction. Any increase in value as a result of the reconstruction should be disregarded. The purchase money must be paid to the member before the company is dissolved.

A shareholder who has not dissented, or required the liquidator to purchase his shares, may not wish to become a shareholder in the new company. He cannot be compelled to do so. Should he refuse to become a member, he will not be entitled to compensation and he may lose all rights to his shares. The scheme usually provides that the liquidator may sell the shares of such a member and the amount received for the shares will be paid to the member.

A company may not deprive a member of his right to dissent. In *Payne v. Cork Co. Ltd*, the articles of a company provided that a dissenting shareholder should not have the power to require the liquidator to purchase his shares. It was held that such an article was void.

Rights of creditors

The sale of the old company's assets by the liquidator is binding on the creditors. The transfer agreement will usually provide that the new company will take over the old company's debts, or that the old company will retain sufficient funds to cover its debts. If a creditor accepts the liability of the new company for his debts there is a novation – a substitution of a new debtor for an old debtor – and his claim against the old company will cease.

A company will pay off a creditor who is unwilling to accept a novation, as a dissatisfied creditor may within a year petition the Court for a compulsory winding up order. If such an order is made, any arrangement under IA section 110 is invalid until approved by the Court.

Scheme of arrangement

The third method of achieving a reconstruction or amalgamation is by a scheme of arrangement under sections 425. This section facilitates compromises or arrangements between a company and its creditors, or between a company and its members, or both its creditors and members. It requires the approval of a specified majority of creditors and/or members and the sanction of the Court.

It can be used whether the company is a going concern or is being wound up, and unlike IA section 110 the company need not be wound up to carry out any scheme of arrangement. It has an advantage over IA section 110, in that the decision of a specified majority will overrule the minority, unless the Court rules otherwise. It will not be necessary to purchase the interests of any shareholder or creditor who dissents from the scheme.

It has been used for a wide variety of schemes involving compromises or arrangements with creditors. Creditors and debenture holders have accepted shares in discharge of their debts; other creditors have accepted part shares and part cash in lieu of their debts; secured creditors have given up their security or agreed to the creation of prior charges; debenture holders have agreed to forego their interest for a stated period.

It has also been used to vary the rights of members. Preference shareholders have agreed to the cancellation of arrears of dividend and a reduction in the fixed rate of dividend. Ordinary shareholders have agreed to surrender part of their holdings to preference shareholders, who in turn have agreed to accept ordinary shares in lieu of arrears of dividend.

Other schemes sanctioned by the Court under section 425 have involved the re-organisation of the capital structures of companies. These have included the reduction of a company's share capital and the cancellation of deferred shares carrying a high rate of dividend. Amalgamations involving the re-organisation of the capital structures of the companies involved have also been approved by the Court.

It has been used to alter the class rights of shares where the rights were conferred by the memorandum which made no provision for any variation of class rights.

As the scheme requires the Court's approval the first step is to ask the Court to convene the necessary meetings of the parties affected by the scheme. The application is usually made by the company or its liquidator, but it can be made by any member or creditor (section 425).

Notices of the meetings are sent out to the members and creditors explaining the effect of the proposed scheme and in particular how it would affect the interests of the directors. If the scheme involves a compromise with the debenture holders, it must show its effect on the interests of the trustees for debenture holders (section 426).

If only a certain class of members or creditors is affected, meetings need only be summoned for that particular class; for example, if the rights of ordinary shareholders are to be altered but not those of preference shareholders, only class meetings of ordinary shareholders need be summoned. There are three classes of creditors – secured, unsecured and preferential – and each class must be dealt with separately. The holders of shares paid in advance are a different class from ordinary shareholders. If there are persons who belong to different classes, they may attend and vote at meetings of each class in which they have an interest.

The various meetings are then held. Voting is by poll, and three quarters in value of the creditors or class of creditors, or members or class of members, present in person or by proxy, must sanction the scheme (section 425). This is to prevent a majority of members or creditors with a minor interest in the company out-voting a minority with a large stake in the company.

The scheme is then submitted to the Court for its approval. Before the Court grants its approval it must be satisfied that the necessary statutory requirements have been complied with: that the requisite majority of members and/or creditors have given their approval at the necessary meeting or meetings; that the meetings fairly represented the class interest and that the scheme is one which a prudent businessman would approve (section 425).

When the Court has approved the scheme it binds all the parties concerned. The order sanctioning the scheme is not effective until a copy has been registered with the Registrar. A copy of the order must be attached to every copy of the memorandum subsequently issued (section 425).

Where, as part of a scheme, the whole or part of the undertaking of a company (the transferor company) is to be transferred to another company (the transferee company) the Court may make an order for all or any of the following matters.

1 The transfer of the property or liabilities of the transferor company to the transferee company;
2 The allotment of shares and debentures;
3 The continuation of any legal proceedings by or against the transfer company to be brought in the name of the transferee company;
4 The dissolution, without winding up of the transferor company;
5 Provision for dissentients similar to that provided under IA section 110.

Takeovers

The fourth method of achieving an amalgamation is to acquire sufficient shares in another company so as to exercise control over that company. This can be effected by purchasing all the shares of the other company or sufficient shares to acquire a majority of the voting power.

The number and classes of shares to be acquired will vary according to the degree of control which the acquiring company seeks. It may desire total ownership, or it may require sufficient control to be able to pass extraordinary or special resolutions. In some cases the acquiring company may be satisfied with a degree of control which allows it to pass ordinary resolutions. This will enable it to secure the appointment of the directors of its choice (section 427).

The voting rights of the different classes of shares is another factor to be considered. If the preference shares do not carry votes, or only have voting powers when their dividend is in arrears, a company may regard it as sufficient to acquire control of the ordinary shares.

A takeover bid is an obvious way of merging two or more companies which are similar or complementary businesses. A takeover offer is an offer to acquire all the shares or class of shares in a company (other than shares already held by the offeror) on the same terms at the date of the offer (section 428). There are a variety of factors which may prompt a takeover bid.

The object of the bid may be to secure a particular asset, or to acquire an asset and use it more profitably, as in the Savoy Hotel case where the object of the bid was to acquire a hotel and convert it into offices.

The transferee company may wish to diversify its interests. In recent times many large companies have sought to stimulate growth by expanding into other fields.

The transferor company may have pursued a conservative dividend policy, or it may not have revalued its fixed assets. Consequently its shares are quoted at a price which is well below the actual or potential value of the business.

The transferee company may feel that the management of the transferor company is ineffective or inefficient.

Any one of these factors or a combination of them would make a company an attractive target for a takeover bid.

There are various ways in which the transferee company may acquire the shares necessary to give it the degree of control it seeks. It may be possible to purchase the shares on the open market, or (if there is agreement on the merger between the two companies) the shares may be acquired by negotiation with the principal shareholders, or by arrrangement between the boards of directors of both companies. The usual method is to make a public offer to the shareholders to buy their shareholding for a combination of cash, debentures or shares in the transferee company.

There is often resistance to a takeover bid from the directors of the transferor company, who may not wish to relinquish control of the company, or who believe that the offer is totally inadequate.

The offer is usually stated to be open for acceptance for a fixed time and is made conditional on acceptance by the holders of a specified percentage of shares. Once a shareholder has accepted he is bound to sell the shares, but the transferee company is not bound to purchase the shares unless the conditions in the offer have been fulfilled (i.e. the acceptance of a given percentage of the shares in question).

The consideration offered to the shareholders of the transferor company may be cash, or an allotment of shares or debentures in the transferee company or one of its associated companies. If a cash offer is made, the price offered will be in excess of the current quoted price of the share, so as to induce the shareholders to accept the bid, rather than sell their shares on the market. The same consideration will apply to an offer of an allotment of new shares or debentures, with or without cash.

If debentures are offered as new securities, they will ensure a fixed income and grant greater security, but the holder will have no right to vote at general meetings or to share in any future in the value of the ordinary shares. Companies often offer convertible debentures as an inducement.

Sections 428–430

The interests of the majority and minority are protected by these sections. This provides that where the holders of 90 per cent of the shares involved have within four months accepted the scheme, the transferee

RECONSTRUCTION AND AMALGAMATION

company may, within two months, give notice to any dissenting shareholder that it wishes to acquire his shares. In calculating the 90 per cent threshold the following shares may not be included:

- Shares already held by the offeror;
- shares which the offeror has contracted to acquire;
- shares held by an associate e.g. a nominee, a holding company; *and*
- shares which an associate has contracted to acquire.

Shares acquired by the offeror during the offer period (e.g. purchases in the market) may be included in the calculation, as long as the price paid for the shares does not exceed the price offered in the takeover offer (section 428). The company is then bound to acquire the shares on the same terms as those given to approving shareholders, unless the dissenting shareholder applies to the Court within six weeks for an order to prevent the compulsory acquisition or specifying different acquisition terms. There can be no compulsory acquisition until the application has been dealt with by the Court.

Six weeks after issue of the notice the offeror sends a copy of the notice to the offeree company and pays to it, or transfers to it, the consideration due for the shares, together with an instrument of transfer executed on the shareholder's behalf by a person appointed by the offeror. The offeree company must then register the offeror as the owner of the shares. The money received by the offeree company must be transferred to a separate bank account, and held on trust for the dissenting shareholders (section 430).

If an offeror has failed to reach the 90 per cent threshold because he has been unable to trace one or more shareholders, he may apply to the court for a notice of compulsory purchase, if the total number of acceptances, plus the untraced shareholders, add up to 90 per cent of the total. The consideration must also be fair and reasonable. The court will only make an order if it considers it just and equitable having regard to the number of known shareholders who have rejected the offer (section 730c).

The Court rarely intervenes to prevent the compulsory acquisition of shares but did so in the case of *Re Bugle Press* where two shareholders held 90 per cent of the issued shares in a private company. They offered to buy the third shareholder's 10 per cent shareholding for £14.50 per share, but he refused their offer. They then formed a new company in which they held all the issued share capital and this new company offered to buy the first company's shares for £10 each. The two shareholders accepted the offer and the second company sought to acquire the third shareholder's shares under section 209 (now section 430). It was held that this was an abuse of the section as the transferee company was the same as the majority in the transferor company. For such a compulsory purchase to be approved it would have to be shown to be fair. Having already offered far more for the shares on the first occasion, it was impossible to justify such action.

The power to compulsorily acquire shares is a useful provision that allows the transferee company to avoid the management and administrative problems which can occur where subsidiary companies are not wholly owned.

Section 430 can be invoked by a dissenting shareholder in the situation where the transferee company has acquired nine tenths of the shares in the transferor company, and has not chosen to acquire his shares compulsorily. Within one month of the transferee company acquiring nine tenths of the transferor company's shares it must notify the fact to the dissenting shareholders. Any dissenting shareholder may then require the transferee company to purchase his shares on the terms of the offer, or on such other terms as may be agreed, or as the Court on either party's application may agree. The dissenting shareholder must be given at least three months from the end of the offer period to decide whether he wishes to be bought out.

27
MERGERS AND THE CITY CODE

Mergers

Under the Fair Trading Act 1973, as amended by the Competition Act 1980, the Secretary of State may refer large scale mergers and proposed mergers to the Monopolies and Mergers Commission for their consideration. The Commission will investigate the facts and if they consider that a merger operates or would operate against the public interest, the Secretary of State has the power to terminate or prevent the merger. The Fair Trading Act allows the Secretary of State to make a reference to the Commission in anticipation of a merger. Secretaries of State have preferred to use this power, as it is far easier to prevent a proposed merger, than to terminate an already completed merger. In the case of a referral of an existing merger the Secretary of State must refer it within six months of it taking place.

Notification of a proposed merger may be given to the Director General of Fair Trading. If no objection is raised within twenty-eight days of giving notice, the merger is given an automatic clearance and cannot be subsequently referred to the Monopolies and Mergers Commission. The twenty-eight day period may be extended by the Director General or the Secretary of State.

The Secretary of State may accept undertakings to direct part of a merged business as an alternative to making a reference to the Monopolies and Mergers Commission.

A merger arises when two or more enterprises of which one at least is carried on in the United Kingdom or by or under the control of a body corporate in the United Kingdom, have ceased to be distinct enterprises either by being brought under common ownership or control, or by one of them ceasing to function as a result of an arrangement to prevent competition between them.

The Fair Trading Act is concerned only with mergers which are of economic significance. The Secretary of State may refer a merger only if either the value of the assets taken over exceeds £30 000 000, or it produces a situation in which at least a quarter of all the goods or services of a particular description supplied in the United Kingdom, or a substantial part of the United Kingdom, will be supplied by or to the same person.

When a merger is referred to the Commission it must satisfy itself that the merger falls within the scope of the Act (i.e. the £30 000 000 assets or one-quarter market share) and it must decide whether the merger or proposed merger will operate against the public interest.

The parties to a merger may not acquire shares during the merger reference period without the consent of the Secretary of State.

The Commission must take into account all matters which appear to them to be relevant, including the maintenance and promotion of effective competition in the United Kingdom, the protection of consumers with regards to goods and services, the reduction of costs by development and competition, the maintenance of a balanced industry and employment in the United Kingdom and the maintenance of a competitive market outside the United Kingdom.

The Commission in its report must give its conclusions on the matters raised in the reference, with reasons, and must also give a survey of the background to the merger. Any effects not in the public interest must be specified, together with any recommendations for remedying such effects. If the report states that there is nothing against the public interest, the merger will proceed. If there is an adverse report there are various courses open to the Secretary of State. He may request the Director General of Fair Trading to consult the parties, with a view to obtaining certain undertakings from them to remedy the harmful effects of the merger indicated in the report. If this proves impossible, the Secretary of State has wide powers which include the prevention of a proposed merger, the cancellation of an existing merger, or allowing the merger to proceed but subjecting the new enterprise to various regulations.

A person who provides false or misleading information to the Secretary of State, the Director General or the Monopolies and Mergers Commission in respect of a proposed merger is guilty of a criminal offence and may be subject to a fine and/or imprisonment.

European Community law does not expressly provide for a system of merger control, although the aim of the third directive is the coordination of provisions regulating internal mergers within a member state. The Commission and the European Court of Justice have taken the view that Article 86 of the EC Treaty can be applied, in certain circumstances, to a merger situation. Article 86 prohibits any abuse by one or more undertakings of a dominant position within the Common Market, or a substantial part of it, if this would affect trade between member states. The article contains four examples of abuse, but none of them refers to mergers.

The European Court applied Article 96 to a merger situation in *Europemballage Corp. and Continental Can Co. Inc. v. EC Commission*. An American company, through a subsidiary, obtained control of a German company which had a share of the German market in metal tins and containers. Two years later it obtained control of a Dutch company which was the largest manufacturer of metal containers in the Benelux countries. The Commission contended that the control of the German company gave the American company a dominant position in the German market. As this was a 'substantial part of the common market' within the meaning of Article 86, its subsequent acquisition of the Dutch company was an abuse of its dominant position, as it would eliminate possible future competition between the two companies and would in this way affect trade between member states. The European Court upheld the Commission's interpretation of Article 86, but allowed the company's appeal on the grounds that the Commission had not adequately analysed the product market. The merger was allowed to proceed.

The application of Article 86 to a merger situation has led to certain problems. So far Article 86 has only been applied to a merger situation where one of the parties has been in a dominant position before the merger, and as a result of the merger find themselves in a dominant situation. There are no provisions for allowing the Commission to hold up a merger pending investigation, or for submitting a proposed merger to the Commission for its consideration. Neither is there machinery for granting exemption on the grounds of efficiency or any grounds of public interest.

The City Code on takeovers and mergers

The Companies Act makes no special provision as to the conduct of a takeover bid. This deficiency has largely been made good by the City Code on takeovers and mergers. It has no legal sanction, but is voluntarily observed by stockbrokers and merchant banks who are involved in takeover transactions. The Code is administered by the Takeover Panel which has its own permanent secretariat. Companies or individuals who act in breach of the Code face a private reprimand or public censure and in the most serious cases, withdrawal of Stock Exchange facilities. The Panel may refer certain aspects of a case to the Department of Trade or the Stock Exchange or to any other appropriate body.

The provisions of the Code are divided into two parts: the general principles and the rules.

The general principles

The general principles are concerned with the conduct to be observed in takeover and merger situations. The Code emphasises that the spirit as well as the precise wording of the general principles and rules must be observed.

Some of the most important general principles include the following.

All shareholders of the same class of an offeree company (the company whose shares are the object of a bid or offer) must be treated similarly by the offeror company (the company making the bid or offer).

During the course of an offer, or when an offer is in contemplation, any information must be furnished to all shareholders.

The directors of the offeree company must not, without the approval of the company in general meeting, take any action which could frustrate a genuine takeover bid which is imminent or which has been made. All shareholders must be given adequate information, advice, and sufficient time to allow them to reach a properly informed decision.

Both parties must make every effort to prevent the creation of a false market in their securities. All documents issued in connection with the takeover bid should be drafted with the same degree of care as if they were a prospectus under the Companies Act.

The directors of both the offeror and the offeree company must act in the best interests of the shareholders, creditors and employees. Their actions should not be motivated by self or family interest. The offeror should only announce an offer after careful and responsible consideration, and only if he has every reason to believe that he can implement the offer.

The rules

There are thirty-eight rules dealing with the standards of conduct required from the parties, and the procedures to be followed in the course of a takeover or merger.

The rules are wide ranging and flexible and are designed to deal with the variety of problems and situations which may arise in the course of a takeover or merger. This can be seen from a sample of the following rules.

An offer should first be made known to the board of directors of the offeree company or its advisers. If the offer is made by an intermediary, the identity of the bidder must be stated. The board of directors of the offeree company is entitled to be satisfied that in the event of the bid being successful, the offeror will be in a position to implement the offer in full.

In the case of a firm offer, the directors must immediately publish a press notice and circularise its shareholders informing them of the bid.

An announcement that talks are taking place and a request to the Stock Exchange to grant a temporary halt in dealings is normally expected when negotiations have reached an advanced stage, or negotiations are about to take place in which a wider circle of individuals will be consulted. If, however, there is an 'untoward movement' in either company's shares, indicating a possible leak of information, an announcement must be released at once.

The Panel's consent is required for any partial offer; that is, an offer to purchase part only of the shareholding not already acquired by the offeror. In the case of a bid which would result in the offeror controlling less than 30 per cent of the voting rights, consent will normally be given. If a bid would result in a holding of 30 per cent, but less than 100 per cent of the voting rights, consent will not normally be given if the offeror or persons acting in concert have acquired shares of the offeree company in the previous twelve months.

An offer which would result in an offeror holding between 30 per cent and 50 per cent of a company's voting rights, will normally be conditional on its approval by holders of over 50 per cent of the voting rights not held by the offeror. (As many shareholders do not bother to vote at the meetings, a 30 per cent holding of the voting rights in a public company is regarded as effective control of that company.)

A person acquiring a 30 per cent control of a company's voting rights must, within 12 months, make an offer for the remainder of the shares. A similar offer must be made if a person, in concert with another, already holding between 30 per cent and 50 per cent of a company's voting rights, acquires further shares (in a twelve month period). The price offered must represent the highest price paid, in the previous twelve months, by the offeror company for shares in the offeree company. The offer must be conditional upon the offeror obtaining sufficient acceptances to bring his holding to more than 50 per cent of the voting rights.

An offer must remain open for acceptance for at least twenty-one days. If it is revised, for example by offering an increased price, it must be kept open for a further fourteen days.

An offer, whether revised or not, may not be extended beyond the 60th day after the initial posting of the offer, unless it has previously become or been declared unconditional as to acceptance. An announcement must be made by 5pm on the 60th day, as to whether the offer is unconditional as to acceptance, or has lapsed.

An offer document must show the present shareholding of the offeror company in the offeree company and also the shares owned or controlled by the directors of the offeror company in the offeree company.

A circular by the offeree company recommending acceptance or rejection of the bid must also give the shareholdings of its directors in the offeror company and in the offeree company, and must state whether such directors intend to accept the bid in respect of their holdings. The circular must also give details of the directors' service contracts and must indicate the effect of a successful bid on their emoluments.

Any person in possession of price-sensitive information regarding an offer or contemplated offer, must treat the information as confidential. No such person (except the offeror) may deal in the securities of the offeree company between the time when there is reason to suppose that an approach or offer is contemplated, and the announcement of the approach or offer or of the termination of the discussions. No such dealings may take place in the securities of the offeror company except where the proposed offer is not regarded as price-sensitive in relation to its securities.

During the offer period all the parties to a takeover or merger transaction are entitled to deal in these securities, subject to daily disclosure to the Stock Exchange, the Panel and the press.

When a company, in the course of a takeover, publishes profit forecasts, the basis of the forecast must be stated and the accounting policies and calculations for the forecast must be examined and reported on by the auditors or the consultant accountants. The basis of any valuation of assets must be given and these must have been valued by an independent valuer.

As can be seen the main object of the City Code is to secure fair and equal treatment for all shareholders when a takeover or merger is proposed, and to ensure adequate disclosure of information to all interested parties.

INDEX

Accounts 217
   accounting records 218
   accounting reference periods 219
   auditors' report 233
   balance sheet 220
   directors report 234
   group 229
   profit and loss account 225
   revision of 219
Accounting classification of companies 41
Administration order 274
   discharge of 279
   effect of 276
Administrator 275
   duties 278
   powers 276
   vacation of office 280
Allotment of shares 113
Amalgamations *see* Reconstructions and amalgamations
Annual general meeting 134
Annual return 97

Articles of association 57
   alteration of 59
   contents of 58
   form of 57
   legal effects of 60
   Table A application of 57
Association clause 55
Auditors 236
   appointment of 236
   duties of 238
   liability of 242
   qualifications of 237
   removal of 243
   remuneration of 244
   report of 233
   resignation of 243
   vacation of office by 243
   valuation of shares by 240

Balance sheet 220
Bubble Act 15
Board meetings 156
Bonus shares 115
Borrowing powers 199

Borrowing powers – *cont.*
  rule in *Royal British Bank v.
    Turquand* 200
  securities offered 202
Brokerage 78

Calls on shares 124
Capital *see* Share capital
Capital redemption reserve fund
  102, 131
Capitalisation of profits 115
Certificate of incorporation 24
Charges
  fixed 206
  floating 206
  register of 49, 208
Chartered companies 33
Charters of incorporation 13
City Code 294
  general principles 295
  rules 295
Class rights, variation of 108
Commencement of business 24
Community law 19
  directives 19, 20
  regulations 19, 20
Companies
  chartered 33
  classification of 33
  contrasted with partnerships
    31
  defunct 247
  dormant 235
  European 21
  formation of 23
  limited by guarantee 35
  limited by shares 37
  medium sized 38
  membership of 87

  oversea 40
  partnership 41
  private 37
  public 37
  registered 34
  small 41
  subsidiary 28
  statutory 34
  unlimited 36
Companies Acts
  1862 17
  1908 17
  1929 17
  1948 17
  1967 17
  1976 17
  1980 18
  1981 18
  1985 18
  1989 19
Compulsory liquidation 247
  striking off the register 247
  winding up by the Court 249
Compulsory purchase of shares
  pre-emption rights 120
  takeover, in 289
Consequences of incorporation
  25
Contracts
  allotment 113
  directors' 175
  pre-incorporation 66
  ultrá vires 53
Contributories
  compulsory winding up 250
  voluntary winding up 270
Corporation 25
Creditors in winding up 263
  preferential 264

INDEX

secured 263
unsecured 264
voluntary winding up 269

Debenture holders
  receiver, appointments by 213
  register of 3
  remedies of 212
Debentures 203
  bearer 205
  definition of 203
  fixed charge 206
  floating charge 206
  issue of 204
  irredeemable 205
  late registration 209
  perpetual 205
  redeemable 208
  registered 205
  registration of 208
  secured 205
  trust deed 210
  unsecured 206
Declaration of solvency 268
Deeds of settlement 16
Deferred shares 100
Defunct company 247
Department of Trade
  investigations by 194
  petitioners, as 251
Directives 19, 20
Directors
  agents, as 169
  alternate 153
  appointment of 153
  assignment of office 154
  board meetings 156
  compensation for loss of office 162
  contracts of, with company 175
  dealings in options by 180
  degree of skill 171
  disclosure of business interests 175
  disqualification of 154
  duties of 165
  duties owed to employees by 169
  employees as 170
  interests in shares 182
  loans to 178
  managing 158
  number of 152
  powers of management of 156
  proceedings of 152
  qualification shares 155
  remedies against 173
  remuneration of 159
  report of 234
  service contracts of 180
  shadow 152
  substantial property transactions by 177
  trustees, as 167
  vacation of office 161
Disclaimer 262
Dissolution of a company 266, 269, 270
Distribution of assets by receiver 215
Dividends 129
  declaration of 130
  interim 130
  payment of 129
  profits available for 131
  reserve fund 130
  restrictions on distribution 131
Dormant company 235

Early dissolution of company 249
Elective resolution 148
Employee share scheme 89
Emergence of company legislation 13, 14
Estoppel 117, 118
Extortionate credit transaction 259
Extraordinary general meeting 135
Extraordinary resolution 146
European Company 21
European Court 20, 293

Financial assistance for purchase of shares 89
Fixed charge 206
Floating charge 206
Forfeiture of shares 127
Forged transfer of shares 117
Formation of a company 23
Foss v. Harbottle, rule in 187
Founders' shares 100
Fraudulent trading 260

General meeting 133
Gratuitous payments 52
Group accounts 229
Group, small 42
Guarantee, company limited by 35
Group, medium-sized 42

History of companies 13
Holding company 28

Incorporation
　consequences of 25
　certificate of 24
　veil of 27
Increase of capital 103

Insider dealing 183
Interim dividend 130
Investigation by Department of Trade 194
　company's affairs 194
　company's books and papers 197
　directors' share dealings and interests in shares 197
　ownership of a company 196

Joint stock company 14
Joint Stock Companies Acts 16

Legal personality of company 25
Liability for false statements in prospectus 79
　civil 79
　compensation 82
　criminal 86
　damages 79–82
　deceit 81
　misrepresentation 80
　negligence 85
　rescission 80
Lien of company over shares 128
Limitation of liability 54
Limited liability clause 54
Liquidation committee 256
Liquidator 256
　provisional 253

Majority rule 186
Manager
　appointment of 214, 254
　receiver and 214
Medium sized companies 42
Meetings 133
　adjournment of 144
　annual general 134

chairman at 139
class 136
extraordinary general 135
general 133
minutes of 151
notice of 136
poll at 141
proxies at 143
quorum 138
resolutions at 144
voting at 141
Membership of a company 87
bankrupts 91
companies 88
joint holders 91
lenders 92
method of acquiring 87
minors 91
personal representatives 92
register of interest in shares 96
register of members 94
rights and liabilities 93
subsidiary companies 90
termination of 94
Members' voluntary winding up 268
Memorandum of association 44
alteration of 53
association clause 55
capital clause 55
effect of 60
form of 44
limitation of liability 54
name 46
objects 49
other clauses 56
registered office 48
specimen 45

ultra vires 53
Mergers 291
European Community law, and 292
Monopolies and Mergers Commission 291
Secretary of State, and 291
Minority protection 190, 193
Misfeasance 262
Mortgages of shares 126
equitable 126
legal 126

Name 46
change of 48
dispensing with 'ltd' in 47
misleading 46
passing off 47
publication of 46
restrictions on 47
Notice of general meetings 136

Objects clause 49
alteration of 53
main 51
powers 50
rules in interpreting 50
ultra vires doctrine 53
Offer of listed securities 71
Official receiver 256
Onerous property, disclaimer of 262
Option dealings 180
Ordinary resolution 146
Ordinary shares 100
Overseas companies 46

Partnership companies 41
Partnership, contrasted with a company 31

Petitioners in a winding up 250
Placing 68
Poll 141
Preference 261
Preference shares 101
  cumulative 101
  participating 101
  repayment of capital on winding up 101
Preferential debts 207, 264
Pre-incorporation contracts 66
Primary offer 74
Private companies
  characteristics of 40
  conversion to or from public companies 38, 39
  definition of 37
Profit and loss account 225
Promoters 63
  definition of 63
  duties of 63
  payment of 63
  remedies for breach of duty by 64
Proof of debts 263
Prospectus 73, 76
  contents of 76
  definition of 73
  liability for false statements in 79
  not required, when 74
  supplementary 77
Provisional liquidator 253
Public companies 37
  characteristics of 40
  conversion to or from private companies 38, 39
  definition of 37

Purchase of shares
  by company 106
  financial assistance for 89

Qualification shares 155
Quorum 138

Raising capital 68
  placing 69
  private placing 68
  prospectus 73
  rights issue 69
Receiver 213
  administrative 213
  appointment of 213
  effect of appointment of 214
  distribution of assets by 215
Reconstruction and amalgamation 281
  sale under the memorandum, by 281
  scheme of arrangement, by 281
  I.A. section 110, under 282
  takeover by 287
Redeemable debentures 204
Redeemable shares 102
Reduction of capital 104
Register
  of charges 208
  of directors' interests 182
  of interests in shares 96
  of members 94
  types of 49
Registered company 34
Registered office 48
Regulations 19, 20
Requisition of meeting 136
Reserve fund 130

INDEX

Resolutions 144
  circulation of 149
  elective 148
  extraordinary 146
  ordinary 146
  registration of 150
  special 145
  written 147
Restoration to the register 248
Rights issue 69
Rule in
  Foss v. Harbottle 187
  Royal British Bank v. Turquand 200

Scheme of arrangement 284
Seal 24
Secondary offer 75
Secretaries
  appointment 244
  duties of 245
  qualifications of 99
Share capital
  alteration of 103
  authorised 99
  classes of 100
  clause 55
  equity 100
  increase of 103
  issued 99
  nominal 99
  paid up 100
  raising 68
  reduction of 104
  reserve 99
  uncalled 99
Share certificates 116
  estoppel 117
  forged 117
  issue of 116
Share premium account 115
Share warrant 162
Shares 110
  acceptance of offer to purchase 112
  allotment of 113
  application for purchase of 111
  bonus 115
  calls on 124
  deferred 100
  definition of 111
  forfeiture of 127
  founders 100
  issue at a discount 114
  issue at a premium 115
  lien on 128
  mortgage of 126
  ordinary 100
  preference 101
  purchase of 106
  redeemable 102
  surrender of 127
  transfer of 118
  transmission of 123
  variation of class rights of 108
Small companies 41
South Sea Bubble 15
Special resolution 145
Statutory companies 34
Stock 104
Stop notice 96
Striking off the register 247
Subdivision of shares 104
Subsidiary 26
Surrender of shares 127

Tables A–F 57
Takeovers 287

Takeover bid 287
Transfer at an undervalue 258
Transfer of shares 118
   certification of 122
   forged 117
   form of 121
   implied terms in 121
   pre-emption rights in 120
   procedure on 122
Transmission of shares 123
Trust deed 210
Trusts, notice of 95

Ultra vires doctrine 53
Underwriting 77
Unlimited company 36

Valuation of shares 240
Variation of class rights 108
Veil of incorporation 27
Voluntary arrangement 272
Voluntary liquidation 267
Voluntary winding up 267
   commencement of 267
   creditors' 269
   declaration of solvency 268
   effect of 270
   liquidation committee 270
   liquidator in 268, 269
   members' 268
   procedure 268, 269

Winding up by the Court 249
   completion of 266
   contributories in 250, 255
   creditors 263
   disclaimer 262
   dissolution of company 266
   fraudulent trading 260
   grounds for 251
   liquidation committee 256
   liquidator 256
      appointment of 256
      power and duties of 256
   meetings in 255
   Official Receiver 256
   payment of debts 264
   petition 250, 253
   petitioners 250
   preference 261
   preferential debts 264
   procedure in 254
   provisional liquidator 253
   statement of affairs 254
Written resolution procedure 147
Wrongful trading 260

EMPLOYMENT LAW

COLIN THOMAS

Employment Law is a clear and comprehensive guide to the rights and duties of employers and employees, and to the provisions of legislation relevant to employment in the UK.

This book looks first at the contract of employment and its terms before describing the nature and obligations of the parties to the employment relationship. It deals with the payment of salaries and wages, equal pay, and then examines the circumstances and procedures of the termination of employment and the complex issues of unfair dismissal, redundancy and compensation payments.

Further chapters focus on sex and race discrimination in employment, the role of the trade unions, the law relating to industrial action, and an entirely new chapter on industrial tribunal procedure has been added.

The book contains a selection of questions (with sample answers) and the text is illustrated throughout with actual examples showing how legislation and case law have been interpreted and applied. The text incorporates the provisions of the Employment Act 1990.

Colin Thomas is a senior lecturer in the School of Legal Studies at the University of Wolverhampton.

TEACH YOURSELF BOOKS

OTHER TITLES AVAILABLE IN TEACH YOURSELF

☐	0 340 55939 X	**Employment Law** *Colin Thomas*	£8.99
☐	0 340 56826 7	**Taxation** *David W. Williams*	£6.99

All these books are available at your local bookshop or newsagent, or can be ordered direct from the publisher. Just tick the titles you want and fill in the form below.

Prices and availability subject to change without notice.

HODDER AND STOUGHTON PAPERBACKS, P.O. Box 11, Falmouth, Cornwall.

Please send cheque or postal order for the value of the book, and add the following for postage and packing:

UK including BFPO – £1.00 for one book, plus 50p for the second book, and 30p for each additional book ordered up to a £3.00 maximum.

OVERSEAS, INCLUDING EIRE – £2.00 for the first book, plus £1.00 for the second book, and 50p for each additional book ordered.

OR Please debit this amount from my Access/Visa Card (delete as appropriate).

CARD NUMBER ☐☐☐☐☐☐☐☐☐☐☐☐☐☐☐☐

AMOUNT £ ....

EXPIRY DATE ....

SIGNED ....

NAME ....

ADDRESS ....

....